1986

Public Speaking

Public Speaking

THIRD EDITION

George Rodman

Brooklyn College,
The City University of New York

Holt, Rinehart and Winston
New York   Chicago   San Francisco   Philadelphia
Montreal   Toronto   London   Sydney
Tokyo   Mexico City   Rio de Janeiro   Madrid

To my wife, Linda, and my daughter, Jennifer, who have given me more happiness than I thought possible.

Acquisitions Editors: Anne Boynton-Trigg, Lucy Rosendahl
Developmental Editor: Jackie Fleischer
Senior Project Editor: Lester A. Sheinis
Production Manager: Robin B. Besofsky
Design Supervisor: Louis Scardino

Photo Credits

Pages 3, 27, 82, 89, 91, 148, 189, 209, 262, 298. Photographs by George Bing.
Pages 19, 41, 57, 63, 107, 134, 162, 233. Photographs by Bruce Cotler.
Page 8. Photograph by Dick Doddridge, courtesy of Mothers Against Drunk Driving (MADD).
Pages 281, 288. Photographs by Louis Romano, courtesy of the Brooklyn College Television Center.
Page 149. Official photograph, the White House, Washington.

Library of Congress Cataloging-in-Publication Data

Rodman, George R., date.
    Public speaking.

    Includes bibliographical references and index.
    1. Public speaking.   I. Title.
PN4121.R665 1986   808.5'1   85–8673

ISBN 0-03-002498-6

CBS COLLEGE PUBLISHING
Holt, Rinehart and Winston
The Dryden Press
Saunders College Publishing

Preface

There are many public speaking textbooks — so many, in fact, that the first question for an author or reader is, "Why another?" After all, most of the books (including the last edition of this one) are well written and pedagogically sound, and the content of the course is relatively straightforward.

More than anything else, a desire to reach the student governed the changes in this new edition. Many of the concepts are expanded and clarified, and many new student examples are included.

I also tried to tailor the order of material to a student's receptivity at each point in the semester. For example, students first enter a class with certain expectations about how the course will add to their knowledge. The overview of speech preparation in Chapter 1 organizes the student's existing knowledge and adds a preview of the various new concepts that later chapters develop. An anecdotal approach drives home the points while it holds interest. Now the student is ready for more theoretical considerations, so the second chapter deals with listening, the human communication process, and rhetorical criticism all at once. (These three areas, which are usually dealt with as separate fields of inquiry, fit harmoniously into the beginning student's gestalt.)

This edition has been extensively rewritten with an eye to updating, clarifying, and expanding the most important material. The following major changes have been made:

1. The first chapter is now built around the story of how Candy Lightner, the founder of Mothers Against Drunk Driving, prepared and presented her first press conference.
2. The "focus" chapter has been rewritten to stress topic choice and development.
3. New chapters cover audience analysis and speaking for the electronic media.
4. The chapter on persuasive speaking has been revised to clarify the differences between a strategy to convince and a strategy to actuate.

Each chapter begins with a formal outline and ends with a short summary and questions/assignments, which can be used either for class

v

discussion or formal written assignments. Other questions and assignments are in the Instructor's Manual.

The Instructor's Manual is available from your Holt representative or
from the Communications Editor, Holt, Rinehart and Winston, 383 Madi-
son Avenue, New York, NY 10017. A taped self-study course to accompany
the text and exam questions on floppy disk are also available from the
author, Department of Television and Radio, Brooklyn College of CUNY,
Brooklyn, NY 11210. The self-study course could be placed in your library
or media resource center for students who need extra help outside class.
The exam questions on floppy disk can be used by any instructor who has
access to an IBM-compatible personal computer.

As always, this new edition is a team effort. I wish to thank the
professionals at Holt, Rinehart and Winston, including Anne Boynton-
Trigg, Lucy Rosendahl, Jackie Fleischer, Patricia Murphree, Lester A.
Sheinis, Kristin Camitta Zimet, Robin B. Besofsky, and Louis Scardino.
The changes in this edition are based on the suggestions of reviewers for
all three editions of this book, for which I thank them. The reviewers for
this edition are Sandra Ketrow, University of Florida; Mary Osentowski,
Richland College; Olaf Rankis, University of Miami; Kay Robinson, Barton
County Community College; Gwenn Schultze, Portland Community Col-
lege; Donald Springen, Brooklyn College. Special thanks are in order for
Ron Adler, who has helped me to clarify many concepts.

Brooklyn, N.Y.   **GR**

Contents

Public Speaking

PART ONE

Introductory Overviews

1

Speech
Preparation

Because you begin making speeches early in your public speaking course, you need to know about the process of planning a speech right away; but because the principles of message planning require a depth of understanding, you must explore them in detail. We are going to try a compromise here. We will overview the entire process of creating a speech briefly in this chapter, and develop each major component of that process in detail in later chapters.

An Overview of Speech Planning

The best way to make such an overview meaningful is to relate it to an actual speech, one that was given in "the real world" under circumstances at least as difficult as the ones you face in giving your first classroom speeches. There are literally thousands of such speeches we could use, everything from a politician's election-year plea to a minister's latest sermon; but the most interesting speeches tend to be those presented by "regular people" who are trying to bring about some form of change. Particularly interesting are those speeches given by someone who is trying to correct some injustice so long-standing that people take it for granted. Most interesting of all is one of these speeches that has actually brought about change.

One such speech was given in August of 1981 by a California housewife named Candy Lightner.

The Background

On May 3, 1980, while Candy Lightner and one of her twin 13-year-old daughters were out shopping, her other twin daughter Cari was walking with a friend along a bicycle path near her home. It was a lovely spring afternoon, and Cari was on her way to a church carnival. She would never arrive, however. She was struck and killed by a driver who had been drinking for most of the morning. The driver never stopped.

The driver who killed Cari was eventually arrested. Not only had he been drunk at the time of the accident, but he had a long list of drunk driving violations. Worst of all, he had been out on bail for only two days following another hit-and-run drunk driving offense. The police told Candy Lightner that, because of the state's lenient drunk driving laws, the man who killed her daughter would probably never go to jail.[1]

"I was so angry," Lightner said later, "that I wanted to kill. But I decided to do something constructive instead."[2] What she did was to establish Mothers Against Drunk Driving (MADD), an organization dedicated to finding solutions to the drunk driving problem.

Before she founded MADD, Candy Lightner had little interest in politics. She was not even registered to vote, and she had never spoken in public — in fact, like most people, the thought of public speaking terrified her.[3] But Candy soon discovered that speechmaking was going to be necessary to keep her organization alive. For one thing, the people with the power to make a difference, such as her state legislators, would not pay much attention to her because she did not seem to have much popular support. The governor of the state repeatedly refused to see her. Others told her that her cause was hopeless. Lightner, in her frustration, knew it was time to speak up. She knew that her first speech would have to be a press conference to publicize MADD and its aims.

Getting Started

When Lightner decided to organize MADD, she started "reading everything she could get her hands on about drunken driving." She sought not only all the books on the problem in the library, but everything related to it in current newspapers, in magazines, and on radio and television. When she began to realize the enormity of the drunk driving problem, and how little was being done about it, she began to contact anyone she could think of who might know about the problem or how to correct it. Her contacts included judges, attorneys, political officials, and victims.

When it came time to give her speech, she also made some telephone calls—to the National Highway Traffic Safety Administration, for current statistics on the problem nationwide, and then to the California Highway Patrol, for information on the statewide problem. Finally, she called the state attorney general's office, to find out why local legislators were not making more effort to tighten up lax drunk driving laws.

As part of her research, Lightner did a lot of thinking about her own case and about how she could express her anguish to a group of strangers.

Preparing the Speech

By the date scheduled for her press conference, Lightner had done enough research to speak for hours. However, she had promised a ten-minute statement, so she had to decide how to focus her topic. In order to focus her topic she had to think about her *purpose* in speaking. She knew her general purpose was to tell the public about MADD, of course; but she had to choose a specific goal, a statement of what she really wanted to accomplish—not in her lifetime, or even in the next month, but with this *one* ten-minute speech.

Upon reflection, Lightner was able to state the following purpose:

> After listening to my speech, my audience will write news stories concerning MADD's purposes and goals.

This purpose statement acted as a focal point for all further work on her speech.

Next, Lightner directed her attention to the *content* of her speech. With the help of some friends, she began to formulate a *prospectus,* a list of points she thought she might like to make in the speech:

1. Thousands of people are killed every year by drunk drivers.
2. Drunk driving laws enable many of the violators to return to the streets to kill again.
3. Legislators are ignoring the problem.
4. The parents of children who are killed or crippled by drunk drivers want something to be done about the problem.

There was more. By the time Lightner was done with her list she had several dozen points that she thought she might like to make; but she knew that she had to limit her press conference to a specific, newsworthy event. After all, the press is trained to look for specific, important information that has human-interest value. If she did not get the press's attention, the press would not get the public's attention for her. She decided to announce that her organization was starting a petition to ask the governor to appoint a task force to solve the drunk driving problem.

Once she had homed in on the topic of her speech, the main points began to take shape:

I.   Drunk driving is a serious problem.
  A.   More than 25,000 people a year are killed in alcohol-related crashes nationwide.
  B.   More than 2500 a year are killed in California alone.
II. This problem is not being adequately addressed by the state.
  A.   Drunk drivers have nothing to fear from the system.
    1.   Courts sometimes are not notified about suspended licenses.
    2.   There is inadequate enforcement of drunk driving rehabilitation programs.
  B.   Legislators do not act.
    1.   The Criminal Justice Committee of the Assembly kills all reform bills.
    2.   Defense attorneys who make money defending drunk drivers are also against reform.
III. The governor can help solve the problem by appointing a task force to find solutions to the problem.
    1.   The governors of Maryland and New York have started such a task force in their states.
    2.   The governor recently took the time to save a dog—aren't children just as important?
    3.   The task force should be mandated to come up with solutions that will get the drunk driver off the road.
IV. We must show our support of this task force by signing a petition.

Lightner used her outline as a guide in writing her speech, but as the speech progressed she changed her outline to follow it. The writing process went on like that, from the outline to the speech and back to the outline again.

As she wrote the speech, Lightner had to figure out what she could say to prove those points, and to make them clear and interesting to her audience. She chose statistics and examples carefully, and she thought her arguments out logically. She even decided to read a short article from *Newsweek* (an article about her governor saving a dog's life) to make one of her points.

Those points would make up the body of Lightner's speech. She still had to consider how to begin the speech and how to end it, because the introduction and conclusion are, in many cases, the most important parts of the speech. For her conclusion she needed a good summary statement, something that the press would remember. Because her petition made a strong summary statement, she decided to read it as her conclusion. For an introduction, she needed to get her audience's attention, so she decided to tell her own story of how she had lost Cari to a drunk driver.

Lightner got together with a few of her knowledgeable friends to compose the speech. One of her friends was a free-lance journalist who

Candy Lightner and her daughter Serena at MADD's first press conference.

had a feeling for what would affect an audience of journalists. Her other friends made suggestions about organization, language choice, and strategy.

When the rough draft of the speech emerged, Lightner began to practice it. She practiced by herself, and then in front of her family and friends. She even tape-recorded the speech to see how she sounded. Each time she practiced the speech, she made adjustments, fine-tuning it for effect. She experimented with different styles of delivery: from memory, from notes, and from manuscript. She decided to present it from a manuscript so she could be absolutely sure of the wording of everything she said. After all, if things worked out, she would be quoted in the newspapers and on radio and television. She wanted to make sure the media got it right.

Delivering the Speech

Finally the day arrived. It was less than four months since Cari had died, and Lightner had the chance to do something about it at last. She arrived at the press conference site at the state capital and gave the following speech:

Mothers Against Drunk Drivers

Candy Lightner

1 Good morning.

2 My name is Candy Lightner. I am the president of a newly formed grass-roots organization called M.A.D.D. — Mothers Against Drunk Drivers. The group started in Sacramento as a direct result of the death of my 13-year-old daughter Cari, who was killed in May of this year by a repeat offender drunk driver.

3 Cari was killed at 1:20 in the afternoon while walking inside a bicycle lane on her way to a nearby church. The man who killed her did not stop. He was later arrested and charged with felony hit and run, felony drunk driving, and felony vehicular manslaughter. In fact, the man who killed my daughter was out of jail on bail for only two days from another hit-and-run drunk driving arrest. He had two other drunk driving convictions on his record.

4 Last Friday, this man pleaded "no contest" to the vehicular manslaughter charge, which, by the way, carries no mandatory jail sentence in California. The other two felony charges and two misdemeanor charges from the previous hit-and-run accident were dropped in a plea bargain arrangement with the district attorney.

5 The arrest record of my daughter's killer is not unusual and only represents the tip of the iceberg of the drunk driving problem here in California.

6 Although he hasn't been sentenced yet, the probation department has recommended probation with one year in the county jail. Including his automatic time off for good behavior, he will be out in four months. This for a man who has killed once and was arrested five times for drunk driving since 1976. I think that kind of approach needs to be reevaluated.

7 Following Cari's death I have learned a great deal about the seriousness and urgency of the drunk driving problem in this state. I had no choice — this was the second time my daughter was hit by a drunk driver. This time it cost her life.

8 I want to protect not only my remaining children but other children as well. In the state of California the largest age group affected by drunk driving deaths lies between the ages of 15 and 24. Drunk drivers kill more American people in their teens and twenties than any other cause of death.

9 Drunk driving is a problem that is not being adequately or effectively addressed by the state. This, despite the fact the problem is growing worse and threatens the life and limb of every California citizen every day. We plan to ensure that, in the future, the state will better protect innocent people from drunk drivers.

10 One of the things I have learned from my own personal tragedy and that of others is that drunk drivers in the state of California have almost nothing to fear from the system. Yet we victims are being virtually ignored. I find that appalling.

11   Each year in the United States about 25,000 people are killed in alcohol-related crashes. In the past ten years more than 250,000 have been killed nationwide and millions have been injured — many crippled or impaired for life. Half of all traffic fatalities involve a drunken driver; a new victim is claimed every 23 minutes.

12   Nationwide the economic cost of the drunk driving problem is said to be in excess of four billion dollars a year. In California, surely the cost must run in the hundreds of millions of dollars a year. And these costs do not take into account the devastating emotional and future financial impact on the survivors of drunk driving alcohol crashes — the widows and orphans and the crippled and maimed.

13   I'm asking why this carnage on our highway is allowed to continue unabated.

14   If ten jetliners were to crash in the state of California in a year's time and in each crash, 250 people were to die, you'd better believe that the press would jump all over the issue. Editorial writers would ask why and state legislators and the governor would call for blue ribbon commissions to investigate. And there would be a huge public outcry. Possibly the President of the United States would step in and demand a federal investigation to reduce such a gruesome toll. Corrections would be made.

15   But when the same number of people are killed at the rate of seven or eight a day in drunk driving crashes here in California, the problem is virtually ignored and there is no public outcry for reform. Surely, that is wrong!

16   Drunk driving is the number one highway traffic safety problem in the nation, and according to Commissioner Glen Craig of the Highway Patrol ''. . . it is the number one driving problem, and number one by a very wide margin.''

17   In the past three months I've learned a great deal about the drunk driving problem and I have more to learn. But one thing is clear. No public official, elected or appointed, or other organization has been effective in abating the problem of drunk drivers. I have talked to numerous people in the field, including judges, district attorneys, defense attorneys, directors of alcohol abuse programs, police officials, elected officials, concerned citizens, and victims. Everyone admits there is a serious problem in this state yet nothing effective is being done. It is time to say ''enough'' and develop effective solutions to the drunk driving problem so that the number of lives lost and injuries sustained can be reduced.

18   If a reckless driver's license has been suspended and that driver is caught driving again, he, or she, could get a free ride from the court system, because the Department of Motor Vehicles has no effective way of notifying the courts that someone's license had been taken away. I think that problem should be corrected immediately!

19   If a person shows up drunk or reneges on attending the S.B. 38 program, a program intended to rehabilitate drunk drivers, it takes from one to nine months before that person's license is suspended. That problem should also be corrected immediately!

20   When I ask legislators and members of the attorney general's office why no effective corrective legislation has been passed, I am told they can't get it through the Assembly Criminal Justice Committee. This is supposed to be the "killer" committee on effective reform. I am told this committee is stacked with legislators who are "safe" and do not have to fear reelection problems.

21   I have also been told of special interest groups, namely defense attorneys, who fight effective legislation because they make their money off drunk driving cases.

22   I understand the governor is supportive of corrective drunk driving legislation and there are a number of legislators very concerned about this problem, yet their bills never make it out of the Assembly Criminal Justice Committee. Why? Aren't innocent people worth protecting?

23   Prison inmates have a union and a paid lobbyist. What do we have? Why are we letting a group of special interest people, for monetary reasons or whatever, allow the rest of us to die or be seriously injured by drunk drivers?

24   Someone must be responsible for putting a stop to such utter nonsense and politically criminal behavior.

25   That is why we are calling on Governor Brown, as the highest elected official in the state, to take a firm leadership role and appoint a task force. The purpose of the task force would not be to *study* the problem — that's been done. The purpose of the task force would be to *solve* the problem — that hasn't been done.

26   As governor it is his primary responsibility to protect the health and welfare of the citizens of the state. We call on Governor Brown to appoint a task force charged with the responsibility of developing broad-based measures to address the problem of drinking drivers. The task force should be required to think of any and all possible solutions to this problem, whether it be new legislation, more stringent sentencing by the judges, or more effective prosecution by the District Attorney's office. In short, the task force should be mandated to come up with solutions that will get the drunk driver off the road.

27   The governors of Maryland and New York have started such a task force in their states. They realize the seriousness and urgency of doing something about the drunk driving problem. We ask our governor to do the same.

28   Recently California legislators and Governor Brown took the time to save a little dog. Let me read you a short piece from a recent issue of *Newsweek:*

29   When elderly widow Mary Murphy committed suicide in San Francisco last December, she left an odd instruction in her will: Fearing her dog Sido would be lonely, she ordered the pet killed. But the local Society for the Prevention of Cruelty to Animals took Sido's case to court. Canine-loving Californians joined the cause, hounding legislators to pass a save-Sido bill. Governor Jerry Brown even personally called the judge after signing the bill into law. The judge

duly stayed the canine executioner: "Even stray and abandoned dogs have rights," he proclaimed.

30   That was in the June 30 [1980] issue of *Newsweek*.

31   I hope that Governor Brown and the legislators will also find some time for an issue where the lives of innocent children are at stake. . . . Surely children are at least as important as dogs.

32   At this time we are urging concerned citizens and public officials alike to write to Governor Brown supporting the request for the task force. And we have also started a statewide petition drive asking the governor to appoint a task force. We are not as concerned with what his administration calls "the effort" as we are with the end result. Because the end result means that lives will be saved and fewer innocent people will be injured.

33   We hope that a public outcry won't be necessary for so obvious a problem, but if it is then we will continue to be persistent in our efforts not only for the task force but to get drunk drivers off the road.

34   This is how the petition reads:

35   Dear Governor Brown:

In the state of California, approximately 2500 people a year — that's more than seven people a day — are killed in alcohol-related crashes. Each year over 25,000 people are killed nationally. There are solutions to this problem. We, the undersigned, request you, as governor of this state, to take a leadership role in fighting the drunk driving problem by forming a Governor's State Task Force not to study the problem — it's been studied before — but to solve the problem of drunk driving.

36   Thank you.

After her speech, Lightner answered a few questions. She prefaced the question-and-answer period by saying, "I'm not an expert on drunk driving, but I am an expert on what it's like to be the victim of a drunken driver. I'll be glad to answer a few questions about MADD or about my own case."

The Aftermath

Candy Lightner took a personal stand against a social problem that had been around for so long that people had just learned to accept it. She had told one interviewer:

The public doesn't perceive drunk driving as a crime, yet more people are killed each year in this manner than they are by handguns. Drunk driving is the only socially acceptable form of homicide. Judges, jurors, prosecutors, all drink and drive. They identify with the drunk driver. People look at the defendant and say to themselves, "There but for the grace of God go I." We will not solve the problem until they say the same thing when they all look at the victim.[4]

So Lightner spoke up, and the word went out. Her speech marked the beginning of what was to become a nationwide movement with a long list of accomplishments. MADD's membership reached to all fifty states. California adopted the nation's strictest laws against drunk driving. In fact, over 700 pieces of legislation were introduced in 39 states. President Reagan named a blue-ribbon commission to come up with solutions to the nationwide problem. Several large corporations decided to provide free taxi service home after parties at which alcohol was served. "Safe-ride" programs were established in which teenagers provided rides home for other teenagers who had had too much to drink. The National Restaurant Association made a recommendation to its members that they train bartenders in how to handle drinkers who want to drive. A movie was even made by CBS about Lightner and her accomplishments, and as this book goes to press, the network is considering a sequel. If you ask Lightner what MADD's main accomplishment is, she'll tell you, "I think the biggest accomplishment would be that public attitude is changing, because that is the bottom line. There was a 13 percent decrease in traffic fatalities in 1983, and that was the biggest decrease in 20 years."

The Principles Behind the Speech

Lightner's speech preparation conformed to the same principles that you have to consider as you put together your first classroom speech.

Choosing and Developing a Topic

Lightner's choice of topic was easy for her: Following her daughter's death her only interest was fighting the drunk driving problem through the efforts of MADD; so that, of course, was what her speech would be about. For your first speeches you will do the same thing Lightner did to determine your topic: First you will review your own interests, and then you will compare them to the interests of your audience and the requirements of the occasion (for example, the "occasion" of a classroom assignment).

Next you will determine your *general purpose,* which is usually to inform or persuade. Lightner's general purpose was to persuade: She wanted to get people to change their attitudes about drunk driving, and she wanted them to sign her petition. Her persuasive purpose required her to explain the problem, the solution, and the desired audience response, so she still had to consider the general purpose of informing. She also had to determine her specific purpose, which was to get the press's attention so they would publicize MADD. Finally, she had to develop her topic through a combination of thinking, creativity, analysis, and research, all of which required time and effort.

One student described topic selection and development this way:

As I reviewed my own interests, I came up with a list that included auto racing, U.S. foreign policy, surfing, racquetball, the dating habits of today's college student, how to get good grades, and how to graduate before you go broke. . . .

I then asked myself which of those topics would be of most interest to my audience; that eliminated several topics that they had already heard too much about (surfing, racquetball) and some topics that did not fit into their general realm of experience (U.S. foreign policy). Of the topics that were left, "The Dating Rituals of Today's College Student" seemed most appropriate. After I'd researched the topic for a couple of days, I came up with the following purpose statement:

> After listening to my speech, my audience will recognize at least three similarities between the dating rituals of today's college students and mating rituals of several aboriginal tribes that we like to think of as "primitive."

We will be taking an in-depth look at the process of choosing and developing a topic in Chapter 3. Later, Chapters 10–12 will focus on the specific purposes of informing, persuading, and amusing.

Analyzing and Adapting to the Audience

Like Lightner, you have a "double" audience to contend with. Lightner's immediate audience was a group of journalists, but she was also speaking to the general public. In your speech class you will be speaking to your class members and your instructor at the same time. In Lightner's case, getting through to the general public depended upon having an effect on the journalists. In your case, getting through to your instructor depends upon having an effect on your classmates. In order to ensure this effect, you have to analyze the type of audience your class represents, their purpose in gathering, their attitudes, their expectations, and their needs. Once you analyze them, you have to adapt your message to them: you adapt not only your approach to your topic, but the facts and the language you use to back up your ideas. Adapting does *not* mean that you sacrifice your integrity by telling your audience "what they want to hear." It only means that you tell them what you want to tell them in the way that they are most likely to understand and accept.

One speaker, accepting a scholarship award from the "Sons of Italy Club," analyzed her audience as follows:

My audience consisted of mostly middle-aged and older people. There were about 150–200 of them. Among the special guests were the mayor and some club representatives from out of town. I knew that I had to sound sincere, and yet be organized enough to show that I had a "good head on my shoulders." On the other hand, I didn't want to give the audience the impression that I was superstudious and did nothing but study. For this reason I began the speech by acknowledging the audience's feeling of boredom after sitting through forty minutes of other speeches. I thought this would show that I was one of them. I acknowledged this feeling because from past experiences with this particular audience I know that they are more interested in the festivities and dancing following dinner than with any ceremonies.

Also to get away from the bookworm stereotype I dressed in a very sophisticated (yet not too sexy — I'm a "nice Italian girl!") manner, in a black midcalf dress.

My entire speech supported the idea that I was honored to receive the scholarship by describing my sincere feelings of enthusiasm. I also threw in a few Italian phrases for authenticity and concluded the speech by encouraging everyone to have a great time that evening.

We will be looking at audience analysis and adaptation in more depth in Chapter 4. Chapter 13 will consider adapting to an unseen audience, when you speak through electronic media.

Investigation

Both developing a topic and adapting to an audience require investigation on your part. In fact, all of these principles of speechmaking pertain to all of the stages of speech preparation, so you will find yourself involved in some form of "investigation" from the moment you choose your topic until you sit down after your speech is over. You investigate general ideas and specific facts to support those ideas. You investigate the people who will be in your audience, also. Like Lightner, you can perform your investigation through library research, interviewing, surveying, and just thinking about your own experience. You can also investigate through personal observation, which is why your investigation continues right through your speech, as you observe your audience reacting to what you are saying. We will be discussing investigation in more depth in Chapter 5.

Supporting Material

Investigation helps you uncover material that proves your ideas and helps make them clear, interesting, and memorable. For example, Lightner came up with an *analogy* comparing the carnage of drunk driving to the carnage of airline disasters (paragraphs 14–15). She cited several *statistics* related to the problem (paragraphs 8, 11, 12). She used *quotation* when she read the article from *Newsweek* (paragraph 29), and she used *testimony* when she quoted the commissioner of the Highway Patrol (paragraph 16). She also used her own dramatic case as an *example* (paragraphs 3–4). Such forms of support will be discussed in Chapter 7.

Organization and Structure

The idea of *organization* is to arrange your ideas in the order that will promote the desired effect in your audience. For example, in Lightner's speech, information about the seriousness of the drunk driving problem is introduced at several points (paragraphs 5, 8, 11–12, 16, 35). Lightner could have discussed this idea all at once, but she wanted to reinforce the importance of her topic more than that; hence she chose a repetitive pattern for this point. *Choice* is important here. There are an infinite number of arrangement patterns. Your job is to choose the best one for your speech, given your audience and occasion.

Structure has to do with the parts of your speech. Generally, we divide speeches into the same three parts that are recommended for essays and term papers: the *introduction,* the *body,* and the *conclusion.* As you noticed in Lightner's speech, each part of a speech has its own objectives: the introduction gains the audience's attention and previews the main idea of the speech; the body develops your ideas; and the conclusion reviews the speech and makes your main points memorable. Chapter 6 will help you with organization and structure.

Language

Even though a speech uses the same structural elements as an essay or term paper, there are important differences in the language it uses. Speeches are more personal, less formal, and more expansive than written work. As one expert has pointed out, "Speeches use more words per square thought than well-written essays or reports."[5]

In many other ways, however, the language concerns of a good speech are similar to those of good writing. In wording a speech, you should use language that is clear, interesting, and appropriate. You should experiment with different ways of expressing your ideas as you plan and practice your speech. Your ideas should be expressed directly and simply. Notice how simply and straightforwardly Lightner states her ideas, whether she is recounting an emotionally charged incident that changed her life ("Cari was killed at 1:20 in the afternoon while walking inside a bicycle lane . . .") or stating a statistical fact ("Drunk drivers kill more American people in their teens and twenties than any other cause of death.") We will discuss the principles of language use in more detail in Chapter 8.

Delivery

One of Lightner's main problems in presenting her speech was stage fright. She was, by her own admission, "terrified." In fact, to this day when she speaks in public she has to control her nerves by reminding herself of the importance of what she is saying. Every time she speaks, Lightner thinks about her daughter Cari and says to herself, "This one's for you, babe."

Lightner's involvement with her message is one of the secrets of a successful delivery. In presenting a speech, you have to maintain the greatest possible contact with your audience. You do so with a speaking style that is natural in eye contact, movement, posture, facial expression, and tone of voice. The best way to achieve this naturalness is to care honestly about what you are saying. It also helps to practice carefully and present the speech with the idea that it is important to the audience. We will deal more with the principles of effective delivery in Chapter 9.

Summary

There is a process involved in preparing and presenting a speech. To be successful, you have to devote a certain amount of time to each of the steps in that process. The steps are interrelated: they happen in no set order, and often two or more steps happen at the same time. These steps include preliminary considerations such as choosing and developing your topic, analyzing and adapting to your audience, and investigation. They also include tasks such as choosing the best supporting material, organizing and structuring the speech, and choosing your wording. The final step is practicing the speech.

There are principles that guide the effective completion of all these steps. These principles are basic to all types of message preparation. Understanding their role in public speaking will enable you to use them in *all* forms of communication.

Questions/Assignments

1. How does Candy Lightner's motivation for speaking compare with your own motivation for your first classroom speech? Think of two topics you might present in a speech assignment, in which your purpose would be not just to get a good grade, but to get a favorable response from the class. In other words, what do you *really* want to discuss with your classmates?
2. Do you agree that the steps in the process of message preparation "occur in no set order, and often two or more are necessary at the same time"? Why or why not?
3. Look again at Lightner's speech. What statements, arguments, examples, and so on do you think were probably most effective? What elements of the speech would you change, and how?
4. Think about a time when you had to plan a message — any message. It might have been a request you made to one of your parents, or a friend, or a teacher. (For example, you might have asked a teacher whether you could turn in an assignment late.) How did the process of preparing that message compare with planning for a public speech?
5. As you prepare for your first speaking assignment, keep a "diary" of the message preparation process. Compare the process you went through with the steps involved in the preparation of Candy Lightner's speech. In what ways were the situations similar? In what ways did they differ?

Notes

1. Maria Wilhelm, "A Grieving, Angry Mother Charges That Drunken Drivers Are Getting Away with Murder," *People,* June 29, 1981, p. 24.

2. Interview with Candy Lightner, July 20, 1984. All of Lightner's quotations in this chapter are taken from this interview, unless otherwise noted.

3. David Wallechinsky, Irving Wallace, and Amy Wallace, *The Book of Lists* (New York: William Morrow, 1977), p. 469, lists "speaking in public" as the fear most often reported by adults. A substantial body of research literature on communication apprehension and anxiety has accumulated. See James C. McCroskey, "Oral Communication Apprehension: A Summary of Recent Theory and Research," *Human Communication Research* 4, 1977, pp. 78–96.

4. Mary Barnett, "A Singular Woman," *McCall's,* September 1982, p. v4.

5. Jerry Tarver, "Can't Nobody Here Use This Language?" Tarver's speech can be found in Chapter 10 of this book.

2

Critical Listening

Listening: An Introduction

Chapter 1 was written mostly from the *speaker's* point of view. In your speech class, however, as in life, you will spend more time listening than speaking. Research shows that we communicate in some form about 80 percent of the time we are awake. About 45 percent of this time is spent listening. For college students in the classroom, the proportion of listening time is 60–70 percent.[1] However, even though we spend an enormous amount of time listening, study after study suggests that we are not good at it. Immediately after hearing a speech we forget half of it, and after 48 hours the amount we remember is down to 25 percent.[2]

Learning to listen well can make you more popular (good listeners are always more in demand at gatherings than those who consider themselves the "life of the party") and enable you to learn more. It might even save you from embarrassment. Ralph Nichols, who spent most of his life researching human listening, had an uncanny ability to catch audience members who were not listening. His reaction was typical for a college professor:

> Frequently, as I look into their faces during a lecture, I will see a student, his chin resting on his hand, two unblinking, staring eyes fixed upon me.

Occasionally, just for fun, I stop my lecture abruptly, call the student by name, and ask him: "What do you think of that?" The question has the same effect as throwing ice water in his face. He suddenly jerks to attention and tries to cover up his lack of listening with some hurried remarks: "Oh, yeah, sure, I guess that's a good, err . . ."[3]

As sadistic as this behavior seems, Nichols actually did his students a favor. He pointed out to them that "faked" listening was not *really* listening. Unfortunately, there is no human behavior that is so difficult to do well yet so easy to fake. We all have so much to think about. What are we going to do after class? Is the landlord going to evict us? Will we ever finish that project we started? It takes time to think these matters through. The easiest place to steal thinking time is in a nice, anonymous audience. We spend much time as part of one audience or another. After a while, we learn how *not* to listen, how to turn off what is going on around us so we can concentrate on our thoughts. A problem arises when we do it too often. By blocking out messages, we barricade ourselves against any of the benefits those messages might have had for us.

Ideally, we should learn to listen when we want to hear and *not* to listen when we want to withdraw. Unfortunately, most of us find it easier to learn how *not* to listen. This habit is especially unfortunate in a public speaking class, where listening critically to others' speeches will enable you to improve your own.

Some factors that affect listening are out of our control. For example, research shows that we listen better to effective speakers,[4] and that listening effectiveness partially depends upon our intelligence and information processing ability.[5] All things being equal, however, anyone can learn to be a better listener. The first step in that learning process is to understand what listening is all about. This chapter deals with that question by looking at four topics: (1) the place of listening in the process of communication; (2) the components of listening; (3) methods of enhancing listening; and (4) the objectives of listening.

The Process of Communication

Where can listening go wrong? To analyze the major trouble spots we need to look at the overall process of human communication.

Communication is a complex process. It is easiest to analyze it using a model and an accepted, standard terminology. Communication theorists have borrowed a set of terms from electronics theory that have become standard for discussing communication. The terms include *source, message, channel, receiver,* and *noise.*

A simple model depicting communication between just two people might look like the diagram on page 22. The *source* is anyone who originates a message. In public speaking, the source is usually the speaker. The

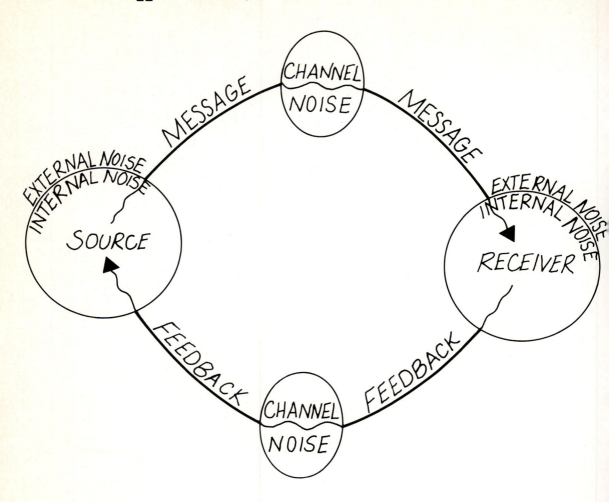

receiver is anyone who takes in that message (a member of the audience in the case of public speaking). *Message* is the general term for the ideas that are shared between source and receiver. *Channel* is the means through which the message moves. The channels of human communication are the five senses. *Feedback* is a message about the original message that travels back to the source from the receiver. In public speaking, feedback includes the audience's reactions during the speech and their questions and criticisms after the speech. Without feedback, communication is incomplete.

The most important term for us here is *noise*. To a communication theorist noise is anything that interferes with the clear reception of a message. Noise can be internal or external. *External noise* is any distraction in the environment: a jackhammer starting up outside the window, a power failure that suddenly dims the lights, or even a friend across the room who catches your eye and mouths a hello. *Internal noise,* sometimes referred to as *psychological noise,* occurs within a source or receiver. In public speaking internal noise consists of daydreams and thoughts that have nothing to do with the speech. Internal noise can affect either the source or receiver. The source might *encode* (put together) an idea in a sloppy, confused way because of internal noise, and the receiver might *decode* (interpret) the idea incorrectly because of internal noise. Limitations in or interference with the source's or receivers' sight, hearing, or other senses create *channel noise.*[6]

In our model, internal and external noise form a bubble around both source and receiver. This bubble impedes effective communication. The process becomes even more complex when the number of receivers is increased, as in a public speaking situation.

What does this model mean for you as a listener? It sets you three challenges:

1. You must break through your own "noise bubble."
2. You must take action to interpret every message, even if it is in your own language.
3. You must give feedback to the speaker.

To meet the first two challenges you should know the components of listening and how to enhance it. To meet the third you should learn more about how to handle speech criticism.

The Components of Listening

Listening is a complex process that contains three major steps: comprehension, interpretation, and evaluation.[7] Understanding these steps will give you a basis for examining your own listening behavior.

Comprehension, the first step, is recognizing the words that are being presented. In order to comprehend a message you have to be able to hear it and concentrate on it.

The second step, *interpretation,* involves translating those words into ideas. When you interpret a message, you mentally assign meaning to the words that are used.

The third step, *evaluation,* requires you to judge the worth of the speaker's ideas. In this step you judge whether the speaker's ideas are important to you.

These three steps might be represented by three questions that could act as listening guidelines:

1. The Comprehension Question: "What did the speaker say?"
2. The Interpretation Question: "What did the speaker mean?"
3. The Evaluation Question: "So what?"

We go through these three steps every time we truly listen, even in the most casual conversations. Imagine that one of your main interests in life is skiing. You have a friend whose main interest is surfing. You are listening to that friend tell you an anecdote about a spectacular "wipeout." To listen you must first *comprehend* what is said. Comprehension will break down if you cannot hear, of if you are distracted by an interruption.

If you do comprehend what is said, you next *interpret* the story in light of your own experience: You liken "wiping out" in surfing to "wiping out" in skiing. Thus you attribute meaning to the surfing terms that your friend uses, even though you are not a surfer.

Finally, you *evaluate* the importance of your friend's story in light of your own interests; you might amend your ideas about "balance" and how it keeps you from falling over while skiing.[8] When you evaluate your friend's message you place a judgment on it: "Good idea," you might think, or "Bad idea," or "Interesting story," or "Dull story." Whatever your judgment, if you have truly listened to what has been said, then you have gone through *all three steps:* comprehension, interpretation, and evaluation.

The listening process continues this way, hundreds of times during the average day. We go through these steps as we listen to radio, TV, friends, strangers, and speeches in class. When we do not want to listen, we cut off the process before the steps are completed. Let us look at some ways to make the most of each step.

Methods of Enhancing Listening

Listening is an active process. It requires effort. You don't just sit there and wait for it to happen. Five methods help make listening happen: being prepared, controlling distractions, withholding judgment, taking notes, and thinking while you are listening.

Be Prepared to Listen

Just as you prepare messages, you can prepare to listen to a message. First, you can practice listening by exposing yourself to challenging messages. Discussing complex topics with friends, attending lectures, and tuning in to documentaries on radio and TV are just a few of the ways that you can exercise your ability to listen. If you exercise this ability regularly, you will be better prepared to listen to a speech in class.

Another way to prepare to listen is to find out what the topic of a speech will be and then do some thinking about it. If one of your classmates is going to talk about nuclear energy, you could consider questions like this in advance: Is nuclear energy safe? Is it economical? Is it practical?

Finally, you can prepare to listen by building up a positive attitude about listening. Remember: You will be listening for your own benefit.

Control Distractions

As we mentioned earlier, "noise" is anything that interferes with the clear reception of a message. An effective listener has to make a conscious effort to overcome noise, whether it be internal in the form of daydreams or personal worries, or external in any of its forms: the sound of a book closing, a whiff of cologne, or the sight of a speaker tripping over the podium.

You can minimize the effect of some noise by planning for it in advance. Recognize those distractions, both internal and external, that you can predict. Are you worried about your neighbors' complaints that your cat has been befouling their children's sandbox? Take note of that worry, and resolve to concentrate on the speech instead. Do you have a social interest in one of your classmates? Take note of that, too. Do you have a cold? Take note: "Possible sniffles." Just recognizing these distractions helps you to fight them. Against some of them you can take preventive action: If you have the sniffles you can take an antihistamine before the speech starts.

You can control other, unexpected distractions *while* you are listening by compartmentalizing them. In other words, put them away, into a separate compartment, and say to yourself, "I'll think about them later. For now I am going to concentrate on this speech."

Withhold Judgment

Although evaluation is especially important in a speech class, you should not judge too quickly. For example, you should not let your *initial* evaluation of the topic get in the way of comprehending a speech. Psychologist Carl Rogers has suggested that human beings have a natural tendency to evaluate a message before they hear all of it.[9] Instead of going through all three steps of the listening process, we often skip the first one, comprehension, and then evaluate what we *think* is being said rather than what really is being said.[10] The character Emily Litella (Gilda Radner) on NBC's *Saturday Night Live* often satirized this tendency by demanding "equal time" for news reports about things like "making a steak out of Puerto Rico." As exaggerated as this example is, it is typical of the type of reaction caused by premature judgment. To truly listen you should withhold your evaluation of the message until your comprehension is complete.

In order to do so, keep two things in mind: First, *do not dismiss a topic as "uninteresting" until you have heard all that the speaker has to say.* Some topics just do not sound interesting at first, but if looked at closely enough they become fascinating. Ask "What is of interest in this topic?" rather than "Is this topic interesting?" The difference between those two questions is crucial, because the first one presupposes that there will be *something* of interest if you listen closely enough. Remember also that the things that will be of interest to you might not emerge until the speaker is well into the presentation.

Second, keep your criticism of the *speaker* separate from your criticism of the *speech*. Recognition of the speaker's delivery or physical appearance will be of use to you in improving your own speeches, but if you hold these things against a speaker you might "turn off" and miss the substance of what is being said. Do not let your feelings about the speaker interfere with your comprehension of the message.

The next method for enhancing listening, taking notes, will also help you to withhold evaluation and control distractions.

Take Notes

A major problem in listening is allowing insignificant details to distract you from the main points of a speech. To keep everything straight during a presentation you should take notes on the main ideas, on the details that you consider important and interesting, and on questions that come up as you listen. It is impossible to keep all these matters in your head and listen at the same time. If you record them in notes you can keep your mind on what is being said *when* it is being said.

One method of note-taking is as follows:

Divide a blank sheet of paper in half. Label one side "Main Ideas" and the other "Details and Questions."

Under "Main Ideas," list the topic or title of the speech, along with whatever seems to you to be a main idea. If these ideas happen to appear in standard outline form, fine; but you do not have to force your notes to follow the formal rules of outlining. In fact, it would be distracting to try to do so. Simply list what seem to be main ideas, as they come up.

Because your first responsibility is listening to the speaker, it is important to keep your notes brief. If you take down too much you will be writing when you should be listening, which will be distracting for both you and the speaker. You have to learn to listen for general ideas, jot them down briefly, and return your attention as quickly as possible to the speaker.

Sometimes you have to figure out the general idea from everything the speaker says. More often, though, the speaker will make a generalization about the idea before developing it. At other times, the generalization will appear after the development or right in the middle of it. It is important to listen for that general idea, no matter where it is. Suppose, for example, that you were in the audience when Attorney General William French Smith gave his speech on "Combating Organized Crime." Smith presented one idea this way:

> Today, organized crime is heavily involved in drug trafficking. Indeed, the drug trade is now the nation's number one crime problem — especially when one considers the criminal activities spawned by drug trafficking. For example, a recent study done of the Baltimore area found that 243 addicts committed a total of almost a half million crimes over an eleven-year period. That's an average of 2000 each — one every other day.[11]

Note-taking helps you keep track of the main points of the speech.

If you were listening actively to that idea, you might reduce it to a brief note such as:

Details and Questions	*Main Ideas*
	Drugs = #1 problem

On the opposite side of the same page under "Details and Questions," list those details that seem interesting to you, especially those that you might want to remember for your own use. Listening to Smith's speech, you might jot down one or two details like this:

Details and Questions	*Main Ideas*
Baltimore: 2,000 addicts, 1/2 million crimes, 11 years	

Also list in this column any questions that come to mind during the speech. If the speaker does not answer your questions in the course of the speech, ask for clarification during the question-and-answer period. Listening to the Attorney General's speech, you might realize that you had recently heard some statistics that seem to conflict with his. For example, you might have read an article that stated, "The average addict can only stay alive and out of jail for three years." How then could they collect crime data on addicts for eleven years? In this case, you might want to question the Attorney General about the source of his statistics. To make a note of that, you simply jot down the statistic with a question mark after it. That way, if the question is answered during the speech, all you have to do is cross out the question mark in your notes.

Using this method of split-page note-taking, notes on a speech about "Communication Between a Horse and Its Rider"[12] might look like this:

Details and Questions	*Main Ideas*
Great quote — where's it from?[13]	Horse-rider communication
Is the Lippizaner School in Austria?[14]	Humans use natural aids (voice hands legs seat) and artificial aids (whips spurs martingales)
Horses get insomnia?[15]	Horse Physiology — sensitive to touch; communicates with movements of ears, nostrils, back, and tail
	Horse psychology — not smart good memory moody sociable

That is just one method of taking notes. There are many others. Nichols, for example, suggests a similar split-page format, with "facts" on one side and "principles" on the other.[16] Other methods commonly used in speech classes include taking notes on an outline provided by the speaker and taking notes on a speech criticism form provided by the instructor. The method of note-taking that you use is not terribly important. Use whatever method you like, but take notes.

The final method of enhancing listening is the most important.

Think While You Listen

We have the ability to *think* at the rate of at least 400 words per minute, whereas on the average we *speak* at only 150 words per minute.[17] This gap between thinking speed and speaking speed is usually detrimental to listening, because we have a tendency to start wandering off mentally in some direction other than the speaker's topic.

Listening experts suggest a number of techniques for turning this gap into an advantage rather than a disadvantage.[18] Note-taking is one of them. Here are four more techniques:

1. *Anticipate the speaker's ideas.* Think ahead of the speaker, and see

whether you can predict the general direction in which the speech will move. Also see whether you can predict what the next point will be.

2. *"Fill in the blanks"* with your own data. When the speaker makes a point, come up with examples or other supporting material from your own experience. Make sure you stick to the subject under discussion.

3. *Summarize* the speaker's ideas: From time to time, review in your mind the ideas that have been covered so far. You can, of course, consult your notes for this purpose.

4. *Evaluate* the speech as you listen to it. Be a critical listener. In order to come up with an intelligent, critical analysis immediately *after* a speech, you have to make some decisions *during* the speech. Luckily, the thought/speech differential will enable you to do it without missing the essence of the speech. What do you listen for? Anything that you can use to improve your own speeches. Listening with this objective enables you to pick out certain "evaluative targets."

Targets for Evaluation

As part of an audience in a public speaking class, you are entitled to be selfish. You are, of course, expected to treat the speaker humanely,[19] but you also have the right to seek out and take away from a speech things of personal importance to you. In fact, it is your responsibility to do so. If you act with what Nichols calls "enlightened self-interest,"[20] you will automatically become a better listener.

The evaluative targets that you should listen for in a speech coincide with the principles of message preparation we summarized in Chapter 1. Questions based on these principles become guidelines for listening to speeches.

Choice of Topic

Did the speaker choose an appropriate topic? Why is it important to *you?* What do you *need* or *want* to know about this topic? Remember that no topic is inherently uninteresting. The topic of the speech might be "Drunk Driving," and you might neither drink nor drive. Still, you *know* people who drink, and as a passenger you share the highway with some of them. Perhaps the speech will show you ways to protect yourself.

Audience Analysis and Adaptation

How has the speaker adapted this topic to this particular audience? Has the speaker figured out *why* the audience needs to listen and stressed those needs in the speech? Has the speaker referred to the audience, and does the speech use ideas and information that they find familiar and interesting?

Investigation

Has the speaker investigated the topic sufficiently? What has the speaker found that interests you? Has the speaker read articles, conducted interviews, or made some personal observations that will help you understand the things you are interested in? To return to the "Drunk Driving" example, perhaps the speech will supply you with some arguments you can use to help get a drunken friend out from behind the wheel of a car next New Year's Eve.

Forms of Support

What supporting material (such as anecdotes, examples, definitions, and quotations) has the speaker used? Is it well chosen? Does this supporting material clarify or prove the speaker's ideas? Does it make those ideas more interesting or memorable?

Organization and Structure

Is the speech well organized? What are the main points? Is the organization of these points easy to follow? Does the speech flow smoothly from point to point, or do the points seem to be unrelated and "forced together"?

Does the speech have a clear-cut introduction, body, and conclusion? Does the introduction gain your attention and establish the main idea of the speech? How about the conclusion—does it summarize the main ideas and make them memorable?

Language

Does the speaker's use of language make the ideas clear and interesting? Can you learn the meaning of new vocabulary from the context in which it is used? Is there vocabulary that you can borrow to develop ideas of your own? Perhaps the speech is on "Sailing," and a few terms are novel to a landlubber. That is the way great vocabularies are built—by determining the meanings of new words through the contexts in which you find them.

Delivery

Does the speaker seem honestly enthusiastic about the speech? If not, what is it about the delivery that causes you to doubt it? Poor eye contact, posture, or vocal clarity might lessen a speaker's contact with the audience.

An important caution is necessary here: Do not allow the speaker's delivery to distract you from what is being said. The main reason you "listen" to delivery is to be able to help the speaker and yourself understand how delivery affects the audience's perception of the message. Make an extra effort to listen for ideas in spite of distracting mannerisms.

Effectiveness

What is the speaker's purpose? How are you supposed to respond? Does the speech cause you to respond that way? If the purpose of the speech is to arouse your interest, does it? If it seeks to explain something, are the ideas clear? If it tries to persuade you, are you given convincing reasons to change your attitude? If the purpose is to entertain, is the speech relaxing and enjoyable?

To evaluate the effectiveness of the speech, you have to do a certain amount of "critical watching" of the audience around you. How are your fellow audience members reacting to the speech?

Evaluating others' speeches in order to improve your own is a "selfish" objective. Nevertheless the feedback that you give as a critical listener (sitting up, looking interested, looking back at the speaker) will help the speaker present a better speech. As Nichols points out, "Nearly all of us have unconsciously developed a special set of senses that, in effect, measure the way people listen when we talk to them."[21] He sums it up this way: "The more we take from the speaker through listening, the more he will give."[22]

Speech Criticism

One of your main responsibilities in your public speaking class will be to offer criticism of your classmates' speeches. Critically analyzing these speeches will improve your own analytical skills as much as the speaker's speaking skills. In order to go about your criticism in a scholarly and effective way, you should keep in mind the traditions of rhetorical criticism and the idea of constructive criticism.

Following Rhetorical Guidelines

Rhetoric is an interesting term. It has come to be used in a variety of ways. In a derogatory sense we say, "That speech was just rhetoric," meaning "That speech was filled with empty slogans and emotional language rather than logical or ethical thought." On the other hand, if we refer to the "lofty rhetoric of poetry," "rhetoric" means the study of figurative language. A look at the historical use of the term is enlightening: Aristotle defined rhetoric as "the faculty of observing in any given case the available means of persuasion."[23] Modern usage broadened that concept of rhetoric to the study of how discourse produces an effect on a receiver.[24] Because language is the main ingredient in discourse, the meaning broadened until rhetoric became "the study of language."[25]

Today in connection with the criticism of speeches, "rhetoric" refers to the study of the speaker's effect on the audience. Therefore rhetorical criticism entails a consideration of the speaker, the audience, and all the aspects of message preparation that we discussed earlier.[26] Rhetorical criticism in a speech class involves an analysis of the entire speaking situation, including the speaker's purpose, the audience's reaction, and even whether or not the speech fulfilled the requirements of the assignment.

John Wilson and Carroll Arnold, two well-known rhetorical scholars, maintain that the basic critical question is, "To what extent, if at all, did the speaker fulfill the requirements of the rhetorical situation he or she faced?"[27] Another rhetorical theorist, Otis Walter, points out that this question does not cover all speech situations:

> Total reliance on questions about the means of persuasion often results not merely in unimportant answers but sometimes in absurdities. What is the best way — the most intelligent way — to view Hitler's anti-Semitic diatribes? Is it to ask, "Did Hitler use all the available means of persuading Germans to hate Jews?" And who would assign to Hitler a lesser degree of significance if we discovered that these diatribes failed to use some way of making men hate, or much admire him if we found he used all of them? Indeed, we ought to note the techniques that the demagogue uses, but however well or ill adapted to the audience these techniques are is somewhat beside the point.[28]

With this objection in mind, Wilson and Arnold offer three points of view from which to approach speech criticism:[29]

The Pragmatic Viewpoint. The first perspective emphasizes the *effect* of the speech. When we judge a speech from this perspective, we ask questions such as, "What was the aim of the speech?" "Was it successful?" and "Did it fulfill its purpose?"

The Ethical Viewpoint. A second perspective emphasizes the *morality* of the speech. It involves questions such as, "Did the speaker tell the truth?" "Was the speech in the best interests of this audience?" and "Did it advocate a morally acceptable course of action?" This point of view would be effective for a consideration of Hitler's speeches in the 1930s — or, for that matter, the more recent speeches of Colonel Qaddafi of Libya or Ayatollah Khomeini of Iran. Wilson and Arnold point out, however, that the nature of "truth" is still being debated among philosophers, and the ethical viewpoint cannot be made "the sole standard of judgment" about most speeches.

The Artistic Viewpoint. A third perspective emphasizes aesthetic criteria such as originality and creativity. It asks questions along the lines of, "Has this speaker expressed original thinking or merely parroted the words of others?" and "Is the speech worded, organized, supported (and so on) in a creative manner?"

Wilson and Arnold prefer the artistic viewpoint in speech criticism, because it can include pragmatic and ethical considerations. However, you would do well to remember all three perspectives, and use whichever ones apply to a given speech.

Making Criticism Constructive

We say that criticism is "constructive" when it helps the speaker improve. To offer this type of criticism you have to be *substantive*. Rather than saying just "I liked this" or "I didn't like that," you have to provide a detailed explanation of your reasons for liking or disliking parts of the speech. The extra effort will be worthwhile, because it will make your analysis far more effective.

Also, be careful to point out what is *right* with the speech as well as what is *wrong* with it. Otherwise, you run the risk of extinguishing the *positive* aspects of the speaker's behavior. In fact, negative criticism without positive criticism is often useless, because the speaker might become defensive and block out your criticism completely. It is a good idea, therefore, to offer your positive criticism first, and then tactfully offer your suggestions for improvement. For example, rather than saying, "Your ideas about horse psychology were completely unclear and unsupported," you might say, "I really enjoyed your explanation of horse physiology. It was clearly stated and well backed-up with examples and details. Your explanation of horse psychology, however, left me a little confused. It might be my own fault, but it just did not seem to be as well supported as the rest of your speech."

To encourage this type of criticism, many instructors have their students use a speech evaluation form like the one on page 34. Notice especially the first two open-ended questions on the form.

Your instructor might prefer a different evaluation form, or you might want to amend this one to your own liking. Whatever type of form you use, make sure it allows for positive, as well as negative, criticism.

Speech Evaluation Form

Name ————————————   Topic ————————————

Assignment # ———————————   Date ————————————

What did you especially like? ————————————

————————————————————————

In your opinion, how could the speech be improved? ————————

————————————————————————

Please comment on any of the following areas:

Choice of Topic
Interesting?
Appropriate?

Introduction
Creates interest?
Previews main ideas?

Investigation
Sufficient information?
New or surprising information?

Forms of Support
Are ideas developed?
Are points proven?

Organization
Easy to follow?
Moves smoothly from point to point?

Language
Clear?
Vivid?

Delivery
Natural?
Enthusiastic?

Conclusion
Summarizes main points?
Makes central idea memorable?

Overall Effectiveness
Carries out speaker's purpose?
Audience reaction?

Summary

This chapter dealt with listening, a human behavior that is as difficult to do correctly as it is essential to the learning that takes place in a public speaking class. We considered the place of listening in the communication process, the components of listening, the methods of enhancing listening, and the targets to evaluate in critical listening.

Methods of enhancing listening include preparing to listen (for example, by practicing), controlling noise (by recognizing internal distractions such as daydreaming and external ones such as noises in the room), withholding evaluation (until your comprehension of the message is complete), taking notes (to free yourself from remembering details, so you can concentrate on what is being said), and using the gap between thinking speed and speaking speed to evaluate the speech while you listen.

To evaluate a speech, you check whether it follows the principles of message preparation. Your targets are the choice of topic, audience analysis and adaptation, investigation, forms of support, organization and structure, language, delivery, and effectiveness. It is important not to let the delivery distract you from what is being said.

After you listen to a speech, one of your responsibilities is to offer criticism. Effective criticism will follow the traditional rhetorical guidelines. It will also be constructive, which means it will include positive as well as negative comments.

Questions/Assignments

1. How do you interpret Nichols's statement, "The more we take from a speaker through listening, the more he will give"? Do you agree or disagree? Why?
2. What do you think *speakers* can do to help the audience listen more effectively?
3. During the next speech presented in your class, take note of the *internal* and *external* distractions that might have hampered your listening. What can you do to avoid being distracted in the future?
4. People often tend to evaluate a message without first comprehending it. Recall an argument you recently had with a parent or a friend. Do you think the other person might have responded to what he or she *thought* you said rather than what you *really* said? If so, what might you have done to help that person hear you more accurately?
5. As you listen to the next two speeches in your class or the next two lectures in one of your courses, compare two methods of taking notes — your own, and the one suggested in this chapter. Which method works better for you, and why?

Notes

1. Lyman K. Steil, *Your Personal Listening Profile* (New York: Sperry Corp., 1980). This pamphlet is available free by writing to Sperry, Dept 6F, 1290 Avenue of the Americas, New York, N.Y. 10104.

2. *Ibid.*

3. Ralph A. Nichols and Leonard A. Stevens, *Are You Listening?* (New York: McGraw-Hill, 1957), pp. 104–105.

4. Larry L. Barker, Kittie W. Watson, and Robert J. Kibler, "An Investigation of the Effect of Presentations by Effective and Ineffective Speakers on Listening Test Scores," *The Southern Speech Communication Journal* 49:3, Spring 1984, pp. 309–318.

5. Michael J. Beatty and Steven K. Payne, "Listening Comprehension as a Function of Cognitive Complexity: A Research Note," *Communication Monographs* 51:1, March 1984, pp. 85–89. A large body of experimental research suggests that numerous other factors, such as our experience, expectations, and attitudes, affect how well we listen or observe. Two classic studies on this topic are A. H. Hastorf and H. Cantril, "They Saw a Game: A Case Study," *Journal of Abnormal and Social Psychology* 49, 1954, pp. 129–134; and G. W. Allport and L. J. Postman, "The Basic Psychology of Rumor," in Eleanor Maccoby, Theodore Newcomb, and Eugene Hartley, eds., *Readings in Social Psychology,* 3d ed. (New York: Holt, Rinehart and Winston, 1958), pp. 54–65.

6. This discussion of communication models and communication as a process is of necessity limited. For an expansion of this topic, see Ronald Adler and George Rodman, *Understanding Human Communication,* 2d ed. (New York: Holt, Rinehart and Winston, 1985), especially Chapter 1.

7. Carl H. Weaver, *Human Listening: Processes and Behavior* (Indianapolis: Bobbs-Merrill, 1972), pp. 144–145.

8. "Evaluative listening" is stressed in this chapter. Listening theorists identify other types, including discriminative, appreciative, and empathic listening. See, for example, Florence I. Wolff, Nadine C. Marsnik, William S. Tacey, and Ralph G. Nichols, *Perceptive Listening* (New York: Holt, Rinehart and Winston, 1983). See especially Chapter 3, "The Kinds of Listening We Do."

9. Carl R. Rogers, *On Becoming a Person* (Boston: Houghton Mifflin, 1971), pp. 331–337.

10. Ample research evidence indicates that the strength of an audience's attitude toward the topic, as well as their initial attitude toward the speaker, will encourage them to evaluate a message before they hear all of it. For example, see S. Asch, "The Doctrine of Suggestion, Prestige, and Imitation in Social Psychology," *Psychological Review* 55, 1948, pp. 250–276. Similar studies are reported in C. Sherif, M. Sherif, and R. Nebergall, *Attitude and Attitude Change: The Social Judgment-Involvement Approach* (Philadelphia: Saunders, 1965).

11. William French Smith, "Combating Organized Crime," *Vital Speeches of the Day,* February 1, 1984, p. 230.

12. Author's notes on a speech by Elizabeth McEvoy, a student in a public speaking class at the University of New Hampshire.

13. The quotation referred to here was: "The equestrian art, perhaps more than any other, is closely related to the wisdom of life. Many of the same principles may be applied as a line of conduct to follow. The horse teaches us self-control, constancy, and the ability to understand what goes on in the mind and feelings of another creature, qualities that are important throughout our lives." The quotation comes from Alois Podhajsky, *The Complete Training of Horse and Rider* (Garden City, N.Y.: Doubleday, 1967).

14. The answer was yes.

15. The answer was also yes.

16. Nichols and Stevens, *op. cit.*, p. 113.

17. Research suggests that a kind of "inner speech" occurs constantly. The goal is to make it contribute to the listening process. See John R. Johnson, "The Role of Inner Speech in Human Communication," *Communication Education* 33:3, July 1984, pp. 211–222.

18. Wolff et al., *op. cit.* See especially Chapter 7, "Thought Speed Can Mean Added Listening Power."

19. Theorists dealing with the concept of communication ethics point out that ethical behavior is not just the speaker's responsibility. See Kenneth E. Anderson, "Communication Ethics: The Non-Participant's Role," *The Southern Speech Communication Journal* 49:3, Spring 1984, p. 219.

20. Nichols and Stevens, *op. cit.*, p. 42.

21. *Ibid.*, p. 36.

22. *Ibid.*, p. 42.

23. Aristotle, *The Rhetoric,* translated by W. Rhys Roberts (New York: Modern Library, 1954), p. 1355b.

24. See, for example, Bower Aly and Lucile Folse Aly, *A Rhetoric of Public Speaking* (New York: McGraw-Hill, 1973), p. 2.

25. Peter Dixon, *Rhetoric: The Critical Idiom* (London: Methuen, 1971). See especially the first chapter, "Introduction: Some Modern Instances."

26. For an analysis of one way rhetorical criticism can be applied to contemporary political oratory, see P. J. O'Rourke, "Oh, Shut Up: A Measured Assessment of This Year's Campaign Rhetoric," *The New Republic,* May 28, 1984, pp. 20–23.

27. John F. Wilson and Carroll C. Arnold, *Public Speaking as a Liberal Art,* 4th ed. (Boston: Allyn & Bacon, 1978), p. 390.

28. Otis M. Walter, *Speaking Intelligently* (New York: Macmillan, 1976), pp. 202–203. Those who would accept Walter's advice to study demagoguery might want to read Hitler's ideas on effective speechmaking, which appear in *Mein Kampf,* translated by Ralph Manheim (Boston: Houghton Mifflin, 1943). The appropriate chapter is reprinted in Haig A. Bosmajian's *Readings in Speech* (New York: Harper & Row, 1965).

29. John F. Wilson and Carroll C. Arnold, *op. cit.*, pp. 330–333.

PART TWO

The Basics of Message Preparation

3

Focus: Choosing and Developing a Topic

Focus: An Introduction

The first problem a student faces in a speech assignment is focusing on a speech topic. *Focus* is an important term here. It means "to concentrate on one thing." The biggest problem for most of us is that we do not look at topic selection as a process of focus. We speak of "finding a topic," as though the world were a barren landscape of limited topics that were carefully hidden. In fact, the world is a writhing confusion of limitless topics, and our problem is simply to focus on one of them.[1]

The process of *developing* your topic involves expanding it, giving it depth, making it interesting, and making sure that it carries out your purpose. There are limitless ways to develop a topic. Developing, too, is a focusing process.

Ways to Generate Ideas

Focus requires thinking, creativity, and analysis, three processes that are essential throughout the speechmaking process.

42

Thinking

The British novelist W. Somerset Maugham once observed that it is important to have lots of ideas so you can throw the unimportant ones away.[2] This process of throwing away unimportant ideas is especially helpful today. Modern people are inundated with more messages than ever before. The electronic revolution has made every one of us a potential publisher or broadcaster, while our highly depersonalized and mobile society has increased our need to communicate. In our rush to express ideas, we sometimes do not wait for the good ones.

"Waiting for good ideas" is also known as thinking. One reason thinking tends to be difficult is that it is sometimes frowned upon in our society. It is also thought of as painful. Try an experiment to see for yourself. Just sit down anywhere and think. Concentrate. Wrinkle up your forehead to increase the intensity of your concentration. See how long it takes for someone to walk up and ask, "What's wrong?"

Thinking is definitely a skill that can be learned. There are even popular courses on the topic.[3] One useful approach is John Dewey's classic paradigm of "reflective thinking."[4] According to Dewey, the process of thinking is divided into five steps, and every time we think we actually go through all five steps, even if we do not realize it. Here is the way Dewey's five steps might work in your topic-selection process:

1. Defining the Problem. First, you recognize and clarify the problem. In this case, you have been assigned a speech. You need to come up with a topic. Where are you to begin?

2. Analyzing the Problem. You have just two sources for potential topics: things you know about and things that you can find out about. To analyze what you know, think about the things you like to do, the things you like to read about (actually go to your bookshelf and look at its contents objectively), the things you like to talk about, and the things you like to daydream about. To analyze the things you would like to find out about, go to the library and leaf through *The Reader's Guide to Periodical Literature* or any other reference work and see what attracts your attention.

3. Proposing Solutions. Make a list of possible topics based on your analysis. For example, one student might draw up this list based on personal knowledge and interests:

First Aid for Household Accidents
Training Animals As Actors
Violence in Sports
National Parks
Active U.S. Volcanoes

Special-Effects Photography
Subliminal Advertising
3-D Television

That same student might make another list based on leafing through *The Reader's Guide.* Here is a sample list from one page of that reference work:

Acid Rain
Adoption Controversies
Adultery
Agent Orange
AIDS
Air Pollution
Air Traffic Safety

A similar list could be generated from a perusal of your daily newspaper or your favorite magazine. Here is a partial list from one issue of *The New York Times:*

Child Abuse
Separation of Church and State
The Space Shuttle
Immigration Reform
Nuclear Disarmament
Asylum for Refugees
Foreign Aid
How to Fight Forest Fires
Killer Jellyfish
Discrimination Against Homosexuals
Asbestos Danger in Schools
Health Preparation for Foreign Travel
Police Corruption
International Terrorism
Nuclear Waste Disposal
Labor Relations
Pro Sports Salary Escalation
How Winning a Lottery Changes Your Life

4. Testing Solutions Against Criteria. Criteria are standards for judging something. In this stage of the thinking process, you ask yourself certain questions about the proposed solutions. The criteria for your speech topic include:

Is the topic interesting to you?
Would it interest your audience?
Does it conform to the assignment?

Is it broad enough, so it is not trivial?
Is it limited enough to explore in depth?

5. Selecting the Final Solution. Out of the possibilities that pass the test of your criteria, choose the best one. But do not agonize trying to choose between the last two possibilities. As experts have pointed out:

> A consistent difference between good and poor college speakers is that the good speakers choose subjects carefully but swiftly and stick to them.[5]

Dewey's paradigm gives us one perspective from which to view the topic-selection and -development process. Another perspective is provided by taking a good look at the process of creativity.

Creativity

Creativity is a popular topic these days. We have best-selling books and franchised training programs on creative management, creative marriage, creative divorce, and even creative dying. In public speaking, creativity is important because it allows both you and your audience to perceive the speech as "new"; therefore, you will be more enthusiastic in giving it and the audience will be more enthusiastic in listening to it.

There are different types of creativity. One type enables you to use available resources to get a job done. Some people are so well endowed with this type of creativity that they can repair practically anything with a can opener and a rock. It is this type of creativity that enables speakers to find a speech topic in their own interests and experiences. Students often experience a creative block in this area. They often fail to see how many facets of their own lives are potentially interesting to their classmates. Every speech teacher has a favorite story about students who come in insisting that they cannot think of a speech topic. When the teacher offers to discuss the problem with them, these students explain that they have no time because they have to get ready for a karate tournament, or they have to go work at a local clinic for autistic children, or they have to go feed a pet ostrich.

Another type of creativity is the discovery of some new relationship between two or more things you already know. If you have recognized a similarity between a child's situation with an abusive parent and a spouse's situation with an abusive mate, you might come up with the topic, "Children should be allowed to divorce their parents." This type of creativity enables you to "brainstorm" and free-associate for new topic ideas. For example, you could make random lists under the headings "People, Places, and Things." Your lists might look like these:

People
President Reagan
Mother Teresa

Babe Ruth
Robert DeNiro
Billy Joel

Places
Los Angeles
China
England
Miami, Florida
New York City

Things
race cars
handguns
nuclear weapons
swimsuits
evening gowns

Any of the items on these lists might be the inspiration for a speech topic. To free-associate, you take any word from any one of those lists and write down whatever word it brings to mind, and then you write down whatever word *that* word brings to mind, and so on. For example, "baseball" might remind you of "springtime," which reminds you of "beer parties," which reminds you of "alcohol problems," "alcoholism," "Alcoholics Anonymous," and so on. Once again, you have generated a list of potential speech topics.

Another type of creativity is the discovery of order in something that appears to be chaotic. This is the type of creativity that Jacob Bronowski, the brilliant poet, scientist, and philosopher, best appreciated:

> Nature is chaos. It is full of infinite variety, and whether you are Leonardo da Vinci or whether you are Isaac Newton or whether you are modestly sitting down thinking about acts of revolt, there comes a moment when many different aspects suddenly crystallize in a single unity. You have found the key; you have found the clue; you have found the path which organizes the material. You have found what Coleridge called "unity in variety." That is the moment of creation.[6]

This is the type of creativity you will experience when your speech finally "comes together." It is also the type of creativity that enables you to organize your speech, something we will have more to say about in Chapter 7.

Obviously, creativity is important in public speaking; but can creativity be learned? Most theorists agree that it can at least be encouraged. It is a natural ability that would be far more prevalent were it not often suppressed (after all, "creative types" are, by definition, a little out of step with the rest of society). The best way to encourage creativity is to recognize it as a process with various phases, and then allow enough time and energy for each of those phases to work.

Most theorists agree that creativity has four phases: *preparation, incubation, illumination, and verification.*[7] An examination of these phases gives us an idea of how they relate to topic selection and development.

1. Preparation. Most experts agree that creativity does not "just happen"; it begins with a period of preparation in which a problem is formulated, its components are defined, and various solutions are considered. The preparation stage is primarily a time of thought and research. In speech preparation, this stage is the time you spend thinking about and investigating your topic. The preparation stage is often slighted by college students because they put things off until the last minute. The result is almost always a noncreative speech.

2. Incubation. The next phase of the creative process is a period of getting away from the problem. You step away from the task at hand and allow your subconscious mind to work on it.[8] In speech preparation, the incubation stage is a short vacation from your work on the speech. This "vacation" might entail putting your notes aside for a day or so, or it might entail a short break, such as going off to a movie or for a cup of coffee. No matter how brief, this vacation will not be possible if you wait until the last minute to prepare your speech. The time set aside for incubation is important because it leads to illumination, the next phase of creativity.

3. Illumination. The next phase of the creative process is often referred to as the "Eureka!" phase. (*Eureka* is Greek for "I have found it.") It is a moment of sudden, concise, and certain insight into the problem. The literature is replete with stories of creative people who experience illumination at unpredictable — sometimes embarrassing — times. Legend has it that in ancient Greece the mathematician Archimedes was in the bathtub when he came upon the method for determining the volume of irregularly shaped solids by measuring the liquid they displace. He had been working on this problem for months with no success, so when the answer came to him he got up and ran naked through the streets shouting, "Eureka!" It is hoped that you will experience the same type of excitement (with less exposure) in the illumination you experience during speech preparation. It might happen when you hit upon the perfect topic, or a special approach to that topic, or an organizational scheme that makes your speech "work." It is also hoped that you will verify your insight before you announce it to the world. That is what the final stage of creativity is all about.

4. Verification. In the fourth phase your insight is validated and you find out whether your "Eureka!" is worth its capital "E" and exclamation point. People who have flashes of inspiration in the middle of the night often write down what they consider to be great ideas at 4:00 A.M., only to be baffled by the meaninglessness of their notes in the more critical light of day.

Verification is accomplished by taking a second look at your insight. Sometimes just reexamining an insight by yourself will do the trick. At other times, you might need to see what someone else thinks about it. It might mean taking your idea for a topic to your instructor or one or two of your classmates and seeing what they think of it.

These phases of creativity suggest that you can — in fact you must — *work* at creativity. One of the things we know about the working habits of most famous playwrights, painters, composers, and other creative people is that they set aside time to work, whether they feel creative or not. Creativity is a habitual way of thinking that must be learned, and the surprising thing is that once you learn it, you can often be creative *without* knowing it. You can experience creativity, in other words, without the "flash."

Thinking and creativity are essential in all stages of speech preparation. *Analysis,* on the other hand, while useful in topic selection, is most useful in topic development.

Analysis

Analysis is the process of taking something apart and systematically looking at each part to understand the whole. That sounds simple, but analysis might be more difficult today than ever before. For one thing, there is an unprecedented amount of information floating around for us to wade through. For another, we have a tendency to watch too much television.

"Now what," you might well ask, "does television have to do with our ability to analyze?" Marshall McLuhan would be glad you asked that question, because he was one of the first to equate the advent of television with a decline in analytical thinking.[9] McLuhan suggested that the TV generation (a group consisting of nearly everyone under the age of 40) has lost its ability to analyze. The print generation that came before them thought analytically; when they had a problem before them they broke it up into simpler parts and examined each one of those parts. Today, McLuhan contends, because of our constant use of media that give us "everything at once," people attempt to look at things and understand them immediately, without taking the time to take them apart.

Robert Pirsig, in his book *Zen and the Art of Motorcycle Maintenance,*[10] agrees with McLuhan. He suggests that people are intimidated by technology because they no longer break up complex things into basic components. If they cannot start a Honda by kicking it, yelling at it, or just staring sullenly at it, they give up. They do not sit down to *analyze* what might be wrong with it.

If McLuhan and Pirsig are right, modern people have to work a little harder at analysis than their grandparents did; but analysis is still worth the extra effort when it comes to speech preparation. Sometimes a speech topic can be selected on the basis of analysis. In looking for a topic that your classmates might find entertaining, you might analyze a typical day in the life of a student. Taking the day apart, you might find that it basically consists of breakfast, classes, lunch, classes, dinner, social functions, and sleep. That breakdown gives you a few topics right away. You might realize that students often get too little sleep and find it challenging to stay awake in some of their classes. That might bring you to the idea of "sleeping problems and how to solve them." You could develop this topic through analysis by taking it apart according to types of sleep problems:

Trouble getting to sleep
Trouble waking up
Quality or depth of sleep

You could analyze one particular sleeping problem and come up with a unique set of "methods of falling asleep in class":

   I.   The Tijuana Quick-Dip, in which the head dips forward and the sleeper is awakened just before hitting the desk top.
  II.   The Rochester Roundabout, in which the head tips backward, rolls to the side, and wakes the sleeper up with a whiplash effect.
 III.   The Prop Failure, in which the head slides off the fist that is propping it up, and the sleeper is awakened as he or she receives that fist in the ear.

Thinking, creativity, and analysis will underlie all the phases of speech preparation. The first place to put them to use is in determining your purpose.

Determining Your Purpose

The English statesman and author Benjamin Disraeli once said, "The secret of success is constancy of purpose." He knew what he was talking about. The best way to achieve a goal — any goal — is to remain focused on what you want to achieve. This maxim is especially true in all forms of human communication. No one gives a speech, or expresses any kind of message, without a reason. Purpose is easy to see in messages that ask for something: "Pass the salt" or "How about a movie this Friday?" or "Excuse me, that's my foot you're standing on." But even in more subtle messages the speaker always has a purpose, which is to evoke a response from the listener.

Sometimes purposes are misunderstood or confused by the speaker. This problem wastes time both in the selection and development of the topic, and if it is not straightened out, the final speech will probably just confuse the audience.

The first step in understanding your purpose is to formulate a clear and precise statement of that purpose. You must focus on both the *general purpose* and the *specific purpose.*

General Purpose

Most students, when asked *why* they are giving a speech in a college class, quickly cite course requirements. After all, in a speech class your general purpose is usually assigned; it will ordinarily be to make a "speech to inform" or a "persuasive speech." It is still necessary to *understand* your assigned purpose to give an effective speech.

If your motive for speaking is to learn effective speech techniques, your main concern should be influencing your audience. That is what effective speaking is all about. The idea of influencing your audience involves *changing* them in some way. All the possible ways you could change an audience boil down to three options, which happen to be the three basic *general purposes* for speaking:

1. *To entertain:* To relax your audience by providing them with a pleasant listening experience.
2. *To inform:* To enlighten your audience by teaching them something.
3. *To persuade:* To move your audience toward a new attitude or behavior.

A brief scrutiny of these purposes will reveal that no speech could ever have only one purpose. These purposes are interrelated because a speech designed for one purpose will almost always accomplish a little of the others; even a speech designed purely to entertain might change audience attitudes or teach something new. In fact, these purposes are *cumulative* in the sense that to inform an audience you have to provide them with "a pleasant listening experience" at least long enough to get their attention, and to persuade them you have to inform them about arguments and evidence.

Deciding your general purpose is like choosing the "right" answer on one of those multiple-choice test items in which all the answers are right to a certain degree, but one answer is more right than the others. Therefore we say that any speech is *primarily* designed for one of these purposes. A clear understanding of your general purpose gets you on the right track for choosing and developing a topic. Understanding your *specific* purpose will keep you on that track.

Specific Purpose

Whereas your general purpose is only a one-word label, your specific goal is expressed in the form of a *purpose statement,* which is a complete sentence that tells exactly what you want your speech to accomplish. The purpose statement usually is not used word for word in the actual speech. Its purpose is to keep you focused as a speaker.

There are three criteria for a good purpose statement:

1. A Purpose Statement Should Be Audience-Oriented. As we mentioned earlier, all communication seeks some response from a receiver. This receiver response should be the focal point of your purpose statement. For example, if you were giving an informative talk on gourmet cooking, this purpose statement would be inadequate:

> My purpose is to tell my audience about gourmet cooking.

As that statement is worded, your purpose is "to tell" an audience something, which means that the speech could be successful even if no one listens. Your purpose statement should refer to the response you want from your audience: it should tell what the audience members will know or be able to do after listening to your speech. The purpose statement above could be improved this way:

> After listening to my speech, my audience will know more about gourmet cooking.

That is an improvement because now you have stated what you expect from your audience. You could improve it more through the judicious application of a second criterion:

2. A Purpose Statement Should Be Precise. A clearly worded purpose statement will stick to one, and only one, specific idea. The following purpose statement contains two ideas, and therefore distorts the true purpose of the speech:

> After listening to my speech, my audience will know how to cook *coq au vin* and appreciate fine food.

To be precise a purpose statement should also be worded with enough detail so that you would be able to measure or test your audience, after your speech, to see whether you achieved your purpose. In the example given earlier, simply "knowing about gourmet cooking" is too vague; you need something more specific, such as:

> After listening to my speech, my audience will be able to cook *coq au vin* at home.

At least now you have limited your purpose to a single dish, rather than the entire world of gourmet cooking. This version is an improvement, but it can be made still better by applying a third criterion:

3. A Purpose Statement Should Be Attainable. You must be able to accomplish your purpose as stated. Some speakers insist on formulating purpose statements such as "My purpose is to convince my audience to make governmental budget deficits illegal." Unfortunately, unless your audience happens to be a joint session of Congress, it will not have the power to change United States fiscal policy; but any audience can write their congressional representative or sign a petition. Similarly, an audience will not "learn how to play championship tennis" or "understand the dangers of business regulation" in one sitting. You must aim for an audience response that is possible to accomplish. In your gourmet cooking speech, it would be impossible for you to be sure that each of your audience members will actually be able to cook a meal. You might have no idea, for example, whether they all have access to a kitchen. So a better purpose statement for this speech might sound something like this:

> After listening to my speech my audience will be able to list the five steps for preparing *coq au vin* at home.

The following purpose statements would be less than effective:

> To tell my audience about day care centers. (not audience-oriented)

> After listening to my speech, my audience will understand solar power. (not attainable)

> After listening to my speech, my audience will know about drunken boating. (not specific)

The following purpose statements would be more effective:

> After listening to my speech, my audience will be able to identify the three basic types of day care centers.

> After listening to my speech, my audience will understand how solar power can be used at home, in business, and in government. (This type of purpose statement can be particularly effective because it shows you what your main points will be.)

> After listening to my speech, my audience members will not operate a boat after having had more than two drinks.

The Thesis Statement

So far we have discussed how to select a topic, how partially to focus that topic through its general purpose, and how to focus it further through its specific purpose. Your next step in the focusing process is to formulate your thesis statement. The thesis statement tells you what the central idea of your speech is. It tells you the one idea that you want your audience to remember after they have forgotten everything else you had to say. The thesis statement for your *coq au vin* speech might be worded like this:

> Cooking *coq au vin* is a simple, five-step process that can start you on the road to gourmet cooking.

Unlike your purpose statement, your thesis statement is often spoken directly to your audience. The thesis statement contains more information than the purpose statement, and it is usually formulated later in the speechmaking process, after you have done some research on your topic. The progression from topic to central idea is therefore another focusing process, as you can see in the following examples:

Topic: Why Must an Injured Horse Be Destroyed?

General Purpose: To inform

Specific Purpose: After listening to my speech, my audience will understand why certain types of equine injuries cannot be healed.

Thesis Statement: If a horse cannot get back on its feet within 48 hours, its digestive and respiratory systems stop functioning, and the horse suffers a slow, agonizing, certain death.

In this example, you might have chosen the topic because it was interesting to you and your audience, and it fit the assignment of "an informative speech." When you picked the topic you might not have known the answer to why injured horses have to be destroyed. You found out why after a considerable amount of research, but once you had your central idea your speech became fully focused.

Topic: The Bottle Bill

General Purpose: To persuade

Specific Purpose: After listening to my speech, at least half my audience members will sign my petition to the governor supporting a state bottle bill.

Thesis Statement: Returnable-container laws reduce litter, create new employment, and save resources.

Once again, this thesis statement evolved after research. This thesis statement is particularly useful, because it reveals the three main points of the speech. Another example:

Topic: Saving Water

General Purpose: To persuade

Specific Purpose: After listening to my speech, audience members will use less water in their daily activities.

Thesis Statement: Saving water is a relatively simple process that we should all start doing *now*.

A Focus Model

Progressively defining topic, purpose, and central idea is one form of focus. Figure 3–1 is a model that represents another kind of focus during topic selection and development. The model points out a similarity be-

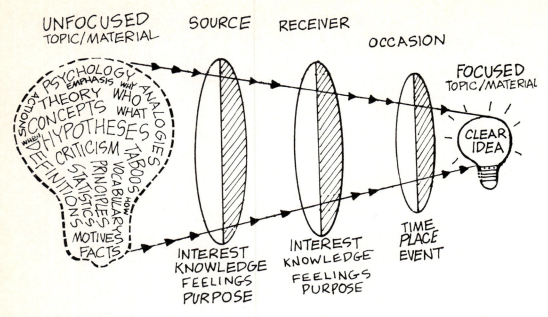

Figure 3–1   Focus Model

tween optical focus and the focusing of your topic. Focusing a topic is like lining up three lenses in such a way that they produce a precise image. In order to focus on an effective topic, you have to align all three lenses simultaneously. The lenses of the focus model include the source of the message (you), the receiver of the message (your audience), and the occasion for which the message is presented.

The model illustrates a procedure for focusing topics and material: View them through the lenses of yourself, your audience, and the occasion. Just focusing from *your* perspective is not enough, but it is a start.

The Source's Perspective

"Above all else," Polonius urged Hamlet, "to thine own self be true." This advice is good to follow in speech preparation. Do not become so involved in finding a "correct" topic or material that you lose yourself. To focus topics or material from the source perspective you have to examine not only your purpose (as discussed above) but also your own feelings, interests, and knowledge.

Your Feelings.   After your purpose has been clarified, examine your feelings about yourself in the specific speaking situation. Your perception of yourself as a speaker will influence you along every step of the speech preparation process. If you have a negative self-image, or if you feel negative about the topic, those feelings will show through in the final product. You will be just a little "off" in terms of the topic you have selected, the information you have gathered, the way you present that information, and every other aspect of your speech. Therefore it is important to look at yourself objectively and to choose a purpose, topic, and material about which you can feel confident and enthusiastic. If you really do not care for gourmet cooking, then that is not an appropriate topic for you as a speaker—no matter how potentially interesting that topic is to your audience.

Your Interests. Until you become famous, a public speaking class will probably be the only place where you are asked simply to "give a speech." In the outside world, topics are usually chosen by whoever asks you to speak. If you are an expert on auto racing, you are asked to talk about auto racing, and so on. In a speech class you are usually called upon to talk without being given a topic. When that happens, it helps to give some thought to your own interests.

Your topic must be one that you are interested in; otherwise, it will be difficult for you to interest anyone else. Your interest in your topic will improve your ability to investigate it. It will also increase your confidence when it comes time to present it.

The same is true for all the material you use in a speech. If it is not interesting to you, it will be difficult to make it interesting to your audience.

Your Knowledge. You will want to choose a topic you already know something about, even though you will have to bolster your own knowledge with new research. However, the main problem for most people is not "knowing something" but knowing *what* they know. Recognizing what you know requires a certain amount of confidence. It is a mistake to think you do not know anything that your audience does not already know. That stance would not only be self-defeating; it would almost certainly be untrue. Your experiences, your thinking, and your investigation will all be unique.

There is also the other side of the coin. Sometimes people think they know things that they do not. Worse yet, sometimes they stand in awe of that which they do not understand. This attitude can cause problems when choosing material for a speech. The temptation to use material that is impressive because of its complexity can be overpowering. By using it, the speaker tries to borrow the intellectual prowess of the source of information. You can avoid this trap by using only ideas, thoughts, and information you understand completely. Carefully collected scientific data you do not understand are much less valuable than ideas you can put into your own words and present from your own perspective. Ideas you have collected from other people must be totally within your control when you use them. You have to leave out those parts that sound good but that you do not understand. If you are interested in archaeology, a college audience will probably be more interested in your personal experience at an excavation site than in a highly specialized, esoteric theory about an ancient Mayan culture—especially if you do not completely understand the theory yourself!

The Receiver's Perspective

In order to analyze topics or material in terms of the receiver of the message, you have to analyze the purpose, feelings, interests, and knowledge of your audience, also. Audience analysis and adaptation is so important in speechmaking that we are going to devote the entire next chapter of this book to it. Suffice it to say here that you should line up your audience analysis with your self-analysis as you focus on a topic.

The Perspective of Occasion

The "occasion" of a speech is determined by the circumstances surrounding it. Three of the most important components of an occasion are *time, place,* and *event.*

Time

The time available for your speech is an essential consideration. You should choose a topic broad enough to be worthwhile but brief enough to fit your time limits. "Sex," for example, might be an inherently interesting topic to a college audience, but it would be difficult to cover the whole topic in a ten-minute speech and still say anything significant. A topic like "How Sexual Stereotypes Are Established Through Television Advertising" conceivably could be covered in enough depth in ten minutes to make it worthwhile. All speeches have time limitations, whether they are explicitly stated or not. If you are invited somewhere to say a few words, and you present a few volumes, you will not be invited back.

Consider time when you focus your material, also. Any idea that takes too long to make clear will have to be dropped, as well as any examples or statistics that take too long to explain fully. If you have too many ideas, you will have to drop all except the ones you have time to develop fully.

Place

Your speech also occupies a physical space. The beauty or squalor of your surroundings and the noise or stuffiness of the room should all be taken into consideration. You can refer to these physical surroundings in your speech if it is appropriate. If you were talking about world poverty, for example, you could compare your surroundings to those that might be found in a poorer country.

Place also affects your choice of a visual aid—a small chart is difficult to see from the back of a lecture hall and so is a pet spider. Where you

Walter Mondale, 1984 Democratic Presidential candidate, adapts to the specific occasion of a speech by taking some last-minute notes.

speak also affects the formality of your work and how hard you have to work to contact the entire audience.

Event

Your speech is an event. It occupies a space in time that is surrounded by other events. For example, the "event" of a speech given in a public speaking class is usually a laboratory experience, before peers, followed by a critical evaluation in which the speakers are expected to learn from experience. This event might call for a learning orientation, a degree of seriousness, and a certain level of thought. The learning orientation could mean that your topic and material will be most effective if it teaches something to the class. To do this, you might want to relate your topic directly to a theory[11] or a set of principles. For example, if you were soliciting contributions to have your cat neutered, you would not want to talk simply about how warm and cuddly your pet is, or how adorably it purrs right before it claws its way up your leg. It would be more appropriate to explain the beneficial relationship humans and cats have enjoyed through the ages (for example, rat control) or the dangers of uncontrolled overpopulation of domestic animals. The seriousness of the occasion might call for material that is well substantiated, and the appropriate level of thought would be one that is challenging enough for college students. If you were speaking at a sports banquet or before a social club, the event would be different, and material that is less serious or challenging might be used.

Sample Speech

The sample speech for this chapter was given by Bobbye Perrin, a student at Central Michigan University. Bobbye's choice of topic demonstrates how an idea that is right in front of us—and never far from anyone's consciousness—can be the topic for an original, creative speech. Her analysis of this topic is informative as well as entertaining.

Bobbye's general purpose for this speech was "to inform." Her specific purpose could be stated as follows:

> After listening to my speech, my audience members will understand the physical reality of sexual chemistry.

Her thesis statement:

> "Sexual chemistry" is a biological fact; understanding it can enhance all our interactions with others.

Bobbye won first place in expository speaking in the 1984 National Forensics Association National Tournament with this speech. Notice how she maintains her focus throughout the speech.

Sexual Chemistry

Bobbye Perrin
Central Michigan University

1 In the autumn of 1954, my mother suffered a severe physical affliction. An affliction that would change her life forever. She was in college at the time and one day her adrenal glands began secreting excessive amounts of unknown substances into her bloodstream. Her pulse rate increased incredibly, her blood pressure soared, and she began talking senselessly. What happened to my mother has the power to affect everyone in this room, and oddly enough, we'd probably welcome its unsettling effects. On that day my mother met my father, and it was "love at first sight." This phenomenon is

something which scientific researchers and research psychologists have labeled "sexual chemistry." In all its strength, sexual chemistry is an internal, emotional sensation that has biological symptoms. For some of us, sexual chemistry may be one of the most pivotal experiences of our lives. For others, social psychologists believe it will enhance our interpersonal dynamics by drawing connections to their physical origins. In any case, it warrants a closer look at its biological factors, physical components, and how chemistry of the sexual kind can work for us.

2   Research psychologists in the United States and Germany have developed a sound biological background for the phenomenon of sexual chemistry. When we meet someone who interests us intensely, there is a moment of understanding. With that, our sympathetic nervous system begins to secrete hormones into our nerve endings and adrenal glands. In our nerve endings, there are more than thirty neurotransmitters that carry impulses to the brain. Two of these neurotransmitters, norepinephrine and dopamine, are responsible for what we feel when we experience "love at first sight": our breath quickens, pulses race, there's an overwhelming compulsion to speak . . . we feel happy and excited, according to Dr. Michael Liebowitz, assistant professor of psychiatry at Columbia University. All these neurotransmitters connect to the limbic system in the brain — our body's pleasure system. Dr. José Delgado, a neurophysicist at Yale University, has done much research on the limbic system by using rhesus monkeys. He concludes that a tiny electrical charge sent through the skull of a rhesus monkey is enough to make the monkey give up food and water for his continued pleasure. I say, "Why let the monkeys have all the fun, let's get in touch with our limbic systems!" Our two neurotransmitters, norepinephrine and dopamine, further act as triggering agents to a naturally occurring, amphetamine-like substance in the brain. It is this elusive substance that makes sexual chemistry so special. It is the moment of awakening within our transmitters that stimulates our nervous system even further. That intensified feeling is sexual chemistry. We are then tuned-in and turned-on in a truly chemical sense of the phrase. Sexual chemistry is not limited to possible sexual relationships only. It forms a special type of friendship. It crosses every boundary of gender, wealth, and origin. But it must be mutual. If only one person feels the attraction, there is no chemistry. However, it can lie dormant in a person, and under the right conditions, suddenly be brought to life, according to Julius Fast, coauthor of the book *Sexual Chemistry*. What sexual chemistry needs, then, is the proper setting: the correct energy, enthusiasm, and strength.

3   Now that we know what happens on the inside for sexual chemistry to take place, let's see what sexual chemistry is composed of on the outside. Well, the eyes have it!, according to Meredith Bernstein, coauthor of *Sexual Chemistry*. It is the instant of recognition, a moment that tells us what we see is good, that arouses sexual chemistry. For every situation, there is a moral looking time. That is, the length of time we can hold someone's eye contact and still be within the bounds of propriety. Violate that time for even a second and a message is sent. In a social setting, the message is usually, "I like

you, I'm interested in you.'' Well naturally, there's more to this than just running around and looking at people. It is important that we become aware of the moral looking time for every situation; if not instinctively, then by learning. A starting point would be having an awareness of the environment in which we're involved. For example, the moral looking time involved in a board meeting of superiors will differ significantly from the moral looking time involved in addressing an audience.

4   The second component of sexual chemistry is an unbeatable smile! After eye contact is made, Fast and Bernstein say, a smile changes the tone of any message previously sent. It's as if we smile and the whole world smiles with us . . . or at least there's a greater chance of it. A smile makes communication official when it's coupled with positive feedback from our viewers. For example, when you nod at me, I know you're listening and that you understand. When we as speakers receive this, although we may not be aware, we feel the other person is sympathetic. Thus, a special bond is established.

5   Lastly, and perhaps most deadly, is the tender touch. In a recent study conducted by researchers to establish just how effective touch was, librarians were asked to touch, or not to touch, the subjects. With only the slightest touch to book-borrowers, the whole functioning system of the library was viewed as a more personal place by those who acquired books. Politicians are also aware of this element during campaign time when they ''press the flesh'' of constituents. Touching can vary in its impact. It can act as a consoling gesture or a deliberate attempt to break down barriers we set up around us. Although it may take time, we can master the components of sexual chemistry.

6   Assuming we have, let's go all the way, well maybe not that far, and see how sexual chemistry can work for us. The advertising aspect of business has always been aware of sexual chemistry to sell a product. Beautiful female models and well-groomed men create just the right rapport with any audience to increase sales. It's in their eyes, their smiles, the overall feeling they generate about the product that stimulates the audience.

7   California salesman Barrie Stein had a record-breaking reputation in sales. When Julius Fast examined his approach, it was realized that he would always touch the arm of the patron, establishing immediate rapport. When we begin to incorporate the components of sexual chemistry into our own lives, the contacts we then experience are heightened to an even greater degree.

8   Sexual chemistry can reflect a positive feeling into our self-images. It's as if we smile and the whole world smiles with us; or at least there's a greater chance. The theory of sexual chemistry says if the image we project can suggest to others a quality or characteristic they see in themselves, or would like to see, the chemical reaction can be readily enhanced by emotional ties: whether it's friendship, respect, or ultimately, love. If we wish to strengthen our self-images, according to Norman Cavoir in a doctoral thesis for West Virginia University, we can imitate the body language of a more self-confi-

dent person. If we do this continually, we will begin to feel more secure and self-confident in ourselves. As this becomes habitual it also becomes easier. So whether it's for business or for pleasure, putting a little chemical fire into our and other people's lives can work to our advantage.

9   Sexual chemistry has the power to stimulate our bodies as well as our minds. Neurotransmitters never lie. Nor do the components of sexual chemistry. The eyes that are the windows to the soul in cooperation with a sweet, simple smile, a nod of approval, and an exciting touch can stimulate new responses. But most important is how all these elements combined can make each human experience fill with the polymers of passion. Sexual chemistry: a chemical explosion and a great feeling!

Summary

This chapter dealt with focus, which is the process of concentrating on one idea that is appropriate to you, your audience, and the occasion of your speech. Focus is essential when choosing a topic, limiting a topic, and choosing material for a speech. Focus requires thinking, creativity, and analysis; therefore it takes time, requires energy, and entails a recognizable process.

Your first step in focusing your speech is to determine your purpose. In a speech class, the general purpose (to inform, to persuade, to entertain) is usually assigned by the instructor. You express the specific purpose in a purpose statement that is audience-oriented, precise, and attainable in your speech situation. Your second step in focusing your speech is to formulate a thesis statement, which is a statement of your central idea, the one idea that you want your audience to remember even if they forget everything else.

This chapter concludes with a model which shows that you should focus topics and material from your own perspective, from your audience's perspective, and according to the occasion.

Questions/Assignments

1. Analyze Bobbye Perrin's "Sexual Chemistry" speech in terms of the focus model. What does the speech tell you about her and about her perceptions of the audience and the occasion?
2. "Do your own thing" is a favorite slogan for some people. Roughly translated, it means do what you do best, or what you are most interested in, or what you most enjoy doing. Using that rough translation, what is *your* thing? How might you develop a speech on "your thing" for a speech class?
3. What, in your opinion, are the three most important interests of the audience in

your public speaking class? In what ways might one or more of your own interests be related to theirs?

4. After you have selected the topic for your next speech, write three specific purpose statements, one for each purpose mentioned in the chapter: inform, persuade, entertain.

5. Select a lengthy news story from a newspaper. Applying the focus model, rewrite the story so that its essence could be presented in a five-minute speech.

Notes

1. For advice on focusing on a topic for *written* communication, see B. F. Skinner, "How to Discover What You Have to Say: A Talk to Students," *Behavior Analyst* 4, September 1981, pp. 1–7.

2. W. Somerset Maugham, *The Summing Up* (Garden City, N.Y.: Doubleday, 1938).

3. One such course is the de Bono Thinking Course. See Edward de Bono and Michael de Saint-Arnaud, *The Learn to Think Coursebook,* 2d ed. (New York: de Bono School of Thinking, 1982). See also Edward de Bono, "Vertical and Lateral Thinking," in William W. Wilmot and John R. Wenburg, *Communication Involvement: Personal Perspectives* (New York: Wiley, 1974), pp. 24–29.

4. John Dewey, *How We Think* (Boston: Heath, 1910). The entire question of how we think—the physiological and psychological processes involved—is highly involved, and theorists are constantly adding to our knowledge in this area. An excellent recent work on this topic is Sir John Eccles and Daniel N. Robinson, *The Wonder of Being Human: Our Brain and Our Mind* (New York: Free Press, 1984).

5. John F. Wilson and Carroll C. Arnold, *Dimensions of Public Communication* (Boston: Allyn & Bacon, 1976), p. 66.

6. Jacob Bronowski, "On Art and Science," in Jack D. Summerfield and Lorlyn Thatcher, eds., *The Creative Mind and Method* (Austin, Tex.: University of Texas Press, 1960).

7. The labeling of these phases is generally attributed to Graham Wallas's classic work, *The Art of Thought* (New York: Harcourt Brace Jovanovich, 1926), pp. 79–95.

8. The role of the subconscious is generally accepted to be important in the creative process. See, for example, Erwin DiCyan, *Creativity: Road to Self-Discovery* (New York: Harcourt Brace Jovanovich, 1978), especially Chapter 15.

9. See, for example, Marshall McLuhan, *Understanding Media: The Extensions of Man* (New York: Signet, 1964).

10. Robert Pirsig, *Zen and the Art of Motorcycle Maintenance* (New York: Morrow, 1974).

11. A theory is a set of statements that seeks to describe, explain, or predict phenomena.

4

Audience Analysis and Adaptation

Audience Analysis and Adaptation: An Introduction

When you choose a gift, it is important to consider the person who will receive it; an ideal present for one person could be a disaster for another. In the same way you need to think about your audience, especially about their interests, when planning a speech. Getting through to a particular audience is what effective speaking is all about. Aristotle recognized this fact when he said, "Of the three elements in speechmaking — speaker, subject, and person addressed — it is the last one, the hearer, that determines the speech's end and object."[1]

Audience adaptation is something that we have a tendency to do naturally. Research suggests, for example, that in everyday conversations what we say to children and the elderly is simpler, more redundant, and less complex than what we say to other adults.[2] The trick to audience adaptation, then, is to take this natural tendency and formalize it, to make it a conscious rather than a subconscious activity.

64

Factors in Audience Analysis

There are several factors to consider in audience analysis, including the degree of willingness, the audience's purpose, and its makeup.

Willingness

There are at least three types of audience you are likely to encounter—"passersby," "captives," and "volunteers." Each type suggests a different degree of willingness.[3]

"Passersby," as the name implies, are people who are not much interested—at least, not in advance—in what you have to say. A crowd milling around the student union or a shopping mall would fit into this category. With this type of audience, your first concern is to make them aware of you as a speaker, either by interesting them in the topic or in you as a speaker. With passersby you might have to pick a really sensational topic or use some device or gimmick to attract attention, such as the loud costumes or wild theatrics on which street speakers often rely.

"Captives" are audience members who have gathered for some reason besides the joy of hearing you speak. Students in a required class often begin as a "captive" audience; so do people at military formations, mandatory work meetings, and other required gatherings. With captives you do not have to worry about devices and gimmicks to make them aware of you as a speaker; you do, however, have to use material that will get them interested and keep them interested in what you have to say. Often captives harbor a special type of hostility, which is caused by their general frustration but which might transfer to you as a speaker. "I hate being here," they seem to be saying, "so just *try* to make me enjoy this speech." You can tap this hostility by showing your audience that you are in the same boat; since you are making the best of the situation, perhaps they could, also.

"Volunteers" are audience members who have gathered together because of a common interest. Students in elective courses, especially courses with long waiting lists, fit into this category; so do members of most clubs, social organizations, and social action groups. Even with an audience of volunteers you have to maintain the listeners' interest; you never lose that responsibility. But when the audience is informed and involved, as volunteers tend to be, you can treat your topic in greater depth without worrying about *losing* their interest.

Most college speech classes are a mixture of captives and volunteers, which means that you do not have to sensationalize your topic or use gimmicks, but you do have to maintain interest and provide depth.

Purpose

Just as you have a purpose for speaking, the audience members have a purpose for gathering. Sometimes virtually all members of your audience will have the same obvious goal. Expectant parents at a natural childbirth class are all seeking a healthy, relatively painless delivery; and people attending an investment seminar are looking for ways to increase their net worth.

There are other times, however, when audience purpose cannot be so easily defined. In some instances, different listeners have different goals, some of which might not be apparent to the speaker. Consider a church congregation, for example. Whereas some members might listen to a sermon with the hope of applying religious principles to their lives, others might be interested in being entertained or in appearing pious. In the same way, the listeners in your speech class probably have a variety of motives for attending; becoming aware of as many of these motives as possible will help you predict what will interest them.

Demographics

Demographics are characteristics of your audience that can be labeled, such as number of people, age, sex, group membership, and so on. In any speech most of these characteristics should affect your planning in some way.[4] Here are some examples:

Number of People. Topic appropriateness varies with the size of an audience. With a small group you can be less formal and more intimate — for example, you can talk more about your own inner feelings and personal experiences. If you gave a speech before five people as impersonally as if they were a standing-room-only crowd in a lecture hall, they would probably find you stuffy. On the other hand, if you talked to 300 people about your unhappy childhood, you would probably make them uncomfortable. Also, the larger your audience, the broader the range of interests and knowledge; with a small audience you can choose material of more specific interest.

Sex. Traditionally, men and women have tended to be interested in different topics. These differences are becoming less pronounced as time goes on because men and women are becoming conscious of sexual stereotypes and are rebelling against them. Still, the differences in interest that prevail are of concern to a speaker in developing a topic. There are still more men than women interested in automotive engineering and more women than men interested in cooking. The guideline here might be: *Do not exclude or offend any portion of your audience on the basis of sex.* Every speech teacher has a horror story about a student getting up in front of a class composed primarily, but not entirely, of men and speaking on a subject such as "picking up chicks." The women in the class, once they realize that the speech is not about methods of handling poultry, are invariably offended. Most of the men will feel the same way.

As with any of these demographic characteristics, the point is to *adapt* your idea (rather than throwing it away) according to who is in your audience. The speaker who wants to speak on how boy meets girl, or vice versa, may still do so; the topic of the speech, however, could be "meeting people." That approach would be appropriate for both men and women. This shift works for topics like "weight lifting" (which can be changed to "body conditioning") and "home economics" (which can be changed to "survival for singles").

Age. In many areas younger people and older people have different interests. Topics such as social security, child rearing, and school success vary in interest with the age of the audience. These differences run relatively deep; Aristotle observed long ago that young people "have strong passions," that "their lives are spent not in memory but in expectation," and that they have high ideals because "they have not been humbled by life or learnt its necessary limitations."[5] Young people have a tendency to be interested in sports cars rather than four-door sedans, fashion rather than durability. Older people, on the other hand, tend to have more practical interests. This fact might make a difference in how you approach a topic. For example, if you were speaking about "The World Food Shortage" to a young audience, the idealism of helping other people might be stressed. With older people, the practical advantages (such as the boost to our own economy that results from international charity) might be stressed. Either way, you have to make a conscious choice based on the best prediction you can make about audience interests.

Group Membership. Organizations to which audience members belong provide more clues to audience interests. By examining the groups to which they belong, you can surmise an audience's political leanings (Young Republicans or Young Democrats), religious beliefs (Christian Youth Organization or Hillel), or occupation (Bartenders Union or Speech Communication Association).

Group membership is often an important consideration in college classes. Consider the difference between "typical" college day classes and "typical" college night classes. At many colleges the evening students are generally older and tend to belong to civic groups, church clubs, and the local chamber of commerce. Daytime students tend to belong to sororities and fraternities, sports clubs, and social action groups.

These four demographic characteristics are important examples, but the list goes on and on. Other demographic characteristics include ethnic background, religion, educational level, economic status, and occupation; demographics that might be important in a college class include home town, year in school, and major subject. In short, any demographic characteristic of the audience that you can identify should be part of your audience analysis.

Collecting Information About Your Audience

There are a number of ways to collect information about your audience. One is personal observation: carefully noticing how your audience dresses, how they behave, what they talk about, and how they seem to spend their time. Another method is simply to interview as many members of the audience as time allows. A third method is to conduct a survey among your audience members — after all, the best way to find out someone's attitudes or interests is to ask. A final method is to go to the library to see what has been written about their community, their school, their extracurricular activities, their clubs, and so on. All of these forms of investigation are covered in detail in Chapter 5.

Information concerning audience type and demographic factors lets you make certain inferences about your audience. The first of these inferences will concern the audience's attitudes, beliefs, and values.

Working Around Attitudes, Beliefs, and Values

Structured in human consciousness like layers of an onion are people's attitudes, beliefs, and values. They are all closely interrelated, but attitudes lie closest to the surface, whereas beliefs and values underlie them. An *attitude* is a predisposition to respond to something in a favorable or unfavorable way. A *belief* is an underlying conviction about the truth of something, which is sometimes based on cultural or religious training. A *value* is a deeply rooted belief about a concept's inherent worth or worthiness. An audience might hold the value that "Freedom is a good thing," for example, which will be expressed in a belief such as "People should be free to choose their political leaders," which in turn will lead to the attitude that "Voting is an important right and responsibility for all citizens." This attitude, in short, leads to a predisposition to vote — in other words, a positive attitude toward voting.

A recent Gallup Poll, conducted nationwide, found that "having a good family life" was the most important social value in the United States. After that came "good physical health," "having a good self-image or self-respect," "personal satisfaction or happiness," and "freedom of choice to do what I want." The same poll found that minority members who have fewer material possessions tend to value material possessions more, and that older people gave a higher rating to "following a strict moral code" than younger people.[6]

You can often make an inference about audience attitudes by recognizing beliefs and values the audience members are likely to hold. For example, a group of religious fundamentalists might hold the value of "obeying God's word." This might lead to the belief—based on their interpretation of the Bible—that women are not meant to perform the same functions in society as men. This belief in turn might lead to the attitude that the Equal Rights Amendment should not be supported.

You can also draw an inference about one attitude your audience members hold from your knowledge of other attitudes they hold. If your audience is made up of undergraduates who have a positive attitude toward sexual liberation, it is a good bet they also have a positive attitude toward civil rights and ecology. If they have a negative attitude toward collegiate sports, they probably also have a negative attitude toward fraternities and sororities. These connections should suggest not only some appropriate topics for each audience, but also ways that those topics could be developed.

For example, a professor who schedules a lecture on obscenity for both daytime and evening classes may have to prepare two separate versions. The daytime students tend to be more forgiving of the use of obscenity than the older evening group. According to the value system of the older group, a person who uses obscene language is untrustworthy. With this group, the professor would have to speak carefully. (Just try to lecture on obscenity without using any.) The lecture would have to work with a system of attitudes that make the evening class more practical and conservative than the younger daytime class.

Such situations make attitudes, beliefs, and values an integral part of audience analysis.

Tapping Your Audience's Needs

Material to capture audience interest is traditionally used in the introduction of a speech, but you would do well to heed this advice:

> The introduction is the first point at which you can try to capture the attention and interest of the listeners, but you do not "capture" it in the sense that it can be securely caged and then left alone. Instead, you will have to use devices to gain attention at the outset of the message and devices to maintain it throughout.[7]

Audience interest is such a fundamental aspect of message planning that we approach it from many angles throughout this book. Chapter 6, on organization and structure, will discuss several devices that are designed to make a speech introduction interesting. The chapter on language will recommend types of language that can maintain audience interest. The chapter on delivery (Chapter 8) makes repeated reference to variety and the speaker's involvement in the message, which also come highly recommended as attention-getting devices. Supporting material, which will be discussed in Chapter 7, and humorous devices, which are covered in Chapter 12, also can hold your audience.

Our concern here is adapting attention-getting devices to a particular audience. Our point of departure is to look at audience *needs.* Relating to audience needs is far more effective than screaming, firing a gun, or blowing a whistle — and far less distracting than any of those ploys. Once the relationship between your audience and your topic is made clear, that audience should be motivated to listen.

The more you know about your audience, the more specific you can be about relating to their needs. If a large percentage of a college audience is graduating soon, they need to hear about future directions. If a large percentage of that audience commutes to school, they need to know how to keep their cars safe and reliable. If most of them live in dormitories, they need to know how to keep from going crazy, and so on.

Sometimes you might not know as much about your audience as you would like. When that happens, the analysis of needs developed by the psychologist A. H. Maslow[8] can be used. In fact, keep these needs in mind for all audiences, because they are common to all human beings.

Playing to each of the needs outlined by Maslow is an effective attention-getting device if handled correctly.

Physiological Needs

Physiological needs are needs for things that enable us to survive. They include our needs for food, drink, and sleep.

We are all concerned with survival. One way to increase audience interest, then, is to relate your topic to your audience's survival or to the improvement of their living conditions. If you gave a speech on food (eating it, cooking it, or shopping for it) you would be dealing with a basic audience need. In a speech on nutrition you could relate to physiological needs by reading the ingredients from the label of a package of food purchased in a local store and explaining what each one of those ingredients can do to a human body. You might even be able to uncover a more specific nutritional need through interviewing or surveying audience members. (A large proportion of your audience might be trying to lose weight, for example.)

Safety Needs

Safety needs center around security in our environment. Whenever you remind your audience of their safety you are tapping their need to feel secure. This need is one reason why we find crime programs on television so enthralling; crime is a threat to security. Also, whenever you relate your topic to your audience's pocketbook you take advantage of their need to feel secure. The president of the American Medical Association reminded his audience at Oregon State University:

> Your interests as patients are at stake in a complicated — and piping hot — debate over a basically simple question . . . which is: *How* should you pay for medical care?[9]

Maslow's Hierarchy of Needs

Thus they were reminded that their medical care was directly related to their financial security.

Social Needs

Social needs include needs for love and affection and the need to belong to worthwhile groups. Everyone needs to feel loved. That explains some of the annoying pets people have. It also explains millions of dollars of advertising that relates just about anything — shampoo, beer, automobiles — to the ability to be loved. People need to feel that they belong to worthwhile groups, too. Those groups might be professional groups, family, or friends. Any one of these groups can be referred to in a speech.

One speaker who recognized his audience's need to belong to worthwhile groups was General Douglas MacArthur. MacArthur was fired by President Truman in one of the most dramatic incidents in American political history. He was invited to explain his side of the story to a joint session of Congress. He responded with his famous speech "Old Soldiers Never Die." In it, he happened to mention:

> I stand on this rostrum with a sense of deep humility and great pride — humility in the wake of those great American architects of our history who have stood here before me, pride in the reflection that this forum of legislative debate represents human liberty in the purest form yet devised. Here are centered the hopes, and aspirations, and faith of the entire human race.[10]

Social needs explain why it is often effective to include personal references about an audience in a speech. If you tell an audience why they, as a group, are important, you help satisfy their need to belong. If you do it well enough, you might even help satisfy their need for esteem.

Esteem Needs

Esteem needs are based on prestige. People have a need to feel that they are respected. The British humor magazine *Punch* once ran a parody of how a tough-guy entertainer like Frank Sinatra might sound speaking before a college audience:

> Hey, you in the third row, what're you majoring in, gum chewin'? Throw the bum out, go on get him out of here before I hit him. An' toss the two guys out on either side of him, too, for being stupid enough to sit alongside a bum like that. Go on, get them out.[11]

A strategy like that would be disastrous. A *good* example of recognizing an audience's need for esteem was demonstrated when the manager of public affairs for *Playboy* magazine spoke before the Southern Baptist Convention:

> I am sure we are all aware of the seeming incongruity of a representative of *Playboy* magazine speaking to an assemblage of representatives of the

Southern Baptist Convention. I was intrigued by the invitation when it came last fall, though I was not surprised. I am grateful for your genuine and warm hospitality, and I am flattered (although again not surprised) by the implication that I would have something to say that could have meaning to you. Both *Playboy* and the Baptists have indeed been considering many of the same issues and ethical problems; and even if we have not arrived at the same conclusions, I am impressed and gratified by your openness and willingness to listen to our views.[12]

This speaker told his audience that listening to him was a measure of their prestige. In the next example, another speaker uses a different twist to the same device by telling his audience that their prestige might be threatened. The speaker is a vice president of Shell Oil, and he is speaking to students at the Greater New Orleans Science Fair:

You students here today are the first generation that has grown up entirely in the space age. And the quality and imagination shown in your projects is evidence that our investment in science education has really paid off.[13]

Self-Actualization Needs

Self-actualization needs are based on the need to accomplish as much as possible with our lives. Maslow points out that whereas the other needs are deficiency needs (people need them to stay healthy), self-actualization is a growth need (it is satisfied by the improvement of an already healthy person). Whenever you relate your topic to your audience's need for self-improvement, you are tapping their self-actualization need.

Self-actualization is particularly important in a college classroom, because of the audience's need to grow *intellectually*. College audiences are thirsty for knowledge. That explains, in part, the popularity of "trivia" games on most college campuses. (What *was* the name of Tonto's horse?) Because of this need, three devices are generally recommended as attention-gaining material:

1. A historical reference.
2. A literary reference.
3. A startling statement of fact.

Any of these three references increase an audience's knowledge, and therefore tap their self-actualization need. For example, Judson C. Ward, vice president of Emory University, used a historical reference in a speech to students. He began this way:

In the year 1760, the same year that George III ascended the British throne and James Wright was named Governor of His Majesty's Royal Colony of Georgia, a red-headed, freckle-faced, lanky boy of 17 enrolled at the college of William and Mary. That boy was Thomas Jefferson. Although he presented no College Board scores, we know that he was already proficient enough in Greek and Latin to read the classics in the original languages. . . .[14]

Most people would consider information like the color of Jefferson's hair to be trivia; yet that type of information grabs our attention. We need to know new things because of our need for self-actualization.

This is true of literary references, also. An insurance executive once began a speech this way:

> An embittered Voltaire put into the mouth of Candide the question: "If this is the best of all possible worlds, what then are the others?" Two centuries later, the American novelist James Branch Cabell added cynically: "The optimist proclaims that we live in the best of all possible worlds; the pessimist fears this is true."[15]

Literature is a vehicle for intellectual growth. When you quote a masterpiece of prose or poetry, you tap your audience's need for self-actualization.

A startling statement of fact also increases your audience's knowledge, and therefore helps satisfy their need to grow. Dr. Thomas Elmendorf, in a speech on television violence (the sample speech in Chapter 7), mentioned the following data:

> By the time a child is 18 years old, he has spent more hours in front of a television set than he has in school. Over TV he will have witnessed by that time some 18,000 murders and countless highly detailed incidents of robbery, arson, bombings, shootings, beatings, forgery, smuggling and torture — averaging approximately one per minute in the standard television cartoon for children under the age of ten.[16]

This startling statement does more than add to our knowledge; it also affects our security. You can relate to many needs at once. You can also use more than one device. Consider the following introduction to a speech by a professor of philosophy at the University of Michigan:

> Of all that was done in the past
> You eat the fruit
> Either rotten or ripe
>
> (T. S. Eliot)

> We are a daring civilization. An adventurous civilization. But in the last analysis, we are a stupid civilization. We are a civilization afflicted with a death wish. We are destroying (not just using, but destroying) natural resources, ecological habitats, the tissue of which society is made. We are destroying, by the increasing number and magnitude of various stresses, individual human beings. We are destroying life at large. The civilization which intentionally or unintentionally does all these things cannot be called either judicious or wise. We are a stupid civilization.[17]

The professor used a literary reference by quoting lines of a poem by T. S. Eliot, and thereby fed his audience's self-actualization needs. He enhanced the audience's esteem ("We are a daring civilization") and threatened that esteem ("We are a stupid civilization"). He also tapped his audience's safety needs ("We are destroying . . . individual human beings").

In short, none of the needs stipulated by Maslow is ever completely satisfied, and you can tap them by either enhancing or threatening them. Either way, a sensitivity to these needs results in a sensitivity to human interest. That is what audience interest is all about.

Sample Speech

This sample speech was given by a college professor, Rebecca C. Jann, as an address for Senior Recognition Day at Queens College in Charlotte, North Carolina.[18] Notice how she adapts the speech to her audience.

What They Should Have Told Me When I Was a Senior

Rebecca C. Jann
Professor, Queens College

1 Greetings to you, seniors, who invited me to address you today and who soon will be able to decide whether that was a mistake. Greetings to you, colleagues, and to you, freshmen, and most special greetings to anyone who came even though you were not required to.

2 When I was facing my senior year, I needed some good answers fast, and nobody would give me any. I was just beginning to be a little bit receptive to some good answers . . . because I had conscientiously avoided following any advice at all for a couple of decades and now I was facing some of the consequences.

3 For example, since I had changed my major six times, the only way I could graduate with a major in my new and true calling was to schedule six labs per week during my last year. Having six labs is pretty bad, but what was worse was that several of the required courses were not about anything I really needed to know.

4 I realized that even if I managed to graduate, I was going to be facing the hard, cruel world knowing practically nothing about the really important parts of science — like volcanos and dinosaurs and, of course, sex.

5 I went to the library and checked out a lot of books on volcanos and dinosaurs and, of course, sex. I couldn't read the books during lab and get them all smeared with substances you would rather not hear about, and I couldn't read them in the evening because I had some critical extra-curricular activities to maintain [it was a co-ed school]. We weren't allowed to cut lectures; so I just sat toward the back in most of my irrelevant classes and read the books about volcanos and dinosaurs and . . . whatever.

6 Naturally, then I had some problems about QPAs and letters of recommendation and so forth.

7   When I was a senior I was about ready to admit my mistakes and be more receptive to advice for the future, like how to cope with the real world after graduation and whether I should go to graduate school, and if so, where? Or maybe should I get a job, and, if so, what and how? Or should I just get married and if so, to whom?

8   I wanted those answers fast. That's when I got the bad news: there were no answers after graduation. But that was a long time ago, and now . . . we still don't have any answers.

9   I could end with that message, but I won't. I'm tempted to. Maybe there are no absolute truths to help you make decisions about life during your senior year and after graduation, but I have compiled two lists of nearly indisputable certainties.

10   My first list comes from my professional knowledge as a biologist. These are ten facts which I think everybody could find useful in making decisions about the future. These are facts important especially for those of you who are going to escape without taking my courses. These are facts which are 99.9 percent certain.

11   [1] The human brain will function properly only within a healthy human body because the brain depends on a critical balance of natural psychoactive drugs which the body makes. Without the proper chemical balance, the brain tries to make you do the wrong things.

12   [2] The human body is designed for regular activity. Without regular exercise, its natural drug balance gets messed up and your brain tries to make you do the wrong things.

13   [3] There is no way to lose weight quickly and safely.

14   [4] You can't keep frogs alive in captivity for more than two weeks.

15   [5] Smoking is bad for you. Actually it doesn't matter what you are smoking or even sniffing; it is bad for you.

16   [6] Carbohydrates are good for you.

17   [7] To keep your houseplants healthy, try to give them a home which closely imitates their natural habitat. Unfortunately, this means you have to find out where they came from.

18   [8] We do have a real problem with the environment — accumulations of toxic pesticides and industrial wastes in our country and overpopulation in many parts of the world and dwindling energy sources everywhere. If we don't make the right decisions about the environment now, you won't have much of a future to worry about. The very least you can do about it is to learn as much as you can about these problems and then to vote responsibly and to write your legislators.

19   [9] Women really are different from men, not just in the obvious anatomical features but also in the way our brains work. For many years, I didn't want to believe this fact, but now I see that the fact that our brains work differently is a compelling reason to insist that we gain a larger role in running the world.

20   [10] This fact is known to students in my physiology class as Jann's second law: You are what you think you are. I already told you that your body controls the drug balance of your brain. Equally important is knowing that

your brain controls the hormones and nerves of your body. If that sounds like Catch-22, it is. The worse you feel, the worse you feel, and vice versa. On the other side of the coin, this means that the human brain is capable of helping you overcome disease and anatomical deficiencies. Miracle cures do exist, but only if you believe in them, and you can be one of the world's most beautiful women or one of the world's most successful women or one of the world's greatest minds only if you believe in yourself.

21   My second list of ten near-absolute certainties comes from personal experience. Actually, I am only 97.5 percent sure of some of these certainties, and those of you who have more personal experience than I are not required to listen.

22   [1] You don't have to learn everything from first-hand experience. Many 99 percent certainties can come from the experience of others as revealed to you through conversations with friends and through great literature, visual art, and music and maybe even soaps. If I didn't believe this certainty, that you don't have to learn everything from first-hand experience, I wouldn't be making this speech.

23   [2] The only valid reason to get married is for love.

24   [3] The way you can tell if it's really love is to try to live without being with him. If you survive, then you know it wasn't really true love.

25   [4] The only valid way to choose a career is for love.

26   [5] The way you can tell that you have a career is if you can hardly wait to get to work. If you dread going to work most days, then you don't have a career; you have a job . . . and you might as well look for another job which is easier or which pays better. For many very happy and successful people, jobs are just ways to finance their true callings. Their real careers are what they do in their spare time.

27   [6] If you dread going to class but you're doing it so you can have a career or even a job, you'd better be prepared for a big disappointment. There were people who liked the classes I dreaded, the classes where I sat in the back and read books. The people who liked the classes I dreaded ended up in careers very different from mine. The classes and subjects and activities and people you like are very good predictors of the type of career you will love. If you have never liked any of your classes, there's good news. There are very few jobs available in those fields anyway. According to several reliable sources, the only college graduates who are virtually guaranteed of careers for the rest of this century are those of you who are majoring in nursing. For the rest of you, it's too late to change your major. The other top ten employment opportunities for the rest of this century are in fields like retail sales and driving trucks and fast foods. So your best bet is to find out what you like and make a career of it, even if your job is just your way to finance your true calling.

28   [7] The most important job skill in any career suitable for a college graduate is good writing. If you really want to go for it, use your senior year wisely. Beg your instructors to assign term papers and urge them to write critical comments in the margins.

29   [8] Honesty is the best policy.

30   [9] It's very humiliating to have taken a whole lot of math courses and have a Ph.D. in science and then have to admit in front of a large audience that you can't count. I don't have a ninth point.

31   [10] Careers are less important than personal relationships. However, the people I know who have great personal relationships are the ones who have real careers, either in their jobs or in their spare time.

32   In summary, here is my advice for you to use during your senior year: Eat right, get lots of exercise, don't inhale anything except the cleanest air you can find, and don't make any decisions until you are sure your brain's drug balance is stable.

33   Next semester, take as many courses as Dean Thompson will allow. Find out what you like, and then spend your time learning so much about it that your brain convinces you and the rest of the world that you are A-one, top-notch, and totally awesome.

34   Learn to spell and write. Please.

35   If you are married or insist on getting married, remember that for centuries men have neglected their personal relationships and their health and their brains' natural drug balances to pursue their careers. Now that you have the opportunity to make the same mistakes, don't.

36   For those of you who are curious about what happened during and after my senior year, I did finally graduate. I turned down a graduate fellowship and got married and had 2.2 children. I read all my husband's textbooks for the courses I didn't get to take. I had brief careers as a carpenter and as a semi-pro musician and a fairly long career as a nearly full-time volunteer. Then I got another graduate fellowship and became a retread. I had limited careers in teaching various sciences to people of various levels of ability and interest; and I had brief careers in biological research and in environmental consulting. I'm still happily married to a very fine man who finances my many careers and supports me in many other ways. Now here I am happily being what I think I am.

Analysis of the Speech

Jann, a popular biology instructor, had been asked to speak at Senior Recognition Day by the seniors themselves. She did a quick demographic analysis: The audience would be composed almost entirely of women (Queens is a women's college), many of whom would be college seniors 21 years old, give or take a year. The seniors, freshmen, and faculty of the college were all required to attend. That made them a type of "captive" audience, although not a hostile one. The campus community generally enjoys Senior Recognition Day. Some other students and friends of the college were also in attendance. The chapel was reasonably full, with about 500 people. Except for the freshmen, Jann knew most of her audience. In her words, "It's a small, friendly place."[19] Her speech was to be in honor of the seniors, so the occasion called for the seniors to be the primary audience.

This is part of Jann's description of her audience:

The students at Queens are mostly extremely pleasant and polite, conservative, reasonably talented, affluent (or at least aspiring to appear so) Southern women. We are all sensitive to and politely assertive about women's issues.[20]

The seniors were a diverse lot, but Jann knew something about their values: These young women were part of a generation that placed a high value on both a career and a family life, and many of them felt torn between the two worlds. They held many conflicting beliefs and attitudes, some of which could be addressed in her speech.

Jann also knew that audience expectations would require that her speech have something to do with biology, because that was her field of expertise. Still, this occasion was no time for scholarly examinations of esoteric scientific theories. Because of their specific needs these audience members would be most interested in some universal truths and nuggets of wisdom that they could take with them into the world.

Jann described the ceremonies as follows:

Senior Recognition Day is a formal convocation held in the chapel. It begins with an academic procession with organ prelude and the works, faculty and seniors wearing academic regalia. The seniors all sit in the front directly under the speaker's podium. The faculty sits in the front but on the other side of the chapel. There is a prayer, some introductory welcomes, a choir piece or solo, introduction of the speaker, the speech, the honorary degree presentation, the college hymn, another prayer, and the recessional.[21]

Under the influence of such formal ceremonies, it is easy for a speaker to slip into impersonal, high-flown rhetoric. Jann knew she would have to avoid this tendency for the sake of her primary audience.

Jann made reference to her audience types in her introduction — she welcomed both the volunteers and the captives. Then she gave an anecdotal outline of her own college days, and the concerns she felt as a student: what to major in, how to handle required courses, sex, marriage, career, and so on. This part of the speech (paragraphs 2–9) helped her to establish rapport with her audience — it showed the audience members that the speaker had once experienced many of the concerns they were feeling that day.

Jann then enumerated ten "99.9 percent certain" facts from her "professional knowledge as a biologist." Points 1, 2, 3, 5, 6, and 8 dealt directly with physiological needs, point 9 with esteem and social needs, and point 10 with self-actualization. Notice that these numbered "facts" dealt with these needs *as adapted for this particular audience.* Point 4 was provided as comic relief, which is another form of audience adaptation.

Jann then listed ten "near-absolute certainties" from her personal experience. Once again, these items are heavily weighted in terms of specific audience interests: marriage, love, and career. Point 9, according to Jann, "was a result of panic at the podium. After extensive cutting and pasting, I couldn't believe I was facing 500 people with only nine points after having promised ten."[22] Jann had to adapt to her audience on the spot for this one, and she appears to have pulled it off well. She concludes with a summary of her main points (paragraphs 32–35) and a personal note to make those main points memorable.

Summary

This chapter dealt with the process of analyzing and adapting a speech to a particular audience. To analyze your audience you look at their level of willingness, their purpose, and demographics such as number of people, sex, age, and group membership. You also analyze the attitudes, beliefs, and values that the audience members are likely to hold. Perhaps most important, you pay heed to audience interests. One way to look at audience interests is through the needs outlined by Maslow: physiological, safety, social, esteem, and self-actualization needs are common to all human beings. Adapting your speech to address these needs in a particular audience will keep the audience interested.

Questions/Assignments

1. Three different "audience types" are mentioned in this chapter. How would you vary the material in your next speech for each of these types?
2. Suppose you were trying to persuade your class to accept a social or political change (for example, the Equal Rights Amendment). What advantages could you stress? Which advantages would you cite if you were addressing an older audience, consisting of people in business and their spouses? Give reasons for any differences.
3. Do you think Maslow's needs are common, *to the same extent,* to all human beings? If so, why? If not, how does the importance of these needs vary from person to person?
4. Some television commercials seem to grab our attention more than others. What commercials do you pay attention to? Why? Do they appeal to one or more of your needs? Explain your answers.
5. In the sample speech, Jann appears to have given a highly personal, light-hearted speech in the middle of some very formal ceremonies. In light of this fact, was her speech, in your opinion, a good example of audience analysis? Why or why not?

Notes

1. Aristotle, *The Rhetoric,* translated by W. Rhys Roberts (New York: Modern Library, 1954), p. 120.

2. Gwen Asburn and Alice Gordon, "Features of Simplified Register in Speech to Elderly Conversationalists," *International Journal of Psycholinguistics* 8:3, 1981, pp. 7–31.

3. The classic modern analysis of audience types is in H. L. Hollingworth, *The Psychology of the Audience* (New York: American Book Company, 1935), pp. 19–32.

4. An example of how demographics such as race, age, and union membership affect an audience's perception of messages is Carl H. Botan and Lawrence R. Frey, "Do Workers Trust Labor Unions and Their Messages?" *Communication Monographs* 50, September, 1983, pp. 233–244.

5. Aristotle, *op. cit.,* pp. 122–123.

6. Peter Kerr, "Rating the Things Americans Value," *The New York Times,* January 28, 1982, p. C3.

7. Gary Cronkhite, *Communication and Awareness* (Menlo Park, Calif. Cummings, 1976), p. 333.

8. A. H. Maslow, *Motivation and Personality,* 2d ed. (New York: Harper & Row, 1970), pp. 35–47.

9. Max H. Parrott, "HMOs versus Fee-for-Service," *Vital Speeches of the Day* 42, June 15, 1976.

10. From *Congressional Record, House,* April 19, 1951, pp. 4123–4125.

11. Stanley Reynolds, "Professor Blue-Eyes Is Back," *Punch,* November 17, 1976, p. 917.

12. Anson Mount, speech before Southern Baptist Convention, in Will A. Linkugel, R. R. Allen, and Richard Johannessen, eds., *Contemporary American Speeches,* 3d ed. (Belmont, Calif.: Wadsworth, 1973).

13. C. L. Blackburn, "Progress, Pollution, and Parallel Technologies," *Vital Speeches of the Day* 42, May 1, 1976.

14. Judson C. Ward, Jr., "The Practical Liberal Arts," *Vital Speeches of the Day* 43, December 15, 1976.

15. J. Carroll Bateman, "The Best of All Possible Worlds," *Vital Speeches of the Day* 34, December 15, 1967.

16. Thomas Elmendorf, "Violence on TV," *Vital Speeches of the Day* 43, October 1, 1976.

17. Henryk Skolimowski, "The Last Lecture," *Vital Speeches of the Day* 43, January 1, 1977.

18. Rebecca C. Jann, "What They Should Have Told Me When I Was a Senior," *Vital Speeches of the Day* 50, November 1, 1983.

19. Personal correspondence with Professor Jann, September 24, 1984.

20. *Ibid.*

21. *Ibid.*

22. *Ibid.*

5

Investigation

Investigation: An Introduction

Why Investigate?

You investigate people, ideas, and facts early in speech preparation.

You investigate the *people* who will be in your audience. You try to learn as much as possible about their interests and attitudes, so you can make your message appropriate for them. You do not want to tell denture jokes at a senior citizens' club, where the audience is likely to be offended.

You investigate your *ideas* to improve their quality. This work is important at each stage of speech preparation, from choosing your topic to fine-tuning your arguments. You begin with an idea that interests you and that you consider important. You limit that idea to what you can effectively deal with, given your audience and the time limitations of the speech. During the process of investigation you will mold that idea, take it apart, put it back together, expand it here, streamline it there. When you have finished, your investigation will be one of the differences between an idea that is clear and one that is gibberish.

You investigate *facts* to substantiate and help develop your ideas. Expert testimony, statistics, and examples support the substance and importance of your ideas.

Investigation is another one of those practices that is becoming more difficult because of our overabundance of information. People often do not bother to investigate because they think it requires too much energy; they do not know where to go for the answers without investing more time than those answers are worth. People who feel that way are missing out on the most interesting part of their work. The answers are there, waiting to be uncovered with less time and energy than you would think. You can investigate without pain through library research, interpersonal research, and personal observation. Some practical guidelines for each of those methods will be discussed in this chapter. First, though, consider the following word about taking notes.

Taking Notes

Chapter 2 presented a system for taking notes on someone else's speech (pp. 26–28). You will also have to take notes when you are researching your own speech. Everyone has a different system for taking notes. As you research you will be struck with ideas. You should take notes on these ideas, no matter how earthshaking and unforgettable they seem at the time. Half the time you will realize that your ideas are illogical or insufficient if you express them in writing. At other times, ideas that do not quite seem to make sense will jell on paper and become quite valuable. Write your notes as if you were writing them for someone else. Then leave them for a while. When you come back to them, if you still think they are worthwhile, you can transcribe them onto index cards. You should also take notes on ideas, quotes, and facts that you get from other sources. Each note card should list a topic, the note, and a source, if necessary. For example, if you are researching the idea of cybernetics (communication between humans and machines), you might be struck with an idea such as

Robots

Could robots eventually be made to *think*, like R2D2 in *Star Wars*?

"Robots could eventually be taught how to think, like the one they called R2D2 in *Star Wars*." If, after you have researched the topic for a while, this thought still seems valid, you might transfer it to an index card (page 84).

Later, you might find other items that relate to this idea:

Robots—Can they be made to think?

"Rapidly, we approach the final phase of the extensions of man—the technological simulation of human consciousness . . ."

—McLuhan, *Understanding Media,* p. 19.

Robots—Made to think?

"Everything a computer does is based on three functions: (1) Math computation, (2) storage of information, and (3) retrieval of information. It will never be able to do more."

Smith, Interview
4/5/85

Placing your ideas and research on index cards in this manner will make the analysis and organization of that material easier later on, but if you do not feel like using index cards, do not let that discourage you from taking notes. Take them on anything. The clean side of computer printouts, for example, is fine for investigative scribbling. Printouts can usually be obtained free at the computer center, and they will impress those who tend to be intimidated by the technology they represent.

Library Research

It is important, in this age of communication saturation, to understand that your intake of information is a form of nourishment. You have to approach information in the same way you approach food. You should try to take in a certain amount of high quality. If you take in too much, you should diet for a while. If you have a deficiency, you should correct it, and if you are preparing for a special exertion, you should alter your diet accordingly. Getting ready for a speech is like getting ready for a sports event; you not only have to make special preparations, you have to be in shape to begin with.

Staying in shape, in this sense, means regularly exposing yourself to stimulating ideas. One way to do so is to converse as much as possible with people you consider knowledgeable. Another way is through the selective use of the mass media. For example, when watching television you might see what is available in educational programs or documentaries before settling down to an evening of repeated plots and gratuitous violence on weekly entertainment programs. When listening to the radio you might spin the dial to an interview with one of our "great minds" rather than listen to a DJ's mindless prattle in between hit songs and hyped advertisements. Most important, you should expose yourself to stimulating ideas through daily reading. You should, for example, keep generally informed by reading a good newspaper and a selection of magazines. At least one of the magazines should be a national newsweekly such as *Time* or *Newsweek,* which you should read from cover to cover and discuss with your friends and neighbors.

Even if you keep yourself in top shape, though, you will need a special workout or two to prepare yourself for a speech. That is where the library comes in. It is full of special pieces of equipment for communication athletes. The most important piece of equipment there is probably the card catalog.

The Card Catalog

The card catalog is an ancient and noble information-storing device. It is your key to all the books in the library; they are filed there according to subject, author, and title, so you can look for general topics as well as specific books or authors. Once you find a book, you need not read the whole thing. You can check the table of contents and index for sections relating specifically to your topic.

Usually it pays to locate as many books as you can in this manner, and then select the one or two that have the best sections related to your topic. It is a good idea to give an in-depth reading to a limited number of pages. Do not concentrate on bulk. In order to read for understanding, read slowly and carefully. Pause from time to time to think about what you have read, and take notes as you read.

The card catalog can be used to find more than one book at a time. As a general rule, if you choose just one book from the catalog and then run to the shelves to locate it, it won't be there. There is no way to tell why that happens. It is just one of life's little mysteries, like the way toast always seems to fall jelly side down. You can guard against this heartbreak by locating, through the card catalog, a section of the stacks that holds more than one book related to your topic. Once you find the general area, you can review the tables of contents and indexes of all the books there. If several of them seem to be important to your topic, choose the one or two that seem to be written the best and/or have the most recent copyright data. Remember to limit your reading and do it in depth. Read for understanding.

Reference Works

Reference works will also be listed in the card catalog, but it would be a better idea to spend some free time wandering through the reference room yourself. There are wonders there that could turn you into a trivia expert. There are encyclopedias galore, even specialized ones like *The Encyclopedia of Social Sciences* and *The Encyclopedia of American History;* there are statistical compilations, like *The World Almanac, Facts on File,* and *The Guinness Book of World Records;* you can even find out *Who's Who in America* or *Who Was Who.* You can collect a lot of facts in a short time in the reference room.

Periodicals

Periodicals (magazines, journals, and newspapers) are good resources for finding recently published material on interesting topics. Indexes like *The Reader's Guide to Periodical Literature* will enable you to find popular magazine articles on just about any subject. Specialized indexes like *The Education Index* and *Psychological Abstracts* can be used to find more specific, technical articles, and newspaper indexes, most noticeably *The New York Times Index,* can be used to find microfilmed newspaper articles.

Both the microfilm machines and the indexes themselves are designed to be easy to use. Although you will need specific instructions for operating the microfilm machine in your library (your librarian will be glad to give you those instructions), there are general guidelines for using indexes. To investigate a general subject area using an index, use the following procedure:

1. List four or five possible titles or "headings" for your topic.
2. Arrange these headings from most to least specific.
3. Look up the most specific headings first.
4. If at first you do not succeed, look for your topic under one of the more general headings.

For example, if you decided to investigate the new "Star Wars" space weapons that the government is proposing, you might formulate the following list of possible headings:

1. "Star Wars" proposal
2. Laser Weapons
3. Satellite Weapons
4. Space Warfare
5. U.S.–Soviet Space Relations

If you turned to *The Reader's Guide to Periodical Literature* with this list, you would find no articles under the first heading. Your second heading would lead you to "Lasers — Military Use." Under that heading you would find three articles, but they would be highly technical and probably not much use to you. Under "Satellite Weapons" you would find a cross-reference, "See *Artificial Satellites*." Under "Artificial Satellites — Military Use" you would find nothing on your topic, but you would find another cross-reference: "See also *Anti-Satellite Weapons*." Unfortunately, under that heading you would find only one article, and that one is so technical you need an advanced degree just to read it.

At this point nonsystematic researchers would probably forget what they had been looking for in the first place; but you have your list to consult, to keep you organized. Now you try your fourth heading, "Space Warfare," and you hit a bonanza: eighteen articles, including several from popular magazines such as *Time* and *Newsweek* (which is a good thing, because you would not have found anything under your fifth heading).

Once again, be selective. Pick the one or two articles that seem to be the most directly related to your topic, and digest them.

Nonprint Materials

The library is also a treasury of nonprint and audiovisual materials. Films, records, tapes, and videotapes can be used not only as research tools but as aids during your presentation. Your library probably has an orientation program that will acquaint you with what it has to offer. Take the tour! Do not be proud — even experts take an orientation tour before using a particular library. In fact, if you have not taken the orientation tour at your library, do so immediately. It may be the most productive hour you ever spend!

On-Line Databases

A growing number of libraries have access to on-line databases, computerized collections of information that can be searched by a telephone link. One popular collection of databases is Dialog Information Retrieval Service. Dialog contains over 80,000,000 records from news services, magazines, scholarly journals, conference papers, books, and other sources. With the right "key words" to help the computer locate the material you

Many libraries are now equipped with on-line databases.

want, you can obtain scores of citations on your topic in just a few minutes rather than spending hours or weeks looking manually. Once you have located the items you want, it is possible to read abstracts or even entire articles on the screen of the library's computer terminal — or even have printouts mailed to you. For more information on databases, see your librarian.

Library Gnomes

Once you have done everything mentioned above, if you still cannot find exactly what you need, seek out the gnome in your library. Every library has at least one. In folklore, garden-variety gnomes (the word comes from the Greek word meaning "to know") are ageless dwarfs that guard precious ores and treasures. The library variety are real, though they may stand over six feet tall. These people seem to know where everything is, and they are enthusiastic and generous in sharing their knowledge. They can usually be found behind the reference desk, but they might be anywhere. Find the gnome in your library, and you have half the battle won.

Talking with a library gnome is one way of using interpersonal communication as a method of investigation. That opens up a whole new realm of possibilities.

Interpersonal Communication

Interpersonal communication can be used for investigation through *brainstorming* and *interviewing*.

Brainstorming

Brainstorming is a technique for generating ideas. It involves the spontaneous contribution of ideas from each member of a group.[1] When the technique works, the contributed ideas lead to the creation of new ideas.

There are a number of ways to explain the creative effect of brainstorming. One is the idea of free association; when we associate one idea with another, we retrieve ideas that would otherwise be too deeply stored away to use. Freud, however, would insist that creativity stems from the "freely rising" fantasy that noncreative people suppress and creative people accept. If you happen to be a Freudian, brainstorming might work because you are encouraged to entertain "wild" ideas. Finally, there is the Gestalt view, which is that creativity is a reaction to "psychological incompleteness." You build *Gestalten,* or patterns, by a restructuring of the whole rather than a careful step-by-step analysis of components. Brainstorming, by stressing quantity, could help in building *Gestalten.* For our purposes here, however, it is only necessary to point out that brainstorming does work, and it can work either formally or informally.

Informal Brainstorming

"Brainstorming informally" means brainstorming in everyday conversations, using communication to generate ideas rather than just to kill time. When you go out for a beer after class, do not ask your friend whether the Dodgers will win the pennant or whether Erica and Lance will get back together on your favorite soap opera. Ask a question based on your topic instead. Informal brainstorming leads to the discovery of new and different materials, including films, television programs, popular books, magazines, or newspaper articles that might relate to your topic.

Formal Brainstorming

In formal brainstorming, you meet in a group of three to five people, pick a general topic, and start spilling out ideas. There are three rules for formal brainstorming, all of which are designed to facilitate the free flow of ideas:

1. No criticism of ideas — just get them out, record them, and go on to the next idea.
2. The wilder the idea the better.
3. Quantity, rather than quality, of ideas is stressed.

Later, after you have had the chance to cool down, review the ideas for quality. Throw the unimportant ones away.

Formal brainstorming is often an excellent procedure for generating speech topics and generating ideas about those topics. When you need more specific information, you might want to take advantage of an interview or two.

Interviewing

The interview is an especially valuable form of research on a college campus, where experts abound. The information-gathering interview allows you to view your topic from an expert's perspective, to take advantage of that expert's years of experience, research, and thought. You can use an interview to collect facts and stimulate your own thinking. Often the interview will save you hours of library research and allow you to present ideas you could not have uncovered any other way.

An interview is more than a brainstorming session or a hunt for specific facts and quotes. It is a face-to-face interaction with an expert, in which many ideas that otherwise would be unclear can become more understandable. Sometimes you can guide the expert on to new discoveries. This is the prospect that professional interviewers find most exciting. Digby Diehl (author of *Supertalk,* a book of celebrity interviews) has stated:

Interviewing members of your audience is one way to learn about them.

I've become vaguely aware that what I'm searching for in some loony, unfathomable manner, are not the answers, but The Answers. Somewhere, sprinkled out amongst the best minds of the century, are clues. And someone's tongue is bound to slip.[2]

Conducting an Interview

To have a successful interview, you have to carefully plan out what to do before, during, and after the interview.[3]

Before the Interview. First, determine who the best available expert is. If you are truly ambitious, you might decide to visit or telephone a well-known celebrity. Unfortunately, you generally have to contact well-known people, at least at first, by mail. Even then the proportion of those who accept interviews to those who are contacted is small, and much time can be wasted. Usually it is more practical to find successful authors, teachers, or administrators on your campus or in your community and contact them either personally or by phone. If your expert is willing to be interviewed, set up a specific time. Don't schedule the interview late in the afternoon or right before lunch, unless there is a chance that the expert might take you along.[4] Make sure you schedule a sufficient amount of time. Try to arrange for the least possibility of distraction.

After you have scheduled the interview, prepare the questions you would like to ask. Review these questions immediately before the interview so they are fresh in your mind, and keep them with you in case you need to refer to them during the interview.

It is a good idea to know as much as possible about both the person you are interviewing and the topic of the interview. If possible, collect background material that you could refer to during the interview.

Finally, consider the kind of person the expert is. Remember that everything you do has some effect. Try to plan for positive effects. The way you look (including the clothes you wear) and the way you act (including whether or not you seem to enjoy what you are doing) will influence the response you receive. Plan to dress and act in a way that your expert will consider appropriate.[5]

During the Interview. During the interview, it is important to make the expert feel as comfortable as possible. When you begin, state the specific reason for the interview, explain what the answers will be used for, and ask if it is all right if you take notes or use a recorder (you should definitely do one or the other, even if you have a fantastic memory). Some interviewers suggest that you use the expert's name as often as possible. Others stress that the person being interviewed will be more comfortable if he or she can remember *your* name. They suggest that you give the expert a 3×5 card with your name on it.

Make sure you understand the expert's responses to your questions: Ask him or her (tactfully) to speak clearly, repeat, clarify, or use examples

SITTING ACROSS FROM SOMEONE WITH A DESK IN
BETWEEN IS GOOD FOR VERY FORMAL INTERVIEWS.

SITTING SIDE-BY-SIDE IS VERY INFORMAL AND WILL
PROBABLY MAKE AN INTERVIEWEE UNCOMFORTABLE
UNLESS HE OR SHE WANTS TO BE INFORMAL.

Figure 5-1

if necessary. Summarize or rephrase the answers yourself, if you have any
doubt. Do not ask leading ("Don't you think . . . ?") questions or questions that can only be answered yes or no. Do not get nervous about
periods of silence; use them to collect your thoughts.

When you arrive at the scene of an interview, you should arrange
yourself, in relation to the expert and whatever furniture is present, so that
you will encourage communication. Try to make yourself and the interviewee as comfortable as possible.

Try to be sensitive to the nonverbal cues the interviewee gives you.
Everyone has a need for a certain amount of personal space.[6] Your expert
will probably tell you with a raised eyebrow, a smile, or fidgeting behavior
whether or not you have gotten too close. Figure 5-1 (pages 93 and 94)
represents four ways you could sit during an interview. Different physical
arrangements will work best with different people.

REMOVING THE DESK REMOVES SOME OF THE FORMALITY.

LEARN TO RECOGNIZE AND USE THE APPROPRIATE
SEATING ARRANGEMENT.

Figure 5–1 (continued)

Do not refer to your notes during the interview unless you have to. Try to let the conversation run naturally. The questions you have prepared in advance are "lead" questions, to be used when the natural flow of conversation falters. "Follow-up" questions relate directly to something the interviewee has said, to keep ideas flowing naturally. They cannot be made up in advance.

If you feel you have to guide your expert back to an important idea that has been rambled away from, do so by supplying a transition. For example: "Yes, indeed, Professor Smith. Those are beautiful pictures of your grandchildren. Tell me — is it possible that computers might be able to think by the time those kids grow up?"

Make good use of the time you have scheduled. If one expert cannot answer your questions, see whether he or she knows someone else who can. When experts give you printed material, ask them to point out the exact sections that would be most helpful. Make sure you have enough time so that you do not have to end abruptly; the best information is often saved for the end of the interview.

After the Interview. Review your notes and/or recording as soon as possible after the interview. The more time you allow to elapse, the less sense your notes will make to you. Transcribe the main points and the important quotations onto index cards (or whatever system you prefer).

By now you should have a pretty good idea where your research is leading you. You might need some firsthand observation to bolster your evidence. The next section will deal with the collection of that type of data.

Personal Observation

Personal experience is one of the basic ingredients of any speech, but unsupported personal *opinions* can be detrimental. Personal observation, as a form of investigation,[7] gives some extra weight to your personal opinion. For example, if you were suggesting to an audience that the TV sets should be removed from the lounges of the dormitories at your college, you might say this:

> I think people in dormitories here would interact more if the televisions were removed from the dormitory lounges.

All you have there is personal opinion, which could be based on anything from scientific research to a purely emotional hatred of television — or of college students.

The use of personal observation, however, might allow you to say this:

> Last Wednesday, I spent 7:00 to 10:00 P.M. in the lounge of a dormitory here. Only three times during the evening did anyone attempt to start a conversation. Two of those attempts were met with a request for silence in deference to the television.

If you really wanted to prove your point, you could take personal observation one step further:

> This Wednesday, I received permission from the dormitory supervisor to remove the television from the lounge. During those same hours, 7:00 to 10:00 P.M., I observed the following behavior in that lounge, this time without television:
>
> 1. Thirty conversations were begun.
> 2. Twenty-four of these conversations continued, in depth, for more than ten minutes.

3. Seven groups of students decided on alternate entertainment for the evening, including table games, singing, dancing, and going to the library.
4. Four new acquaintanceships were made, one of which resulted in a TV date for the following Wednesday night.

This example illustrates a type of investigation known as *behavioral observation*. Behavioral observation is used to collect information about human beings. Since your job as a public speaker is communicating with human beings, and since human beings love information about themselves, observing behavior can be an extremely valuable form of investigation.

Depending on the behavior you intend to observe, your investigation can become quite involved. For example, some researchers in New York City wanted to see whether juvenile delinquents were responsible for stripping abandoned automobiles, so they left a car on a city street with the hood up and the license plates removed. They they hid and waited to see what would happen. They observed (in an amazingly short time) that the auto strippers were predominantly middle-class adults.[8] Students in Oregon collected data on wasted foods by measuring garbage from school cafeterias.[9] They were able to document an appalling amount of waste, and officials were forced to make changes in the school lunch programs. Admittedly, it takes a strong stomach for this type of research, but the results are sometimes worth it.

Survey Research

Survey research involves asking a number of people an identical set of questions.[10] One advantage of this type of research is that it gives you up-to-date answers concerning "the way things are" in a fast-moving, constantly changing world. Survey questions can be asked of a specific group, also. This fact can be particularly important in public speaking. Consider the following ideas, which might be presented in a speech on "How to Handle Stress":

According to a *Time* magazine article published in 1976, five out of ten college students will suffer from stress-related illness during their stay in college. (Library data)

According to a survey I conducted last week, nine out of ten students in this class have experienced symptoms of stress within the last two weeks, and fully half of you can expect to suffer from a stress-related illness by the end of this term. (Survey data)

The second statement would probably be of more immediate interest to an audience of students. That is another advantage of conducting your own survey. The major disadvantage is that your survey, being unpublished, may not have as much credibility as evidence found in the library.

Types of Surveys

The three most popular means of surveying people are in-person surveys, printed questionnaires, and telephone surveys.

In-Person Surveys

A list of questions or *questionnaire* can be helpful as part of any interview, but such a list is especially helpful when several people will be interviewed about the same topic. A prepared set of questions could therefore enable you to "interview" several members of your class quickly and efficiently. In-person interview surveys have the advantage of spontaneity. If new questions arise during the interviewing process, you have the freedom to ask them. Because you survey your respondents one at a time, you also have the advantage of observing their nonverbal reactions. In-person surveys are time-consuming, however. If you need to survey *all* the members of your class, a printed questionnaire is probably more appropriate.

Printed Questionnaires

Printed (mimeographed, photocopied, or otherwise reproduced) questionnaires have the advantage of *standardization;* that is, you can be reasonably sure that each respondent has been asked the same question, without benefit of verbal or nonverbal urgings from the survey taker. Printed questionnaires can be mailed, but for the purposes of undergraduate research it is often quicker and easier to hand out the questionnaires and have them completed immediately. If you are looking for answers within a small group, like your public speaking class, it is possible to prepare a questionnaire for every member. For larger groups it may be necessary to take a *random sample*. A random sample is one in which every member of the group has, at least theoretically, an equal chance of being questioned. If you wanted to randomly sample a population like the freshman class at your university, you could not do so at your favorite tavern or on one floor of a dormitory. You could, however, pass out questionnaires randomly during an orientation session that all freshmen attend.

Telephone Surveys

Telephone surveys can make random sampling a bit more systematic, if you happen to have a telephone directory that lists everyone in the population you want to sample. You need only call one person on each page. Theoretically, which name you call should be decided by a random drawing; that is, if there are 100 names on each page of your student directory, you should put the numbers 1 through 100 in a hat and pick out a number at random. (For example, if you picked the number 10, you would call the tenth person on every page.) The main disadvantage of telephone surveys is that after all that work you might get no answer at all.

Types of Survey Questions

There are basically three types of survey questions: those that can be answered yes or no, multiple-choice questions, and open questions that can be answered any way the respondent wants.

Yes-or-No Questions

The yes-or-no question is best asked when you need a quick statistic: "Seventy-five percent of the students in this class have, at one time or another, suffered from a stress-related illness." A yes-or-no survey question produces responses that can be tabulated and expressed as percentages easily. However, it also requires you to "lead" the respondent and does not encourage detail which might be important. For example, if you asked the question "Have you ever experienced symptoms of stress? Yes___ No___," the respondents would not have the opportunity to tell you their definition of "stress" or what they consider its symptoms to be. Yes-or-no questions are especially valuable when you are trying to avoid a long-winded response. You might need to avoid this type of response in a controversial question of opinion, such as "Do you believe in the death penalty for convicted murderers?" Full answers to a question like that might be too lengthy for your purposes.

Multiple-Choice Questions

As a general rule, the more detail you ask for in your questionnaire, the more difficult the answers will be to tabulate and explain. One way to ask a question so the respondent can give some detail, without making tabulation difficult, is to establish the choices yourself. You might follow up a yes-or-no question such as "Have you ever smoked marijuana?" with a multiple-choice item such as

If so, how often?
___ Once
___ A few times
___ Regularly
___ Other

and you might follow that one up with

If regularly, how often?
___ Once a month
___ Once a week
___ Daily
___ Other

You should arrange your choices so only a minimum number of responses will appear in the "other" slot, because those responses will be the most difficult to tabulate.

One useful type of multiple-choice question is the *scale question*.

These questions are particularly useful when you are investigating the strength of your respondent's attitude on something. Scale questions allow the respondent to answer anywhere along a continuum, such as

Do you agree or disagree that marijuana should be legalized?

Strongly Agree	Mildly Agree	Undecided	Mildly Disagree	Strongly Disagree

----------------/----------------/-----------------------/---------------------/-----------------

Notice that scale questions will always have an odd number of choices (usually five or seven) so there will be a point "in the middle" to represent neutrality on the question.

Open Questions

To encourage detailed, complete responses, you might want to use open questions: "What do you think is the number one health hazard in the United States today?"

It is a good idea to provide a limited amount of blank space after a question like this one, to limit long-winded responses.

Surveying for Audience Analysis

Survey research is often the best way to investigate your audience. For example, imagine that you have just arrived at Honeysuckle State University, and before you really have a feel for the place, you are given a week to prepare a presentation for one of your classes. Just to make it interesting, make the class "Introduction to the Family" and your topic "Divorce." To get a better feel for your audience, you might run to the library and find the pamphlet "Student Life at Honeysuckle State," the magazine article "Honeysuckle State: Hotbed of Horticulture," or last year's most obscure master's thesis, "Student Attitudes at Honeysuckle State." If you examine that information carefully, you will probably find that it refers to a more general audience than the one you will face. The information might also be out of date. You might interview your instructor or one of your classmates. Unfortunately, if you rely on only one or two people to speak for the entire class, you may get a limited and incorrect view of that class. It would be more effective, therefore, to conduct a survey in the class and find out some pertinent information, such as the members' family backgrounds (were parents divorced?), marital status (maybe some of the class members are divorced themselves), religion, and attitude toward divorce.

Divorce is not a particularly controversial topic these days. It is not like talking about dropping the bomb on Nicaragua or instituting capital punishment for landlords who refuse to return damage deposits. Still, audience investigation is immensely important. It will make the difference between talking about divorce in general and talking about how divorce affects *that particular audience*.

As you investigate, remember that it is the *quality* rather than the *quantity* of the research that is important. The key is to determine carefully what type of investigation will answer the questions you need to have answered. Sometimes only one type of research will be necessary. If you use some of the guidelines suggested here, your answers will probably be worth the energy you exert.

The Ethics of Investigation

There are ethical considerations to keep in mind at all stages of speech preparation, and the investigation stage is no exception. This matter came vividly to public attention when the "Carter Briefing Book" scandal broke out in 1983.[11] By most accounts, Ronald Reagan trounced Jimmy Carter in the 1980 presidential debates. Following these debates, people felt that Reagan had proved he was knowledgeable about "the issues." Three years later Reagan lost several public-relations points when it was discovered that someone on his staff had stolen Carter's briefing book, which contained all the questions that Carter was going to bring up as "issues" in the debate.

There are also more subtle forms of theft, as when library materials "disappear" about the time that students are preparing for speeches. This behavior is particularly insidious, because it handicaps all other students who subsequently want to investigate that topic.

Other ethical considerations include preserving anonymity on surveys or at an interviewee's request, not falsifying or stretching data to make a point, investigating through unbiased sources, and giving credit where it is due.

Ethical considerations are also important in behavioral observation. The "subjects" of behavioral observation are human beings and deserve to be treated as such. Always think ahead to the possible consequences of your research. Not too long ago some faculty members at a large midwestern university told their students in the basic communication course to "go out and create a communication event and observe the reactions to it." It was not long before the little campus town was in a state of near-panic because a group of students had faked a "shooting" on campus — carefully orchestrated with a blank-firing pistol and splattered-ketchup wounds. State police were called in, the wire services were alerted, and the communication faculty was dragged onto several administrative carpets. The faculty members put all their communication skills to work and quieted things down in about a week. Some even say the whole thing would have been forgotten if only another student group had not decided to throw a dummy off a high-rise dormitory.

Both groups had failed to control the detrimental effects of their research, and therefore had ignored their ethical responsibilities.

Sample Speech

The following speech was given by Chris Wallace, a student at the University of Nebraska-Lincoln. Chris placed third in the 1984 Interstate Oratorical Association Annual Tournament with this speech. She was coached by Kate Joeckel and Jack Kay. As you read the speech, see whether you can recognize the kind of investigation that went into it. Then check the comments that follow the speech.[12]

The Big Mac Attack

Chris Wallace
University of Nebraska – Lincoln

1 Massive is the best word to describe Mac. Tall, wide, and heavy, he packs power in every pound. Hurtling toward you, Mac is truly an imposing sight.

2 Chances are that you have met Mac within the past 24 hours. Depending on your driving habits, he may be a daily acquaintance of yours. But you are among the lucky. You have not been Big Mac's victims.

3 Seven travelers on the Connecticut Turnpike were not so fortunate last year. Mac crashed into them as they waited at a tollgate, turning their cars into a sickening accordion. All seven died, including three children.

4 Clearly, this is not a typical "Big Mac Attack." Rather, it is an attack visited upon us by Mac and his friends: White, Peterbilt, GMC — America's leviathan heavy trucks. Although not all trucks or truck drivers are menaces, the carnage wrought by some has reached proportions we can no longer afford to ignore, as we will see by looking at the trucks, the drivers, and their unsafe trucking practices.

5 The problem begins with the trucks. Put simply, Mac and his pals are out of shape, as a 1979 study by the Department of Transportation's Bureau of Motor Carrier Safety dramatically demonstrated. A one-week inspection program by the Bureau at ten checkpoints along the Mississippi River resulted in 44 percent of the trucks stopped being placed out of service because of severe safety violations. The Bureau further reported that 42 percent of the trucks it stopped in routine inspections that year were classified as "imminently hazardous," meaning that they were an open invitation to driving disaster. The mere fact that over 40 percent of all trucks inspected by the BMCS were potential juggernauts is frightening enough. However, BMCS Deputy Director Kenneth Pierson provided even more chilling testimony to the gravity of the problem when he said that the vehicles stopped represented only 1 percent of those heavy trucks currently on our roadways.

6 Mac and his out-of-shape pals are enough of a menace, but the risks to us are compounded when unprofessional drivers sit behind Mac's wheel. These drivers continue to literally run us over because there is no way any

agency can regulate them. They may have two or more licenses — each from a different state. Thus if they lose one license, they simply drive on the license from another state, according to the July 21, 1983, edition of ABC News "20/20." The National Transportation Safety Board has made available the results of its investigation of 44 such problem drivers. Between them, they had 63 different licenses, 98 license suspensions, 104 accidents, 456 traffic convictions, and most significantly, 53 fatalities.

7   One of these unprofessional drivers was responsible for flipping his rig near Los Banos, California, in December 1982. His cargo spilled across the highway. It consisted of 14 missiles . . . armed with nuclear warheads. It was later discovered that the driver had 14 previous driving convictions, including driving while intoxicated and reckless driving. On this occasion, he admitted that he had been drinking again, and had fallen asleep at the wheel.

8   Why does such unprofessionalism continue to exist? One answer is provided by ABC News "20/20." They indicated that 85 percent of the truckers involved in fatal accidents had no formal driver's training. The explanation is painfully simple. There is a regulation which says that a driver must take an exam before she/he can drive; however, the test is a travesty.

9   The test contains 66 questions. However, in contrast to the exam you and I take to get a car operator's license, this one is not administered by a law enforcement agency. Instead, the company that wants to hire you conducts the exam. Or, if you are an independent driver, you merely test yourself. Oddly enough, no matter who does the testing, you can always use the answer book and simply copy the right answers onto your test. If you can't pass even with the answer book, you can still be hired to drive an 80,000-pound, 18-wheel truck. The regulation only says truckers must complete the exam; it doesn't require that they pass it.

10   Not surprisingly, these unprofessional drivers often engage in unsafe trucking practices, ranging from the use of controlled substances to driving while physically exhausted. The Ralph Nader group conducted a study of substance abuse among truckers in the early 1970s, and discovered that 80 percent of the 1300 polled believed amphetamine use was widespread in their ranks. Another 80 percent admitted to having dozed at the wheel despite the so-called pep pills. These figures assume even greater significance in light of a 1976 Department of Transportation study, which revealed that physical exhaustion on the part of the trucker played a major role in 32 percent of all serious trucking accidents from 1973–76. Drained by sleep deprivation, yet bolstered by the false bravado of controlled substances, it is little wonder that these drivers begin to commit disastrous errors.

11   The results are nothing short of tragic . . . and terrifying, according to Ben Kelly, Senior Vice-President of the Insurance Institute for Highway Safety in Senate Committee testimony on June 14, 1983. Kelly pointed out that while large trucks account for only 1 percent of all highway traffic today, they are responsible for a disproportionate 12 percent of all fatal highway crashes. Unsafe trucks, unprofessional drivers, and unsafe trucking practices provide a three-fold explanation.

12   Mac has literally become "hell on wheels," largely because jurisdiction over truck safety has been delegated to a powerless agency, the Department of Transportation's Bureau of Motor Carrier Safety. Howard Anderson, Policy Director for the Bureau, explains that the agency is sorely understaffed and debilitated by a lack of funds. Thus weakened, the agency is powerless to enforce current regulations, much less pursue needed reforms.

13   For this reason, our initial response to the Big Mac Attack must be to "beef up" the BMCS through an infusion of personnel, funds, and reform responsibilities.

14   First, as Anderson suggests, the agency should be provided with the 1000 new inspectors currently needed and a budget hike commensurate with this increase.

15   Thus empowered, the BMCS should secondly undertake a number of reforms. Immediately, it should outlaw multiple driver's licenses and promulgate regulations to strip drivers of their licenses after the second major law violation, such as drinking and driving, or reckless driving. Finally, the BMCS should mandate that license exams and yearly truck inspections be administered by state law enforcement authorities.

16   To enforce these regulations, the BMCS should incorporate the use of a computer clearinghouse to include all data regarding heavy trucks and their drivers. State officials would be required to submit reports of all applications for licenses, all law violations, all failed license exams, and all failed truck inspections. Problem drivers could then be identified with greater efficiency by the BMCS, and state officials could be informed and instructed to take corrective measures. In addition, the BMCS could use its 1000 new inspectors to conduct road-inspection spot checks with greater frequency.

17   Most importantly, this type of solution works. A similar demonstration program conducted in four volunteer states from 1979–82 proved that the federal/state partnership I have outlined can address truck safety. Positive and substantial reductions in truck-related accidents were reported in all four states, with a reduction of over 30 percent in Utah, according to Kenneth Pierson, Director of the BMCS. Congressional reluctance to appropriate funding seems to be the only obstacle to widespread implementation of the program.

18   Until Congress acts, we can all participate in an immediate solution. After all, when we face Mac one-on-one on a lonely stretch of road, all the bureaucracy in the world counts for very little. So when you see a truck headed toward you remember four little words: assume and make room. Assume the trucker is tired and ill-equipped to drive; assume his truck is overloaded. Then make room. If you are in the driving lane, stay there and maintain a consistent speed. If you're in the passing lane, get over as soon as possible and maintain your speed. Above all, don't make any sudden moves a tired driver in an overloaded truck can't compensate for.

19   Mac has been a very bad boy lately. Per one million miles driven, he is involved in almost twice as many fatalities as cars. Unsafe trucks, unprofessional drivers, and unsafe trucking practices provide an explanation. Until

some solutions such as those I have outlined are implemented, our nation's roadways will continue to be terrorized by these behemoths. The chances are that you will meet one during the next 24 hours. Assume and make room. Remember that when Mac and a car do battle, 97 percent of the fatalities occur in the car. That's the kind of Big Mac Attack we can all live . . . without.

Comments on the Speech

Chris used a variety of types of investigation in this speech. She got the idea for the speech from a television program. Some of the information in the speech (paragraphs 6 and 8) came from that program. Then she found several newspaper articles (paragraphs 3 and 7) and magazine articles (paragraphs 10, 17, and 19) on her topic. She also interviewed two officials of the Department of Transportation's Bureau of Motor Carrier Safety (paragraphs 5, 12, and 14). Because Chris was giving this speech for a tournament, she was not able to survey the members of her audience in advance. However, if she were giving this same speech in a class, she could have surveyed the class members to see how many were drivers, whether they had ever been involved in a truck accident or known anyone who had, how they felt about truck safety, what percentage of accidents they thought involved trucks, and so on.

Summary

This chapter dealt with the process of investigation, which includes the investigation of *ideas,* to improve their quality; the investigation of *facts,* to substantiate ideas; and the investigation of the *audience,* to make the message appropriate to its receivers. Investigation is aided by generally "staying in shape" by exposing yourself to stimulating ideas. It is also aided by understanding the functions of the library, brainstorming, interviewing, personal observation, and surveys.

The library is a labyrinth if you do not understand it, but it is a supermarket of speech material if you know how to shop. Getting to know your library involves making the acquaintance of the card catalog, the available reference works, the periodicals, the nonprint materials, on-line databases, and a library gnome or two.

Brainstorming is a technique for generating ideas in a group. It can be done informally, in everyday conversations, or formally, in a group assembled for that purpose.

Interviewing is especially useful on a college campus. This technique requires the selection of an expert, the preparation of questions, and a sensitivity to the nonverbal cues of the interviewee.

Personal observation, in order to be valid, should be done in a controlled manner. Personal observation as a form of investigation can make your personal opinions more valid in a speech.

Survey research is a useful way to gather up-to-date information about your audience. Survey methods include printed questionnaires and telephone sampling. Survey questions can be worded for yes-or-no answers, multiple-choice answers, or open answers.

Any or all of these methods can be used to investigate a speech topic. The important skill is using the appropriate type of research, rather than using as many types as possible. The appropriate investigation will make your information more valid and your speech more effective.

Questions/Assignments

1. In your opinion, is it true that people often do not bother to investigate because it requires too much effort? Based on your experiences with people such as auto mechanics, teachers, registrars, store clerks, and waitresses, how willing are people to look into a situation thoroughly? How willing are *you*?
2. You are advised to help yourself investigate a speech topic by regularly "staying in shape." What people and/or media events do you, or could you, use to stay in shape? What are the particular benefits you can gain from each source?
3. Select any topic of interest to you. It could be JFK's assassination, the Loch Ness monster, U.S.–Cuba relations, King Tut, or anything else. If you were going to use an index to find sources of information, what headings might you list, and in what order of specificity? Pursue these headings. Which ones are most helpful in locating articles?
4. Imagine that you have the opportunity to interview a particular famous person. What background information would you find helpful before the interview? What questions would you prepare in advance? What questions would you definitely avoid? Explain your answers.
5. What three questions could you ask your class, in survey form, to measure the students' attitudes toward your next speech topic? Which type of questions (yes-or-no, multiple-choice, or open) would you use? Why?

Notes

1. Alex Osborn, *Applied Imagination* (New York: Scribner's, 1959).
2. Digby Diehl, *Supertalk* (New York: Doubleday, 1974), p. ix.
3. The advice of noted television interviewers, such as Barbara Walters, David Frost, and Mike Wallace, is offered in "Some of TV's Best Interviewers Reveal the Tricks of Their Trade," *TV Guide* 25, Aug. 13, 1977, pp. 6–10.
4. Only go to lunch if the interviewee invites *you*. Do not do the inviting yourself. Besides the obvious financial advantage, if your interviewees invite you, the burden of entertainment will be theirs. They will talk more. For other practical hints on interviewing, see John Brady, *The Craft of Interviewing* (New York: Random House, 1977).
5. Those who are interested in the effect of clothes will want to read John F. Malloy, *How to Dress for Success* (New York: Warner, 1975).
6. For a more thorough discussion of nonverbal cues and personal space, see

Mark L. Knapp, *Nonverbal Communication in Human Interaction,* 2d ed. (New York: Holt, Rinehart and Winston, 1978), or Albert Mehrabian, *Silent Messages: Implicit Communication of Emotions and Attitudes,* 2d ed. (Belmont, Calif.: Wadsworth, 1980).

7. A more detailed analysis of personal observation as a form of investigation is in William L. Rivers, *Finding Facts* (Englewood Cliffs, N.J.: Prentice-Hall, 1975), pp. 56–75.

8. This study is reported in Floyd L. Ruch and Philip G. Zimbardo, *Psychology and Life,* 8th ed. (Glenview, Ill.: Scott, Foresman, 1971), p. 547.

9. David J. Johnson, "Trash Tells a Tale," *The National Observer,* Dec. 20, 1975, p. 1.

10. Survey research, as well as other forms of behavioral observation, can be far more complex and rigorous than what is suggested here for speech investigation. The complexity and potential of this type of research is covered more fully in books such as Fred N. Kerlinger, *Scientific Behavioral Research: A Conceptual Primer* (New York: Holt, Rinehart and Winston, 1979).

11. For a sampling of editorial opinion on what came to be known as "Debategate," see *Editorials on File* 15, May 16–31, 1984, pp. 548–555.

12. Chris Wallace, "The Big Mac Attack," *Winning Orations, 1984* (Interstate Oratorical Association, 1984), pp. 58–61.

6

Organization and Structure

Organization: An Introduction

"Starting tomorrow I gotta get organized," reads the sign over the office worker's desk. The desk is littered with files, letters, papers, and half-eaten sandwiches, so you *know* the worker will be too busy trying to do the job in an unorganized way to ever get truly organized. Speech preparation is like that, too. If you take some time in the beginning to organize, and if you devote some time to staying organized, you can save a lot of time in the long run. Then, of course, when it comes time to give your speech, your audience will understand you better if your ideas are presented in an organized way.

Organization is the process of arranging something according to a plan. In speechmaking, the importance of organization is based on the limitations of human information processing. The fact of the matter is this: the human mind can deal with only a small number of ideas at any one time. Psychologist Jerome S. Bruner articulates the problem this way:

> One of the most notable things about the human mind is its limited capacity for dealing at any one minute with diverse arrays of information. It has been known for a long time that we can deal only with about seven independent items of information at once; beyond that point we exceed our "channel

108

capacity," to use the current jargon. We simply cannot manipulate large masses of information.[1]

The scientific research upon which our knowledge of information processing is based began over 100 years ago with the experiments of a logician named Jevons. His experimental procedure was laughable by today's standards: he simply had an assistant throw various numbers of beans into a box. He would then, with a glance, estimate the number of beans for each throw. Jevons continued his experiment, faithfully recording his estimates, until he wore out three assistants and had produced the following percentages of correct guesses for various numbers of beans:[2]

No. of Beans	3	4	5	6	7	8	9	10	11	12	13	14	15
Percent of Correct Estimates	100	100	96	82	73	56	62	43	38	42	23	28	18

Jevons interpreted these results to mean that between four and five beans (or "pieces of information") could be dependably "processed" by the human mind at one time. In the last hundred years this experiment has been repeated hundreds of times with increasingly sophisticated electronic equipment and statistical techniques,[3] but the results have remained stubbornly the same. Psychologist George A. Miller summarizes his years of research in this phenomenon as follows:

> My problem is that I have been persecuted by an integer. For seven years this number has followed me around, has intruded in my most private data, and has assaulted me from the pages of our most public journals. This number assumes a variety of disguises, being sometimes a little larger and sometimes a little smaller than usual, but never changing so much as to be unrecognizable. The persistence with which the number plagues me is far more than a random accident. . . . Either there really is something unusual about the number, or else I am suffering from delusions of persecution.[4]

The number that so tormented Miller as the irrefutable limits of human information processing was "the magical number seven, plus or minus two." Because ideas expressed by a speaker are more difficult to keep straight than beans in a box, speakers have traditionally limited themselves to seven minus two (rather than plus two) ideas for a full-length speech. Because classroom speeches are generally shorter than full-length speeches, three to five main points seem to be the rule for classroom speeches. In this case tradition and science heartily agree that if we are going to be able to communicate a reasonable amount of information at any one time, we have to break it up into a limited number of ideas. Speech organization is basically a process of breaking up information into a limited number of related chunks.

Organization will result in two major benefits for you as a public speaker. First, if your speech is organized, it will be easier for you to remember everything that you want to say. One point will lead smoothly into the next, and you will be able to transmit more information than you would in a hit-or-miss, unorganized manner. Second, your audience will understand more and remember more of what you say, if it is organized in a logical manner.[5]

Recent research suggests that organization is especially important for an audience of people who, like your classmates, might have to speak soon themselves. Apparently the distraction of thinking about their own speeches causes what researchers call a "next-in-line" effect, which is partially eliminated by careful organization.[6]

Three procedures are used to organize a speech: structuring the speech with an introduction, transitions, and a conclusion; outlining; and roughing out the speech.

Speech Structure

In a structured speech your thesis is established in the introduction, developed in the body, and reviewed in the conclusion. The basics of speech structure can be summarized in the aphorism, "Tell what you are going to say, say it, and tell what you said" (see Table 6–1). This sounds redundant, but it is necessary: In Chapter 2 we discussed research in listening that suggests an audience will remember only 50 percent of a typical message immediately after hearing it; a few days later that figure will drop to 25 percent.[7] Clear organization can improve these gloomy statistics for you.

Structured messages seem to be especially important for an audience composed of college students. Minds wander. There is not much you can do about that. Several researchers have tried to discover why minds wander. One study suggests that first-year college students spend about 25 percent of their class time daydreaming about sex.[8] Trying to compete with sexual fantasies is a difficult task, but when you repeat your central idea at three different points in your speech, you *more* than triple the chances that your audience will remember it, because audiences have a tendency to listen more carefully during the beginning and end of a speech.[9]

TABLE 6–1   Basic Speech Structure

I. Introduction	II. Body	III. Conclusion
A. Attention-getter	**A.** ⎤	**A.** Review
B. Preview	**B.** ⎥	**B.** Memory Aid
	· ⎥— Main points	
	· ⎥	
	· ⎦	

Let us take a look at the three components of a speech in the order in which you would prepare them. You begin by organizing the body of the speech, because it is impossible to know the best way to introduce your content before you have decided what that content is to be.

Developing the Body of the Speech

The body makes up the bulk — usually 70 to 80 percent — of the speech. The first step in organizing the body is to develop a *prospectus*.

Developing the Prospectus

A prospectus is a list of points that you might want to make in your speech.[10] You can begin developing a prospectus as soon as you decide on a topic, because several points may occur to you at that time. Then, as you investigate and think about how you, your audience, and the occasion of your speech relate to that topic, other points will come to you. You should write ideas out (even if only on a random scrap of paper) whenever they come to you.

For example, if your local city council decided to cut off funds to the American Society for the Prevention of Cruelty to Animals (ASPCA), you might want to prepare a speech with the following purpose:

> After listening to my speech, my audience will write to the city council supporting funding for the ASPCA.

After a few days of research and note-taking, your prospectus might look like this:

1. The ASPCA is of great benefit to the city.
2. It cannot operate without city funding.
3. The city has decided to stop funding it.
4. The city has also recently rescinded the ASPCA's tax-exempt status on the grounds that the society's charity is not directed at human beings.
5. The city should provide funds through license fees.
6. The license fees could be higher for animals that are not neutered.
7. The ASPCA protects us against packs of strays.
8. Packs of strays litter the streets, yowl at night, and may attack children or pets.
9. The ASPCA helps us care for our pets.
10. It provides the community with education programs.
11. It protects against mistreatment of all animals, even commercial livestock.
12. It provides shelter for lost pets.
13. It provides emergency treatment for pets that have been injured in accidents.

14. Because of the ASPCA the city does not have to employ dog catchers or operate pounds.
15. Because it is a humane society thousands of animals are saved each year.
16. The ASPCA operates more cost-efficiently than a similar municipal agency could.

The list goes on. By the time you have finished your prospectus, you might have two or three times as many items.

You can see that this list is a record of random thoughts, not presented in any logical order. That is fine. When you have completed your prospectus, you can review it and exclude all those points that, upon reflection, you do *not* want to cover in your speech. When you have done that, you should have about fifteen or twenty points left. You can review the remaining points and formulate a thesis statement containing *one* idea that covers all of them. In this case, the thesis statement might be:

Our city cannot afford to lose the ASPCA.

The next step will be to organize the rest of your prospectus into an outline.

Types of Outlines

After developing a prospectus you are ready to build an outline for your speech. This outline is the skeleton that provides the necessary framework and basic form of the speech. It contains the main ideas, and it shows how these ideas are divided. Outlines come in all shapes and sizes, but they can generally be classified as either formal outlines, working outlines, or speaking notes.

Formal Outlines. A formal outline generally uses the following symbols:

I. Main point* (Roman numeral)
   A. Subpoint (capital letter)
      1. Sub-subpoint (standard number)
         a. Sub-sub-subpoint (lower-case letter)

A formal outline can be used as a visual aid (on posterboard, for example, or distributed as a handout) or as a record of a speech that was delivered (many organizations send outlines to members who miss meetings at which presentations were given; instructors in speech classes often use outlines to analyze student speeches).

A formal outline contains only the structural units of a speech—

---

*In speech outlines, roman numerals are often used to separate the main divisions of the speech: introduction, body, and conclusion.

main points and subpoints (the divisions of main points, including sub-subpoints and sub-sub-subpoints). In formal outlines main points and subpoints always represent a division of a whole. Because it is impossible to divide something into fewer than two parts, you always have at least two main points for every topic. Then, if your main points are divided, you will always have at least two subpoints, and so on. Thus, the rule for formal outlines is, never a "I" without a "II," never an "A" without a "B," and so on.

If you were speaking on the topic "The Causes of Modern Illness," you might divide your topic into the following main points:

  I. Poor Diet
 II. Pollution
III. Stress

Each of these ideas might be further divided into subpoints:

  I. Poor Diet [main point]
    A. Lack of Nutrition [subpoint]
    B. Chemical Toxins [subpoint]
    C. Irregular Intake [subpoint]
 II. Pollution [main point]
    A. Air Pollution [subpoint]
    B. Water Pollution [subpoint]
    C. Noise Pollution [subpoint]
III. Stress [main point]
    A. Work-Related Stress [subpoint]
    B. Day-to-Day Stress [subpoint]

Supporting points, or material that develops the ideas you present, are not usually listed on a formal outline. When they are, they are not given one of the standard symbols.[11] They are identified by type:

Definition:
Example:
Visual aid:
Quote:

Thus, if supporting points were included, the outline for the first main point of the "Modern Illness" speech might begin as follows:

 I. Poor Diet
    A. Lack of Nutrition
       Example: Breakfast cereals
    B. Chemical Toxins
       Visual aid: Chart showing use of chemical preservatives
    C. Irregular Intake
       Definition: Meal schedule
       Quote: Adelle Davis

Transition statements also sometimes appear on formal outlines. They also are not given standard symbols. Because supporting points and transition statements are not divisions of ideas, it *is* possible to have only one of them under a particular point on a formal outline.

Formal outlines can be full-sentence outlines or key-word outlines. The examples above are in the form of key-word outlines. This type of outline is often used for speaking notes, but it is sometimes too brief to communicate the structure of the speech to someone else (as when an outline is used to substitute for a speech that someone missed). When a more complete model of the speech is necessary, a full-sentence outline is usually more appropriate

A full speech outline should also include the points to be made in the introduction and conclusion. Many instructors prefer that a formal speech outline include a purpose statement, a thesis statement, and the various transitions and internal summaries, also. With these features added, a full-sentence outline for the "Modern Illness" speech might look like this:

Topic: "The Causes of Modern Illness"
Purpose: After listening to my speech, my audience members will be able to list at least three ways to avoid typical modern illness.
Thesis: The three main causes of modern illness are poor diet, pollution, and stress, all of which can be controlled to some extent by each of us.

I. Introduction
    A. Do you ever feel like this?
       Quotation: Adelle Davis on exhaustion.
    B. You *can* make yourself feel better.
       Transition: The first step is to recognize what causes us to get sick.
II. The Body
    A. Modern people often suffer from poor diets.
       1. Too many convenience foods can cause malnutrition.
       2. Too many chemical preservatives can cause toxic reactions.
       3. Irregularly scheduled meals can cause gastric disorders.
         Internal summary: What to do about it.
         Transition: Diet is only one form of "pollution."
    B. Modern people are subjected to more pollution than ever before.
       1. Air pollution contributes to respiratory diseases.
       2. Water pollution contributes to digestive diseases.
       3. Noise pollution contributes to nervous disorders.
         Internal summary: What to do about it.
         Transition: Noise pollution is only one cause of stress.
    C. Modern people are subjected to more stress than ever before.
       1. Work-related stress contributes to nervous disorders.

2. The day-to-day stress of modern living contributes to circulatory diseases.
   Internal summary: What to do about it.

III. Conclusion
   A. Review the problem.
   B. Review what we can do about it.
   C. One final thought.
      Quotation: John Hargood on the pleasures of good health.

Working Outlines. Working, or "scratch," outlines are construction tools used in building your speech. Unlike a formal outline, a working outline is a constantly changing, personal device. You begin organizing your speech material from a rough working outline; then, as your ideas solidify, your outline changes accordingly.

A working outline is for your eyes only. No one else need understand it, so you can use whatever symbols and personal shorthand you find functional. In fact, your working outline will probably become pretty messy by the time you complete your speech.

Speaking Notes. Like your working outline, your speaking notes are a personal device, so the format is up to you. Many teachers suggest that speaking notes should be in the form of a brief key-word outline, with just enough information listed to jog your memory but not enough to get lost in.

Many teachers also suggest that you fit your notes on one side of one 3×5 card. Your speaking notes for the ASPCA speech, then, might look like this:

I. ASPCA Services
   1. Strays
   2. Pets
   3. Livestock
II. Cost Efficiency
   1. Labor
   2. Facilities
III. Financial Condition
   1. Costs
   2. Revenues
IV. Solutions
   1. Real Estate Tax
   2. Licensing Fee

Principles of Outlining

There are three principles that relate to all outlines, working or formal. A good outline will follow all three: division, coordination, and order.

Division. Plato recognized the importance of the principle of division. He said:

> First, you must know the truth about the subject you speak or write about; that is to say, you must be able to isolate it in definition, and having so defined it you must understand how to divide it into kinds, until you reach the limit of divisions.[12]

Plato had the right idea. The first principle of outlining is to divide your topic into main points that completely cover your thesis. Correct division is said to be *exhaustive* and *focused*. "Exhaustive" in this sense means that those points are the most important parts of your central idea. If you are speaking on jury selection and are explaining that lawyers are able to recognize certain biases in prospective jurors, you might divide the idea of bias like this:

A.   Racial bias
B.   Sexual bias

If those are the two most important parts of the idea of bias, then it can be said that the divisions of that idea are "exhaustive." If, however, you divided the idea into "racial bias, sexual bias, and lawyers' biases," that third point would probably *not* be essential to the idea of biases in prospective jurors.

"Exhaustive" also means that all the necessary information can be included under one of the divisions of that idea. For example, if you also want to discuss the fact that some jurors are biased in terms of the defendant's age, you might have to divide the idea of bias like this:

A.   Racial bias
B.   Sexual bias
C.   Age bias

If everything you want to say could be included under one of these three subpoints, then the idea is properly divided. If not, the division of the idea would not be exhaustive.

"Focused" means that each division should contain one, and only one, idea. If you were discussing hangover cures, your topic might be divided incorrectly if your main points looked like this:

I.   "Preventive cures" help you before drinking.
II.   "Participation cures" help you during and after drinking.

You might actually have three ideas there, and thus three main points:

I.   Preventive cures (before drinking)
II.   Participation cures (during drinking)
III. Postparticipation cures (after drinking)

It is important for all messages to be divided in an exhaustive, essential, and focused manner; but speeches have one further requirement: They should have no more than five main points (three or four is considered ideal), and each point should be broken up into no more than five subpoints (and so on for sub-subpoints). As we saw earlier, this number will allow for maximum comprehension within the limits of human information processing.[13]

Coordination. Coordination is the state of being equal in rank, quality, or significance. The principle of coordination requires that all your main points be of *similar importance* and that they be *related* to one another. The principle of coordination is reflected in the wording of your main points. Points that are equal in significance and related to one another can easily be worded in a similar manner. Because of this ease the principle of coordination is sometimes referred to as the principle of "parallel wording." For example, if you are developing a speech against capital punishment, your main points might look like this:

   I. Crime did not decrease during the 1950s, when capital punishment was enforced.
  II. The Eighth Amendment to the U.S. Constitution protects against cruel and unusual punishment.
 III. Most civilized countries have abandoned the notion of capital punishment.

The relationship of those points might seem obvious to you as a speaker, but chances are they would leave the audience confused. Similar, parallel wording of main points helps to guard against this confusion:

   I. Capital punishment is not effective: It is not a deterrent to crime.
  II. Capital punishment is not consitutional: It does not comply with the Eighth Amendment.
 III. Capital punishment is not civilized: It does not allow for a reverence for life.

Order. An outline should demonstrate a logical order for the points you want to make. The way you divide your ideas sometimes helps determine the order in which you present them, but not always. The general rule is this: You must make a conscious choice about the order in which you present your points, based upon the purpose you want them to accomplish. Different organizational patterns will be most effective for different purposes.

Patterns of Organization

You should divide, coordinate, and order your points according to a pattern: The audience will tend to understand and remember more that way. There are a great many patterns that you can use. The most common patterns, and therefore the ones that are most often used as examples, are time, space, topic, problem-solution, cause-effect, and climax.

Time Patterns. Arrangement according to periods of time, or chronology, is one of the most common patterns of organization. The period of time could be anything from centuries to seconds. The "hangover cures" example on page 116 is an example of a time pattern. In our ASPCA example a time pattern might look like this:

   I.   Early attempts by the city to control animals, 1900–1920.
  II.   The ASPCA takes over, 1920–present.
 III.   The outlook for the future.

Arranging points according to the steps that make up a process is another form of time patterning. The topic "Getting That Big Date" might use this type of patterning:

   I.   The first step: Choosing an appropriate person.
  II.   The second step: Breaking the ice.
 III.   The third step: Asking for the date.

Space Patterns. Space patterns are organized according to area. The area could be stated in terms of continents or centimeters or anything in between. If you were discussing the ASPCA in New York City, for example, you could arrange your points according to borough:

   I.   Manhattan
  II.   Queens
 III.   Brooklyn
 IV.   Bronx
  V.   Staten Island

Topic Patterns. A topical arrangement is based on types or categories. These categories could be either well-known or original; both have their advantages. For example, a division of college students according to well-known categories might look like this:

   I.   Freshmen
  II.   Sophomores
 III.   Juniors
 IV.   Seniors

Well-known categories are advantageous because audiences are generally more receptive to ideas that they can associate with their present knowledge. Familiarity also has its drawbacks. One disadvantage is the "Oh, this again" syndrome. If members of an audience feel they have nothing new to learn about the components of your topic, they might not listen to you. To avoid this turnoff you could invent original categories that freshen up your topic by suggesting an original analysis. For example, original categories for "college students" might look like this:

I. Grinds — the students who go to every class and read every assignment before it is due, who are usually seen in dormitories telling everyone to turn their stereos down.

II. Renaissance students — the students who find a satisfying blend of scholarly and social pursuits. They go to most of their classes and do most of their assignments, but they do not let school get in the way of their social life.

III. Burnouts — the students who have a difficult time finding the classroom, let alone doing the work.

Problem-Solution Patterns. The problem-solution pattern, as you might guess from its no-nonsense title, describes what is wrong and proposes a way to make things better. It is usually (but not always) divisible into these two distinct parts. One variation of the problem-solution arrangement contains five steps and has come to be known as the motivated sequence:[14]

1. **The Attention Step.** The first step draws attention to your subject. ("For example, "Have you ever gotten all dressed up to go out for a meal in a nice restaurant, and then sat down and been choked by smoke from the table next to you?")

2. **The Need Step.** Step 2 establishes the problem. ("Ambient smoke — that is, smoke from someone else's cigarette, cigar, or pipe — is a threat to your health as well as a general nuisance.")

3. **The Satisfaction Step.** Step 3 proposes a solution. ("The State Clean Air Act will provide for separate smoking and nonsmoking areas in restaurants.")

4. **The Visualization Step.** Step 4 describes the results of the solution. ("Imagine — clean air in every public place, without denying smokers their rights in any way.")

5. **The Action Step.** The last step is a direct appeal for the audience to do something. ("Sign this petition, and you will have done your part.")

Cause-Effect Patterns. Cause-effect patterns, like problem-solution patterns, are basically two-part patterns: First you discuss something that happened; then you discuss its effects. For example, many speakers feel that the topic of inflation is amenable to this pattern. The reason people tend to misunderstand inflation is that they confuse causes with effects. These speakers would organize a speech on inflation as follows:

I. Causes
    A. Government budget deficits
    B. Increase in money supply
II. Effects
    A. Rising prices
    B. Rising wages

A variation of this pattern is reversing the order and presenting the effects first and then the causes. Effect-to-cause patterns would work well with a topic such as "rising gasoline prices"; the audience would presumably already be interested in and knowledgeable about the effects, and discussing them first might increase interest in your analysis of the causes.

Climax Patterns. Patterns that build to a climax are used to create suspense. For example, if you wanted to create suspense in a speech about military intervention, you could chronologically trace the steps that eventually led us into World War II, or Korea, or Vietnam in such a way that you build up your audience's curiosity. If you told of these steps through the eyes of a soldier who was drafted into one of those wars, you would be building suspense as your audience wonders what will become of him.

This pattern can also be reversed. When it is, it is called *anticlimactic* organization. If you started your military-intervention speech by telling the audience that you were going to explain why so-and-so was killed in such-and-such a war, and then you went on to explain the things that caused him to become involved in that war, you would be using anticlimactic organization. This pattern is helpful when you have an essentially uninterested audience and you need to build interest early in your speech to get them to listen to the rest of it.

Once you have organized the body of your speech, you can turn to your introduction and conclusion.

Developing the Introduction

As pointed out earlier in this chapter, the introduction of a speech provides an attention-getter and a preview (of your thesis and perhaps of your main points). Your introduction should perform other functions, too, such as setting the mood and tone of your speech and demonstrating the importance of your topic to the audience. Let us start with gaining audience attention, the first thing you will want to accomplish in your introduction.

Gaining the Audience's Attention

Your audience will have many other things on their minds when they come to hear your speech. Your first job will be to cut through all those distractions and help the audience members focus on what you have to say. There are several ways to do it. Here is a list of attention-getters, along with examples of how they might be used to introduce a speech on "Communication Between Plants and Humans."

1. **Refer to the Audience.** A reference to your audience is especially effective if it is complimentary, such as "It is great to have the opportunity to address a group of America's brightest young scholars . . ." Of course, to be effective the compliment has to be sincere.

2. **Refer to the Occasion.** A reference to the occasion could be a reference to the event of your speech, such as "We are gathered here today, as we are on every Tuesday and Thursday at this time, to examine the phenomenon of human communication . . ." You might also refer to the date: "On this date, just five years ago, a little-known botanist made a breakthrough that set the scientific world on its ear . . ." This type of reference naturally must relate to the topic.

3. **Refer to the Relationship Between the Audience and the Subject.** "My topic, 'Communicating with Plants,' ties right in with our study of human communication. We can gain several insights into our communication with one another by examining our interactions with our little green friends."

4. **Refer to Something Familiar to the Audience.** If you are discussing a topic that might seem new or strange to the audience, attention will be attracted to the familiar among the new, in much the same way that we are able to pick out a friend's face in a crowd of strangers. For example, "See that lilac bush outside the window? At this very moment it might be reacting to the joys and anxieties that you are experiencing in this classroom."

5. **Cite a Startling Fact or Opinion.** A statement that surprises an audience is bound to make them sit up and listen, even to a topic that they consider old hat. If the audience members think they have heard it all before about plant-human communication, you might mention, "There is now actual scientific evidence that plants appreciate human company, kind words, and classical music."

6. **Ask a Question.** A rhetorical question causes your audience to think rather than to answer out loud. "Have you ever wondered why some people seem to be able to grow beautiful, healthy plants effortlessly, while others couldn't make a weed grow in the best soil you could get?" This question is designed to make the audience respond mentally, "Yes, why is that?"

7. **Tell an Anecdote.** A personal story perks up audience interest because it shows the human side of what might otherwise be dry, boring information. "The other night, while taking a walk in the country, I happened upon a small garden that was rich with lush vegetation. But it wasn't the lushness of the vegetation that caught my eye at first. There, in the middle of the garden, was a man who was talking quite animatedly to a giant sunflower."

8. **Use a Quotation.** Quotes sometimes have a precise, memorable wording that would be difficult for you to match. Also, they allow you to borrow from the credibility of the quoted source. For example, "Thorne Bacon, the naturalist, recently said about the possibility of plants and humans communicating, 'Personally, I cannot imagine a world so dull, so satiated, that it should reject out of hand arresting new ideas which may be as old as the first amino acid in the chain of life on earth.'"

9. **Tell a Joke.** If you happen to know, or can find, a joke that is appropriate to your subject and occasion, it can help you build audience interest: "We once worried about people who talked to plants, but that is no longer the case. Now we only worry if the plants talk back." Be sure, though, that the joke is appropriate to the audience, as well as to the occasion and to you as a speaker.

Stating Your Thesis and Main Points

A well-planned introduction will usually preview the structure of a speech by telling the audience what your thesis is and/or what your main points will be. This preview tells them what to listen for and gives them an idea of what your method of organization will be. For example, Katherine Graham, the chairman of the board of the Washington Post Company, addressed a group of businessmen and their wives this way:

> I am delighted to be here. It is a privilege to address you. And I am especially glad the rules have been bent for tonight, allowing so many of you to bring along your husbands. I think it's nice for them to get out once in a while and see how the other half lives. Gentlemen, we welcome you.
>
> Actually, I have other reasons for appreciating this chance to talk with you tonight. It gives me an opportunity to address some current questions about the press and its responsibilities — whom we are responsible to, what we are responsible for, and generally how responsible our performance has been.[15]

Thus, Graham previewed her main points:

  I.   To explain whom the press is responsible to.
 II.   To explain what the press is responsible for.
III.   To explain how responsible the performance of the press has been.

Sometimes your preview of main points will be even more straightforward. This is how one student previewed her ideas in the introduction of a speech on the hazards of inaccurate credit checks:

> . . . The issue I would like to explore today is that of the accuracy of credit reporting. In exploring this topic, I think we need to try and identify some of the shortcomings involved in the current practices of credit reporting, identify why these shortcomings come about, and, finally, identify some measures we might take to improve the credit reporting system.[16]

Sometimes you will not want to refer directly to your main points in your introduction. Your reasons might be based on a plan calling for suspense, humorous effect, or stalling for time to win over a hostile audience. In that case you might preview only your thesis:

"I am going to say a few words about ____."
"Did you ever wonder about ____?"
"____ is one of the most important issues facing us today."

Setting Mood and Tone

Notice, in the example above, how Katherine Graham began her speech by joking with her audience. She was speaking before an all-male organization; the only women in the audience were the members' wives. That is why Graham felt it necessary to put her audience members at ease by joking with them about women's traditional role in society. By beginning in this manner she assured the men that she would not berate them for the sexist bylaws of their organization. She also showed them that she was going to approach her topic with wit and intelligence. Thus she set the mood and tone for her entire speech. Imagine how different that mood and tone would have been if she had begun this way:

> Before I start today, I would just like to say that I would never have accepted your invitation to speak here had I known that your organization does not accept women as members. Just where do you Cro-Magnons get off, excluding more than half the human race from your little club?

Making the Audience Care

Your audience will listen to you more carefully if your speech relates to them as individuals. Based on your audience analysis, you should state directly *why* your topic is of importance to your audience. This importance should be related as closely as possible to their specific needs, at that specific time. For example, if you were speaking to your class about why they should help support the Red Cross, you might begin like this:

> Lives have been lost in the time it takes an ambulance or doctor to reach the victims of accidents. Too many people have died from accidentally severed veins, drowning, choking on food, or swallowing iodine, plant spray, arsenic, or other poisons.
>
> If someone on the scene had known what emergency measure to take, tragedy could have been averted.
>
> The Red Cross, with vast experience in the latest, most successful life-saving techniques, has put together a handy, easy-to-follow manual, *Standard First Aid and Personal Safety*. The information it contains could save your life — or that of someone dear to you. This book is available only through the Red Cross, and [they will] send it to you *free*.[17]

This introduction establishes an immediate importance: the audience members do not have to wait until they need blood or until an emergency or a disaster strikes. Acquiring the free booklet is something that is important to them right now as healthy, reasonably secure members of a college class.

Developing the Conclusion

The conclusion, like the introduction, is an especially important part of your speech. Your audience will have a tendency to listen carefully as your speech draws to a close; they will also have a tendency to consider what you say at the end of your speech as important. Therefore the conclusion has two important functions: to review the thesis and to leave the audience remembering your speech.

Reviewing Your Ideas

You can review your thesis either through direct repetition or by paraphrasing it in different words. Either way your conclusion should include a short summary statement:

> And so, after listening to what I had to say this afternoon, I hope you agree with me that the city cannot afford to lose the services of the ASPCA.

You might also want to review your main points. You can review directly: "I made three main points about the ASPCA today. They are. . . ." You can review artistically, instead. For example, first look back at that introduction by Katherine Graham; then read her conclusion to that speech:

> So instead of seeking flat and absolute answers to the kinds of problems I have discussed tonight, what we should be trying to foster is respect for one another's conception of where duty lies, and understanding of the real worlds in which we try to do our best. And we should be hoping for the energy and sense to keep on arguing and questioning, because there is no better sign that our society is still healthy and strong.[18]

Let us take a closer look at how and why this conclusion was effective. Graham posed three questions in her introduction. She dealt with those questions in her speech and reminded her audience, in her conclusion, that she had answered the questions.

Introduction	*Conclusion*
I. Who is the press responsible to?	I. To its own conception of where its duty lies.
II. What is the press responsible for?	II. For doing its best in the "real world."
III. How responsible has the press been?	III. It has done its best.

Making Your Speech Memorable

Because of the importance of the conclusion of your speech, remember the following list of "don'ts":

1. **Do not end abruptly.** Make sure that your conclusion accomplishes everything it is supposed to accomplish. Develop it fully. You might want to use a "pointer phrase" such as "and now, in conclusion . . ." or "to sum up what we've been talking about here . . ." to let your audience know that you have reached the conclusion of the speech.
2. **Do not ramble, either.** Prepare a definite conclusion and never, *never* end by mumbling something like "Well, I guess that's about all I wanted to say. . . ."
3. **Do not introduce new points.** The worst kind of rambling is "Oh, yes, and something I forgot to mention is. . . ."
4. **Do not apologize.** Do not say, "I'm sorry I couldn't tell you more about this," or, "I'm sorry I didn't have more time to research this subject," or any of those sad songs. They will only highlight the possible weaknesses of your speech, and there is a good chance those weaknesses were far more apparent to you than to your audience.

Instead, it is best to end strongly. You can use any of the attention-getters suggested for the introduction to make the conclusion memorable. In fact, one kind of effective closing is to refer to the attention-getter you used in your introduction and remind your audience how it applies to the points you made in your speech.

You can use elements of surprise or suspense to make a point memorable; you can also use mnemonic devices, which are often formulated as collections of meaningful letters:

> Think of recycling in the same terms as you think of gas mileage: MPG. Only in recycling MPG stand for *metals, paper,* and *glass,* the three materials you stand to conserve.

Whatever device you use, end with a flourish, as John F. Kennedy did when he said, "Ask not what your country can do for you, ask what you can do for your country," in the conclusion of his inaugural address, or as General MacArthur did when he said, "Old soldiers never die; they just fade away."

Tying Your Ideas Together

You should tie all your ideas together through the use of transitions, which show how one idea relates to another. They keep your message moving forward; they tell how the introduction relates to the body of the speech; they tell how one main point relates to the next main point; they tell how your subpoints relate to the points they are part of; and they tell how your supporting points relate to the points they support. Transitions, to be effective, should refer to the previous point and to the upcoming point and relate both of them to the thesis. They usually sound something like this:

". . . Like *(previous point),* another important consideration in *(topic)* is *(upcoming point)."*

". . . But _____ isn't the only thing we have to worry about. _____ is even more potentially dangerous."

". . . Yes, the problem is obvious. But what are the solutions? Well, one possible solution is . . ."

Sometimes, a transition includes an internal review and/or a preview of the next point(s):

". . . So far we've discussed _____, _____, and _____."

"Our next points are _____, _____, and _____."

As you can see, the process of organizing a speech usually takes place in the order outlined in Table 6–2.

Roughing Out the Speech

"Roughing out" means shaping in a preliminary manner. There are a number of ways to rough out a speech. It can be done in the form of a complete written rough draft, in the form of brief notes, or in your head. The form depends largely on the type of delivery you will use. Extemporaneous speeches are generally roughed first in outline form, and then out loud. The "roughing out loud" is generally done alone at first, and then later in front of a small sample audience such as one or two trusted friends.

All the time you were investigating, analyzing, and organizing your speech material you were "roughing out" little sections of the speech in your head. That shaping process will continue right up until the time you actually present your speech. However, there will be one point in your speech development in which your main concern will be sitting down, in

---

TABLE 6–2   Steps in Speech Organization

   I. Formulate thesis statement
 II. Organize body of speech
     A. Divide points
     B. Coordinate points
     C. Order points
III. Organize introduction
     A. Gain audience attention
     B. Preview thesis and/or main points
     C. Set mood and tone of speech
     D. Make the audience care
 IV. Organize conclusion
     A. Review thesis and/or main points
     B. Plan memorable ending
  V. Check transitions from point to point

an environment that is suitable for quality thinking, and figuring out what goes where. That is when most of your roughing out is done.

Roughing out is a process of discovery. It is at this time that you test your ideas, your organization, and your potential audience appeal. Once you are before your audience, it is too late to test. A common plea of a beginning public speaker is: "Oops—forget I said that." Unfortunately, even if (indeed, *especially* if) the audience tried to forget that they heard something, they would remember it. A speech presentation is not well suited to trial and error. Roughing out is. It is easy to deal with an idea that falls apart in mid-development when you are alone. It is impossible to do the same thing when you are speaking in front of an audience.

You should rough out your speech and your working outline at the same time. Start with either the speech itself or the outline, but move back and forth, changing both the outline and speech as you go. As long as you maintain some form of organization, as evidenced by your outline, you can pour out your ideas as they come to you. The structure supplied by your outline gives you the freedom to experiment with new ways of expressing your ideas.

When you have finished roughing out and outlining your speech, you should have various trophies to show for your efforts. You should have a final outline. You should have (in your head, if nowhere else) a speech which you have been constantly trying out, changing, and generally fiddling around with during the entire time you worked with it. You should have a mass of scribbled notes, largely indecipherable, which will include several scratch outlines. The notes could, at your discretion, be written up as a manuscript, reworked into a term paper, or kept as a memento. Generally, however, they should just be shipped off to your nearest recycling center, to relieve tomorrow's public speaking student of the responsibility of killing a tree to complete an assignment.

Sample Speech

Not long ago Paul Urbanek, a student at the University of New Hampshire, expressed some suspicions about the simplicity of the basic principles of message preparation. "It can't be that simple," he said to his instructor. "Do you mind if I try to prove in my next speech that some types of messages *don't* conform to those principles, but are still effective?"

His instructor agreed, on the condition that the speech would have to be based on investigation rather than personal opinion.

Paul agreed and went to work. He began investigating with three main ideas in mind:

  I. Television Commercials
 II. College Lectures
III. Political Speeches

It did not take him long to realize that he was attempting too much. After consulting the focus model (Chapter 3) he narrowed his topic to college lectures. As he continued his investigation, though, his original idea changed in some fundamental ways.

Paul did an admirable job of researching his topic. In fact, because of the condition stipulated, he began organizing his speech around the various types of research he had done: the survey research he had found, his interviewing, and his library research.

As Paul roughed out his speech, he recognized that his most important ideas concerned the principles of message preparation that he was trying to debunk. The main points in his working outline, therefore, became the following:

I.   Are effective lectures focused?
II. Are effective lectures based on investigation?
III. Are effective lectures organized with an introduction, body, and conclusion?

As he continued to rough out his speech, he arranged his main points for effect. He felt he should begin with the principle with which he had found the most agreement, and end with the principle with which he had found the most disagreement. He felt that this ordering would increase audience interest as his speech progressed.[19] He also experimented with different ways of expressing each idea, and he roughed out an introduction, a conclusion, and some transitions from point to point.

By the time Paul gave his speech it was nothing like the speech he had originally intended. He titled his speech:

Do the Profs Practice What Our Prof Preaches?

Paul Urbanek
University of New Hampshire

Comments

Paul first establishes audience interest in his introduction.

1 How many times have you heard students say of one of their professors, "He's obviously brilliant, but I can't understand a word he says"? Richard Calish, writing in *The English Journal*, suggests that the communication gap between student and professor is a fairly common one. He blames it on (and I quote here) "the heartbreaking, headaching, agonizing, scandalizing inability of the average pedagogically inclined, university-trained preacher, teacher, or educational creature to convey a message clearly, briefly, succinctly, openly, understandably, interestingly, in quasi-grammatical and pseudo-punctuational, intelligible, semi-formal, and close-to-normal English from the aura of his own consciousness to that of his thirty or so questioning,

Comments

searching, listening young knowledge-intake organisms — the students.'' (Unquote).

2   It was statements like these that led me to today's topic. I wanted to find out if good lecturers use the principles we learn about in this class.

3   First I needed to find some of our best lecturers. I dug up the faculty evaluation surveys that are on file in the library. These forms are completed by students in each class each semester, and then filed in the library. Anytime you want to find out about your professors, you can look them up there.

4   One question on this survey seemed to be a good measure of a student's evaluation of his professor's ability to communicate. This item is ''The instructor communicates well.'' The possible responses from students range from 5 (highly descriptive) to 1 (not at all descriptive). I chose three professors who were consistently rated as ''5s'' on this item: Professor Wheeler, the physics professor renowned for his in-class demonstrations of exploding gases; Professor Booker, the firebrand of the English Literature Department; and Professor Hartley, Professor of Psychology and Director of the University Counseling Center.

5   I then interviewed these professors. I asked them questions about three of the principles we learn about in this class: investigation, organization, and focus. Specifically, I asked them the following questions:

1. Do you investigate new material for each lecture?
2. Do you organize each lecture with a clear-cut introduction, body, and conclusion?
3. Do you focus on one idea in your lectures?

6   Believe it or not, my model professors did not completely agree with these principles as we have learned them. They did agree, in reference to the first question, that a good lecture had to be based on investigation. But they generally found that their day-to-day research, reading, and interaction with colleagues kept them up-to-date enough in terms of the new material they presented.

7   Professor Wheeler summed up the profs' opinion on investigation when he told me, ''The new material is no problem. It is the standard material, like how many aspects of a particular phenomenon I have to cover, that I need to review before a lecture.''

8   In other words, the professors reinvestigated what they already knew. They did that to make sure that the material was fresh in their minds, and also to make sure that it was presented in an organized manner. That brought me to my second question:

9   ''Do you organize each lecture with a clear-cut introduction, body, and conclusion?'' Here the professors divided according to their discipline. Professor Booker of the English Department said, ''Definitely,'' but Professor Wheeler of Physics explained that his introductions and conclusions were developed around ''units,'' and a unit was impossible to cover in one class period. So, although he believed in organization, his introductions and conclusions were often several days apart! Professor Hartley of the Psychology Department gave the most interesting answer to this question. He said that

Comments

he didn't really believe in conclusions. He said that every one of his lectures began with a transition based on the previous lecture and ended with a transition to the next lecture. The course itself, he told me, ended with a transition to practical, everyday uses of what had been learned.

Transition to third
main point   **10**

By this time my faith in our revered principles was beginning to shake. It almost toppled when I asked the final question. That question dealt with focus, which has been introduced to us as a basic tenet of message preparation. All three profs gave me an identical answer when I asked them, ''Do you focus on one idea only throughout a lecture?'' They all told me, ''No.'' They all told me that they concentrated on one idea at a time, but they seldom gave an entire lecture based on one idea only.

11

I was confused, so I returned to the library. I started reviewing what some experts say about public speaking and how it relates to the college lecture hall. It didn't take me long to realize where I had gone wrong. Perhaps Shana Alexander, the well-known journalist, author, and lecturer, summed it up best. In an article entitled ''Unaccustomed As I Am,'' she stated, simply enough, ''A speech is not a lecture. The object of a 'Speech' is not to get points over; it is to try to make people feel something.''

Paul begins his
conclusion by tell-
ing where his
investigation led
him.   **12**

That hit me as such a revelation that I think I'll repeat it for you: ''A speech is not a lecture. The object is not to get points over; it is to try to make people feel something.'' I considered that statement a revelation because it summed up an important point for this course and for this speech: *Good lecturers try to make their audiences feel something.*

He then reviews his
main points.   **13**

That is why professors Wheeler, Booker, and Hartley are such good lecturers. They don't just ''get their points over.'' The make their audiences *feel* something. In order to do that, they make their lectures *a series of related speeches.* Each one of these speeches-within-a-lecture conforms to the principles of message preparation. They are all based on investigated material. They are all individually organized, and they all focus on one idea.

He reaffirms his
central idea.   **14**

So the profs do practice what our prof preaches. I haven't been able to debunk the principles of message preparation yet. In fact, after this experience, I think I'll quit trying.[20]

Paul distributed a formal outline of his speech to the class. It looked like this:

Topic: ''Do the Profs Practice What Our Prof Preaches?''

Purpose Statement: After listening to my speech, my audience members will recognize the relationship between the lectures they hear and the principles of public speaking.

Thesis Statement: An effective lecture is like a series of related speeches, each one of which conforms to the principles of message preparation.

    I.   Introduction
        A.   The Problem
            Quotation: Richard Calish

    B. The Methodology
       1. Surveys
       2. Interviews
          a. Investigation?
          b. Organization?
          c. Focus?

II. Body
    A. The Principle of Investigation: The profs all agree.
        Quotation: Professor Wheeler
    B. The Principle of Organization: The profs are divided by discipline.
       1. Prof. Booker: "Definitely"
       2. Prof. Wheeler: "Units"
       3. Prof. Hartley: "No Conclusions"
    C. The Principle of Focus: The profs seem to disagree.

III. Conclusion
    A. A Speech Is Not a Lecture
        Quotation: Shana Alexander
    B. The Basic Principles Revisited

Summary

This chapter dealt with speech organization, a process that begins with the formulation of a thesis statement to express the central idea of a speech. The thesis is established in the introduction, developed in the body, and reviewed in the conclusion of a structured speech. The introduction will also gain the audience's attention, set the mood and tone of the speech, and demonstrate the importance of your topic to the audience.

Organizing the body of the speech will begin with a prospectus, which is a list of points you might want to make in your speech. These points are organized according to the principles of outlining. They are divided, coordinated, and placed in a logical order. Transitions from point to point help make this order apparent to your audience.

Organization follows a pattern such as that of time, space, topic, problem-solution, cause-effect, and climax arrangements.

Along with reviewing your thesis and/or main points, the conclusion also helps the audience remember these ideas.

Questions/Assignments

1. Do you agree that the working outline is an effective method for developing message organization? What other methods have helped you?
2. It is stated that at times you might *not* want to refer directly to your main points in your introduction. Can you think of any topics and/or audiences for which an initial preview should be avoided? Explain your answer.

3. Select a speech (or written message) from your class, *Vital Speeches, Representative American Speeches,* the local newspaper, or any other suitable source. Decide what you believe to be the message's *purpose,* and observe the method of organization of main points (chronological, spatial, and so on). Do you think the method employed was appropriate for the purpose? Why or why not?

4. Read a speech (from *Vital Speeches* or another source) or listen to one. Evaluate the introduction and conclusion. Did the speaker fulfill the objectives stated in this text? If not, how might these aspects of the message be changed in order to make the presentation more effective?

5. Review the Paul Urbanek speech at the end of this chapter. After thinking about the evidence he presents, do you agree or disagree with his conclusion that "Profs" really *do* practice the principles of message preparation? Why or why not?

Notes

1. Jerome S. Bruner, "Learning and Thinking," in Richard C. Anderson and David P. Ausubel, eds., *Readings in the Psychology of Cognition* (New York: Holt, Rinehart and Winston, 1965), p. 77.

2. Jevons's experiment, conducted in 1871, is reported in Edwin G. Boring, *The Physical Dimensions of Consciousness* (New York: Dover, 1963), p. 195.

3. George A. Miller, "The Magical Number Seven, Plus or Minus Two: Some Limits on Our Capacity for Processing Information," in Anderson and Ausubel, *op. cit.,* pp. 242–267.

4. *Ibid.,* p. 241.

5. Studies have demonstrated that messages are, in general, not only better comprehended, but more persuasive, and the speaker more credible, when messages are well organized. See R. G. Smith, "Effects of Speech Organization upon Attitudes of College Students," *Speech Monographs* 18, 1951, pp. 292–301; E. Thompson, "Some Effects of Message Structure on Listeners' Comprehension," *Speech Monographs* 39, 1967, pp. 51–57; H. Sharp and T. McClung, "Effects of Organization on the Speaker's Ethos, " *Speech Monographs* 33, 1966, p. 182; and J. C. McCroskey and R. S. Mehrley, "The Effects of Disorganization and Nonfluency on Attitude Change and Source Credibility," *Speech Monographs* 36, 1969, pp. 13–21.

6. J. M. Innes, "The Next-in-Line Effect and the Recall of Structured and Unstructured Material," *British Journal of Social Psychology* 21:1, February 1982, pp. 1–5.

7. Lyman K. Steil, *Your Personal Listening Profile* (New York: Sperry Corp., 1980).

8. Study cited in Floyd L. Ruch and Philip G. Zimbardo, *Psychology and Life,* 8th ed. (Glenview, Ill.: Scott, Foresman, 1971), p. 267.

9. Studies indicate that ideas are better recalled by listeners if they are placed *either* at the beginning *or* at the end of a presentation. This research is summarized in G. Cronkhite, *Persuasion: Speech and Behavioral Change* (Indianapolis: Bobbs-Merrill, 1969), pp. 195–196.

10. The term *prospectus* is used in this way in Leon Fletcher, *How to Design and Deliver a Speech* (New York: Chandler, 1973), p. 259.

11. Different experts suggest different procedures for outlining, and often the rules are not this hard-and-fast. However, I have found the procedure presented here to be the most clear-cut and useful for formal outlining.

12. Plato, *Phaedrus,* translated by B. Jowett in *The Works of Plato* (New York: Tudor, n.d.), vol. 3, p. 446.

13. See, for example, George A. Miller, *op. cit.*

14. Alan H. Monroe and Douglas Ehninger, *Principles and Types of Speech Communication,* 7th ed. (Glenview, Ill.: Scott, Foresman, 1974).

15. Katherine Graham, "The Press and Its Responsibilities," *Vital Speeches of the Day* 42, April 15, 1976.

16. Deanna Sellnow, "Have You Checked Lately?" *Winning Orations, 1983* (Interstate Oratorical Association, 1983), p. 58.

17. From Red Cross fund-raising material.

18. Katherine Graham, *op. cit.*

19. The results of survey and experimental studies indicate that a source's credibility and the effectiveness of a message are *both* enhanced if arguments likely to gain audience acceptance are presented first. See J. C. McCroskey and S. V. O. Prichard, "Selective Exposure and Lyndon B. Johnson's January, 1966, State of the Union Address," *Journal of Broadcasting* 11, 1967, pp. 331–337; and P. Tannenbaum, "Mediated Generalization of Attitude Change via the Principle of Congruity," *Journal of Personality and Social Psychology* 3, 1966, pp. 493–500.

20. References: Richard Calish, "Don't Talk, Communicate," *English Journal* 62, October 1973, pp. 1010–1011; Shana Alexander, "Unaccustomed As I Am," in W. W. Wilmot and J. R. Wenburg, eds., *Communication Involvement: Personal Perspectives* (New York: Wiley, 1974), p. 313, originally published in *Life,* May 19, 1967.

7

Supporting
Material

The Functions of Supporting Material

Supporting material is the information you use to develop your ideas in a speech. It comes in various forms, but before we look at those forms we would do well to examine the functions of support, which include making your ideas clear, interesting, memorable, and convincing.

To Clarify

Those who have not made a careful study of communication are apt to believe that meaning is transferred from one person to another the same way physical matter is transferred: you just hand it over, and that is that. Unfortunately, it is not that easy. Meaning, unlike matter, always changes form in the process of being transferred. People attach different meanings to words and ideas because of different experiences they have had.[1] Those different experiences make supporting material necessary.

Most people will admit that everyone has lived through different experiences. Few, however, realize how vastly different our *stores* of experiences are. There is evidence that the human brain works like a high-speed tape recorder, storing all our experiences. Some of the most star-

135

tling experiments to demonstrate the phenomenal recording capacity of the brain were conducted by Dr. Wilder Penfield.[2] Penfield was a neurosurgeon looking for a cure for epilepsy. He believed that he could control epileptic seizures by subjecting the proper section of the brain to electric impulses. To test this theory it was necessary for patients to remain conscious while exposed portions of the brain were probed with an electric current. Each time the probe was inserted, however, the patients began talking about obscure recollections—things that could not otherwise be remembered—in detail so specific that it supported the idea that everything that has been in our conscious awareness is recorded in detail and stored in the brain, either consciously or subconsciously.

Everything is recorded! The ramifications of that are mind-boggling when you consider research that suggests that around 600,000 different "messages" can be received by the average person *each minute*.[3] One psychologist told the story of a bricklayer who, under hypnosis, "described correctly every bump and grain on the top surface of a brick he had laid in a wall 20 years before."[4] Is it any wonder that each one of us attaches meanings to words and ideas in slightly different ways?[5] How could the word "brick" or a statement such as "Brick is the best type of building material" mean the same thing to you that it does to that bricklayer? The answer is that it cannot. You would need to explain your use of the word "best," for example, to make that statement clear to anyone. Would you mean that brick is best for looks, durability, or ease of installation?

The need for quality explanation becomes more severe as modern people become more saturated with messages that demand their attention. Unfortunately, even as the need for quality explanation becomes evident, we are losing our faith in our ability to transmit information clearly. We seem to have developed a kind of communication paranoia. We are suspicious of all the intervening variables and breakdowns that might occur between a source and a receiver of communication. This communication paranoia was demonstrated when many women withdrew their support from the Equal Rights Amendment, even though they were in favor of its basic idea: "Equality of rights under law shall not be denied or abridged on account of sex." *Time* magazine analyzed the reticence of those who withdrew their support as follows:

> . . . The brevity and broad phrasing of the amendment seemed to feed suspicions of hidden meanings. Said (N.Y.) State Senator Karen Burstein, "If someone came away believing there was even a 1-in-100 chance of unisex toilets, then she'd vote against ERA.[6]

With that sort of communication paranoia running around unleashed, it becomes imperative to amplify your ideas in such a way that the receiver can consider those ideas from a specific point of view. For example, if you were explaining to someone ignorant of automobile mechanics where a carburetor is located, it would do no good to explain that it is "on top of the intake manifold" or "next to the fuel pump" or "to the right of the distributor." Those explanations are all from the perspective of someone who already understands what a carburetor is and where it is located. For someone ignorant of the design of an internal-combustion engine, you might have to say, "It's that big greasy thing right on top of the engine" or "It's right under the thing that looks like a metal Frisbee with 'air filter' written on it."

As you can see, quantity of information is not enough. You must pick information that amplifies *and* changes the perspective of what you are explaining. In other words, you have to give your audience a different way to "look at" the idea. For example, if you were talking about recycling, every member of your audience could have a different idea about what you meant. To some, recycling refers just to aluminum beer cans. To others, the term means reusing everything that is normally thrown away as refuse. You could use supporting material to clarify this idea:

> The type of recycling I'm talking about here involves separating from the rest of your trash all glass, metals, newspapers, and magazines. The papers and magazines must be bundled, the containers must be uncapped and washed, and labels must be removed from the cans. The material is then placed in a separate container for removal once a week to a municipal recycling center.

Making your ideas clear is probably the most important function of supporting material, but its remaining three functions will make the difference between effective support and support that is just adequate.

To Make Interesting

A second use of support is to make an idea interesting or to catch your audience's attention. The audience might know what you mean by "recycling" now, but still not care. Supporting material could be used to bolster their interest in your topic.

> Outside New York City, where sewage has been dumped into the ocean for years, a large mass of thick, life-choking sludge is slowly inching its way toward the shore. It might be too late for New York, but we might be able to avoid the same problem here, if we take action now.

To Make Memorable

A third purpose of supporting material, related to the one above, is to make a point memorable.

One way of making a point memorable is to use language (yours or someone else's, in the form of a quotation) that is striking to the ear. Another way is to use facts and information that stress the importance of the point. For example:

> The State Environmental Protection Agency recently measured the air in this area, and what they found suggests that each and every one of us, at this

moment, is breathing poisons into his or her respective system. These are cumulative, carcinogenic chemical toxins, and they are caused by our township incinerator burning garbage that could just as easily be sold and reused.

To Prove

Finally, supporting material can be used as evidence, to prove the truth of what you are saying. For example, if you said, "The way our local landfill area is filling up, it might have to be closed in a year or so," your audience would find it easy to disagree with you. Supporting material makes it less easy to disagree:

> According to Tom Murray, our village chief sanitation engineer and the man in charge of landfill areas, all our landfills will be filled to capacity and closed within one year. This means, in no uncertain terms, that we are not going to have anywhere to put our garbage.

As you may have noticed, each function of support could be fulfilled by several different types of material. An examination of these different types of supporting material follows.

Forms of Support

Definitions

Definitions identify ideas in a brief statement. It is a good idea to give your audience definitions of your key terms, especially if those terms are unfamiliar to them or are being used in a unique way. Do not assume that your audience attaches the same meaning to a key word or phrase that you do. Meanings are in people — not in words.[7] Your definitions should be simple, concise, and stated in such a way that no other terms within the definition need to be defined.

Dictionary definitions are handy, especially for determining the most acceptable meaning for a word, but you should be careful about using them to define your terms in your speech. Your own carefully chosen words are usually more effective than a dictionary definition. For example, someone speaking on the topic of abortion might not want to use Webster's second meaning:

> By abortion, I mean "monstrosity."

Dictionaries are written for very general audiences. If you were speaking on the abortion issue and relying on another dictionary definition, you might be stuck with:

> By abortion, I mean the expulsion of a nonviable fetus.

That might be an accurate definition, but it also might be too technical for a college audience. It might be clearer to say:

> By abortion, I mean the termination of pregnancy before the twelfth week of gestation.

if that is what you mean.

Another thing wrong with dictionaries is that they might give you a definition that includes the term itself, and that will sometimes make it *seem* as if you are clarifying an idea when you actually are not:

> By abortion, I mean the induced abortion of a fetus.

To define "abortion" with the word "abortion" does not change the perspective on the idea enough to make it clear.

One last problem with dictionary definitions is that they have a tendency to change more slowly than the reality they represent.[8] You might use the term "female chauvinist sexist" in a speech about women employers who discriminate against men. However, if you looked those terms up in *The Random House College Dictionary,* 1972 edition, you would find that "female" means "woman" (as you might expect), but "chauvinist" means "patriot" and "sexist" means "someone who discriminates against women." Therefore, a "female chauvinist sexist" would be a woman patriot who discriminates against women!

Remember: To define something, tell what *you* mean by it. There are two ways to do so. You could formulate a traditional definition or an operational definition. A *traditional definition* places a thing in a class and tells how that thing is different from other things in that class. The classic example is proposed by Aristotle: "Man is a featherless biped." (Aristotle considered fur to be a type of "feather.") Man (and woman, too, we might add) is therefore defined as belonging to a class (bipeds) but different from the other members of that class in that he does not have feathers. (It has been pointed out, however, that kangaroos and plucked chickens might also fit this definition.)

An *operational definition* tells you how to experience the thing you are describing. It tells you where you have to go or what you have to do to perceive a thing. For example, we could use an operational definition to define recycling: First you separate glass, metals, newspapers, and magazines from the rest of your trash, and so on. Operational definitions for "man" might sound something like this:

> You want to know what a man is? Go down to the graduation ceremonies for marine boot camp. Those are men.

or:

> You want to know what a man is? Go to the state school for the retarded, and watch the men who work with those kids every day with compassion and unfailing patience. Those are men.

Descriptions

A description forms an image of how something would be perceived through the senses. It is a "word picture," a direct rendering of the details that summarize something from *your perspective*. An abortion, for example, could be described as a simple, painless, safe operation, or as the nightmare of being at the mercy of a hack butcher. This is how Dr. Martin Luther King, Jr., in his speech "I Have a Dream," described the plight of the black American:

> There are those who are asking the devotees of civil rights, "When will you be satisfied?" We can never be satisfied as long as the Negro is the victim of the unspeakable horrors of police brutality. We can never be satisfied as long as our bodies, heavy with the fatigue of travel, cannot gain lodging in the motels of the highways and the hotels of the cities. We cannot be satisfied as long as the Negro's basic mobility is from a smaller ghetto to a larger one. We can never be satisfied as long as our children are stripped of their selfhood and robbed of their dignity by signs stating "for whites only."[9]

King's description helps us to imagine pain and fatigue, as well as the sight of a sign that says "for whites only." These things can be truly perceived only through the senses, but he manages to give us an image of them by capturing their essence in a few words.

One student borrowed a columnist's description of boxing to begin his speech on that topic:

> Up close, it's a stunning sight. The men dancing and ducking, lips swollen, hair matted, skin slick-polished to a glass. There is a shift of weight, an advance of the bodies, a pause, a retreat. Finally one or another finds what he is seeking: a few inches of exposed belly, an eye that can be poked, an unprotected cheek or nose. If the punch is true, fans near the ring will stiffen. If there is a sign that he is hurt, then the arena becomes a wind tunnel — the howling shakes the place. And the fans in the front rows are anointed by a gentle rain, of sweat and blood.[10]

Analogies

We use analogies, or comparisons, all the time, often in the form of figures of speech such as similes and metaphors. A *simile* is a direct comparison that usually uses *like* or *as,* whereas a *metaphor* is an implied comparison that does not use *like* or *as.* If you said, "Student unrest is like psoriasis: it flares up, then subsides, but never quite goes away," you would be using a simile. If you used phrases such as "simmering student unrest" or "an avalanche of student unrest," you would be using metaphors, because you have implied comparison between student unrest and slowly boiling liquid or a snow slide.

Analogies are extended metaphors. We run across analogies all the time. Here, for example, is the way Ingmar Bergman describes old age:

Old age is like climbing a mountain. You climb from ledge to ledge. The higher you get, the more tired and breathless you become, but your view becomes much more extensive.

Here is the way Carl Sagan explains the age of the universe through analogy:

The most instructive way I know to express this cosmic chronology is to imagine the fifteen-billion-year lifetime of the universe (or at least its present incarnation since the Big Bang) compressed into the span of a single year. . . . It is disconcerting to find that in such a cosmic year the Earth does not condense out of interstellar matter until early September: dinosaurs emerge on Christmas Eve; flowers arise on December 28th; and men and women originate at 10:30 P.M. on New Year's Eve. All of recorded history occupies the last ten seconds of December 31; and the time from the waning of the Middle Ages to the present occupies little more than one second.[11]

Here is how a newspaper reporter pointed out how relatively inexpensive bike lanes can be:

The proposed four-mile-long freeway in New York City at $1.6 billion could finance 100,000 miles of rural bikeways. Or, alternatively, ribbon bikeways could be built paralleling the whole 40,000-mile national Interstate System of highways.[12]

Analogies can be used to compare or contrast an unknown concept with a known one. For example, if you had difficulty explaining to a public speaking class composed mostly of music majors why they should practice their speeches out loud, you might use this analogy:

We all realize that great masters often can compose music in their heads; Beethoven, for example, composed his greatest masterpieces after he had gone deaf and couldn't even hear the instruments play out his ideas. However, beginners have to sit down at a piano or some other instrument and play their pieces as they create them. It is much the same way for beginning public speakers. When composing their speeches, they need to use their instruments — their voices — to hear how their ideas sound.

For an audience of music majors, this analogy might clarify the concept of practicing a speech. For a class of electrical engineers who may not know Beethoven from the Beatles, this analogy might confuse rather than clarify. It is important to make your analogies appropriate to your audience.

Anecdotes

An anecdote is a brief story with a point, often (but not always) based on personal experience. (The word *anecdote* comes from the Greek, meaning "unpublished item.") Anecdotes can add a lively, personal touch to your explanation. For example, a minister used the following anecdote to demonstrate the communication problems he sometimes has with members of his congregation.

> I ought not to be surprised by anything at my time of life, but one of my flock did manage to take my breath away. I was preaching about the Father's tender wisdom in caring for us all; illustrated by saying that the Father knows which of us grows best in sunlight and which of us must have shade. "You know you plant roses in the sunshine," I said, "and heliotrope and geraniums; but if you want your fuchsias to grow they must be kept in a shady nook." After the sermon, which I hoped would be a comforting one, a woman came up to me, her face glowing with pleasure that was evidently deep and true. "Oh, Dr. _____, I am so grateful for that sermon," she said, clasping my hand and shaking it warmly. My heart glowed for a moment, while I wondered what tender place in her heart and life I had touched. Only for a moment, though. "Yes," she went on fervently, "I never knew before what was the matter with my fuchsias."[13]

The minister's anecdote contains an analogy, which makes it a good example of how two types of supporting material can be combined. That brings us to our next type of supporting material: examples.

Examples

An example is a specific case that is used to demonstrate a general idea. Examples can be either factual or hypothetical, personal or borrowed. They can also be combined with another type of support. Senator Edward Kennedy, in his speech before the 1980 Democratic convention, wanted to stress economic problems. He relied on an anecdote that contained several examples:

> Among you, my golden friends across this land, I have listened and learned.
>
> I have listened to Kenny Dubois, a glass-blower in Charleston, West Virginia, who has 10 children to support but has lost his job after 35 years, just three years short of qualifying for his pension.
>
> I have listened to the Trachta family, who farm in Iowa and who wonder whether they can pass the good life and the good earth on to their children.
>
> I have listened to the grandmother in East Oakland who no longer has a phone to call her grandchildren, because she gave it up to pay the rent on her small apartment.
>
> I have listened to young workers out of work, to students without the tuition for college and to families without the chance to own a home. I have seen the closed factories and the stalled assembly lines of Anderson, Indiana, and Southgate, California. And I have seen too many — far too many — idle men and women desperate to work. I have seen too many — far too many — working families desperate to protect the value of their wages from the ravages of inflation.[14]

Hypothetical examples can be even more powerful than factual examples, because hypothetical examples ask the audience to imagine something—thus causing them to become active participants in the thought. If you were speaking on the subject of euthanasia (mercy killing), you might ask your audience to imagine that someone they loved was suffering and being kept alive by a machine.

Examples can be effective in clarifying information and making it interesting and memorable. Strictly speaking, however, they do not prove a point because they refer only to isolated instances that might not be representative. To prove an idea with examples, you have to collect a number of them; at that point they become statistics.

Quantification and Statistics

Quantification is the use of numbers to clarify a concept, to make it more specific. One example of quantification comes from a lecture given by a professor at Columbia University. He wanted to develop the idea that inflation lowers the value of paper currency, so he used quantification (developed in an anecdote) in the following way:

> Some time ago, I found a postcard which I had written to my father on November 23, 1923, while I was attending a boarding school in Germany. The card asked that my father send the bursar "immediately 1.2 trillion marks. If the tuition is not paid by the end of the month, you will have to pay four gold marks."

> Those two figures—1.2 trillion paper and four gold marks—illustrate the catastrophic fraud of the great German inflation which resulted in a revolutionary change in the economic and above all the social order of the country.[15]

Statistics are numbers that are arranged or organized to show how a fact or principle is true for a large number of cases. Statistics are actually collections of examples, which is why they are often more effective as proof than are isolated examples. For example, if you wanted to develop the idea that youths in the United States are not well informed about the economic system, the following example would be insufficient proof:

> I asked my younger brother the other day if he knew the difference between collectivism and a free-enterprise society, and he had no idea. He didn't even know that the U.S. economy is based on free enterprise.

If you combine that with proof based on *lots* of young people's responses it would be more effective:

> A 1985 study by the Joint Council on Economic Education showed that 50 percent of high school students could not distinguish between collectivism and a free-enterprise society, and 50 percent did not know the U.S. economy was based on free enterprise.

Because statistics are potentially powerful proof, you have the ethical responsibility to cite them exactly as they were published or tabulated. It's usually all right to "round off" a percentage or other figure, but it's considered bad form to manipulate your statistics so they sound better than is justified. For example, the term *average* is often used to manipulate statistics. As there are actually three measures of central tendency, or "averages" (mean, median, and mode), it is important to be clear about which one you mean. Imagine that you had the following list of annual incomes for a group of five people:

1. $0
2. $0
3. $500
4. $750
5. $23,750

The mode (most frequent value) for that group would be $0, the mean (arithmetic average) would be $5000, and the median (the point at which 50 percent of the values are greater and 50 percent are less) would be $500. Any of these figures could be cited as the "average" by an unscrupulous speaker.

Another responsibility calls for you to cite the complete source of your statistic along with any other information that would have a bearing on its validity. Established professional pollsters such as Gallup, Roper, and Harris, as well as the best magazines and newspapers, have reputations for accuracy. If you cite them, your audience can be relatively sure that your statistics are reliable. Sometimes the source of a statistic will cause it to be suspect, as when, years ago, a cigarette company mailed cartons of cigarettes to doctors and then sent those same doctors a questionnaire asking which brand of cigarettes they were then smoking. Shortly afterward, advertising for the company stated that seven out of ten doctors reported smoking that brand.[16]

A third rule about the use of statistics is based on effectiveness rather than ethics. You should reduce the statistic to a concrete image, if possible. For example, $1 billion in $100 bills would be about the same height as a sixty-story building. Using such concrete images will make your statistics more than "just numbers."

Sometimes an analogy can be used to clarify a statistic or make it more vivid. Candy Lightner used this technique in the sample speech in Chapter 1. She wanted to impress on her audience the enormity of the drunk driving problem, which claims 2500 lives each year in the state of California alone:

> If ten jetliners were to crash in the State of California in a year's time and in each crash, 250 people were to die, you'd better believe that the press would jump all over the issue. . . . But when the same number of people are killed at the rate of seven or eight a day in drunk driving crashes . . . the problem is virtually ignored. . . .

If you are going to refer extensively to statistical data, they could be tabulated on a chart and presented as a visual aid.

Quotations and Testimony

Using a familiar, artistically stated saying will enable you to take advantage of someone else's memorable wording. For example, if you were giving a speech on the pros and cons of personal integrity, you might quote Mark Twain, who said, "Always do right. This will gratify some people, and astonish the rest." A quotation like that fits Alexander Pope's definition of true wit: "What oft was thought, but ne'er so well expressed."

You can also use quotations as *testimony,* to prove a point by using the support of someone who is more authoritative or experienced on the subject than you.

One speaker recently used quotation for this purpose when he began a speech on stage fright:

> According to Professor Hans Larson, a highly respected psychologist and editor of *The Anxiety Quarterly,* speech anxiety is one of the most prevalent fears in contemporary society.

Notice in this example that Larson is introduced as "a highly respected psychologist and editor of *The Anxiety Quarterly.*" If you quote testimony from a source that your audience will not immediately recognize, it is important to identify that source in this way.

You can usually signal to your audience that you are using a quotation simply by pausing or by changing your pace or inflection slightly. If you want to be more formal, you can preface the quotation with some variation of "And I quote . . ." and end it with some variation of "end of quote" (although that technique becomes tiresome if used too often).

Visual Aids

Sometimes information is clearer, more interesting, more persuasive, and more memorable when it is presented visually. Figure 7–1 provides one example. Saying that a billion is a thousand millions is not nearly as effective as demonstrating that fact graphically. (Imagine how you might use this display in a speech on the increasing national debt.)

Visual aids serve several purposes. They can show how things look (photos of your trek to Nepal or the effects of malnutrition). They can show how things work (demonstration of a new ski binding, a diagram of how sea water is made drinkable). Visual aids can also show how things relate to one another (the million-billion example in Figure 7–1; a graph showing the relationship between gender, education, and income). Finally, they can show important information clearly (steps in filing a claim in small claims court, symptoms of anemia).

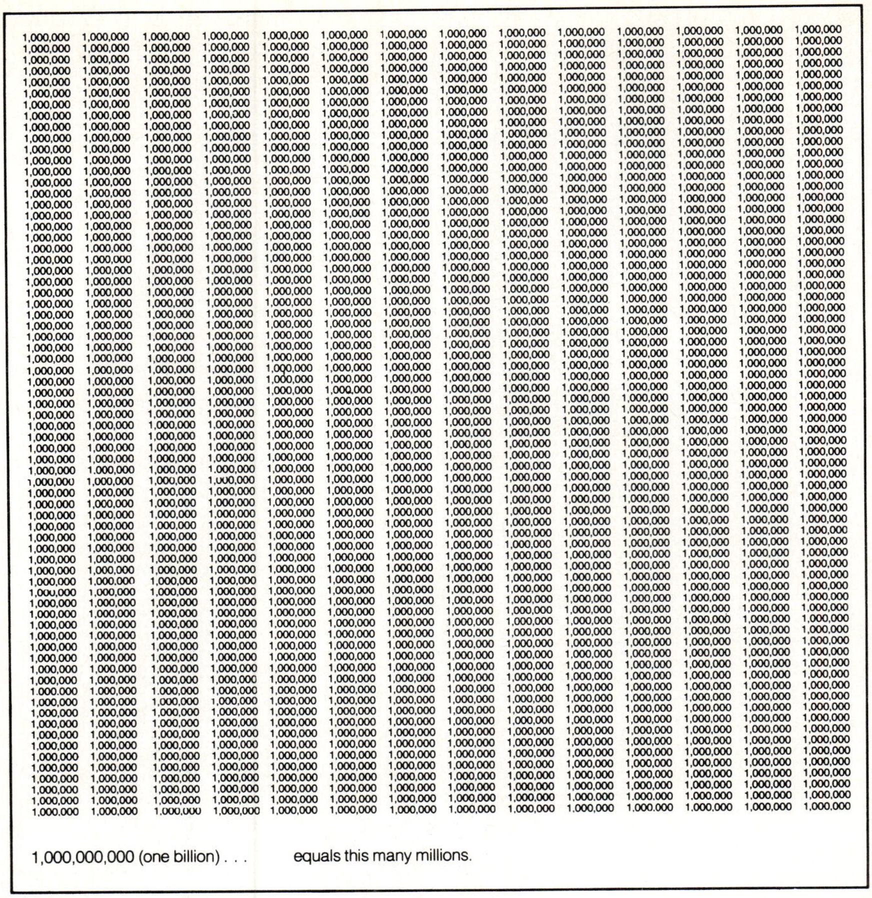

1,000,000,000 (one billion) . . .   equals this many millions.

Figure 7–1

Table 7–1 lists several types of visual aids. Whatever types you use, keep the following points in mind:

1. Keep your visual aids simple. Your goal is to clarify, not confuse. Cover only one idea per aid. Use only key words or phrases, not sentences. Use eight or fewer lines of text, each with 25 or fewer characters. Keep all printing horizontal. Omit all nonessential details.
2. Visual aids should be large enough for your entire audience to see them at one time, but portable enough so you can get them out of the way when they no longer pertain to the point you are making.
3. They should be visually interesting and as neat as possible. If you do not have the necessary skills, try to get help from a friend or at the audiovisual center on your campus.
4. They must be appropriate to all the components of the speaking

TABLE 7–1   Types of Visual Aids

Objects
  Real-life (samples of poisonous plants)
  Models (an architectural plan)
Demonstrations
  Process (first aid procedures)
  Product use (fire extinguisher)
  Behavior (job interview)
Illustrations
  Slides (enlargements of microscopic samples)
  Drawings (blueprints, plans)
  Artwork (portraits)
  Photographs (enlargements)
Tables and charts
  Graphs (sales curve)
  Lists (key personnel)
Handouts
  Lists (addresses and phone numbers)
  Instructions (steps in C.P.R.)
  Outlines
Audiovisuals
  Videotape (excerpt from TV broadcast)
  Film
  Sound-on-slides

situation — you, the audience, and your topic — and they must emphasize the point you are trying to make. Often a speaker will grab a visual aid that has *something* to do with the topic and use it even though it is not directly related — such as showing a map of a city transit system while talking about the condition of the individual cars.

5. You must be in control of your visual aid at all times. Wild animals, chemical reactions, and gimmicks meant to shock a crowd are often too likely to backfire.

6. Talk to your audience, not to your visual aid. It is all right to glance at your chart from time to time to see where you are pointing, but do not become too wrapped up in your props. If you turn your back on your audience, you sacrifice all your eye contact and much of your audience contact.

Two anecdotes illustrate the consequences of improperly used visual aids. The first is supplied by two well-known teachers of speech:

The student's chosen subject was "The Treatment of Snake Bites." Having introduced his subject, he startled his audience by releasing a white rat from a cardboard canister. The speaker announced the rat's name was Maudie, and whipped out a hypodermic needle. Plunging the needle into Maudie, he explained that he was giving the animal a injection of snake venom. Maudie would expire within a few seconds, he said. Meanwhile, he would explain what steps a human being should take if bitten by a poisonous snake. To clarify these steps the speaker now drew grease-penciled lines and circles on

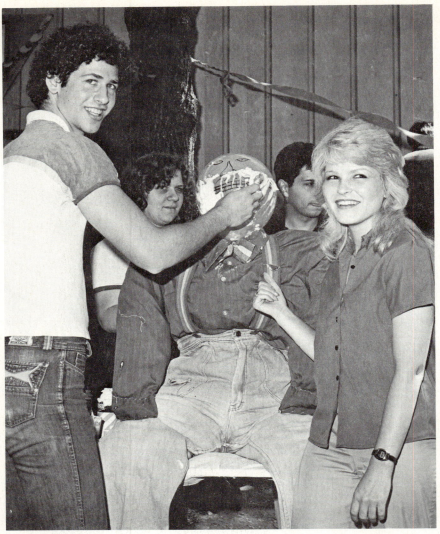

Three-dimensional visual aids can add a lively touch to your presentation.

his forearm to indicate where incisions should be made in cases of snake bite. But Maudie was dragging herself about, gasping her last in full view of everyone. Naturally, her troubles drew even the speaker's attention away from his explanations. He interrupted himself to comment: "Oh yes. Bleeding at the mouth—quite natural at this stage."[17]

The spectacle of a dying mouse made that student's visual aid more of a distraction than a clarification. Comedian Alan Sherman told about a similar experience he had at the University of Illinois:

President Reagan used this chart to clarify one of his key ideas in a speech on the economy.

I walked to the lectern. I hemmed. Then I hawed. I cleared my throat. Then I said:

"I shall give an illustrated lecture on the interior of the human mouth — the teeth, the tongue, the upper palate, the lower palate, and other points of interest."

Then, to illustrate my lecture, I stuck my finger in my mouth, as if to point out the various things I was talking about, and for five solid minutes I spoke totally unintelligible gibberish, never removing the finger from my mouth and sometimes inserting my entire fist.[18]

Aids that extend senses other than sight are also effective in some circumstances. If you were speaking about perfume, skunks, or the effects of a chemical plant on a community, actually producing the appropriate smells might help explain your point. If you were talking about baking brownies or brewing beer, a taste probably would not hurt. You could incorporate something to touch if you were speaking about the texture of good potting soil or the feel of chinchilla fur.

Audio aids such as tape recordings and records can supply information that could not be presented any other way (comparing musical styles, for example, or demonstrating the differences in the sounds of gas and diesel engines), but in most cases you should use them sparingly. Remember that your presentation already relies heavily on your audience's sense of hearing; it is better to use a visual aid, if possible, than to overwork the audio. Of course there are audiovisual aids, including films, videotapes, and sound-on-slide. They should also be used sparingly, however, because they allow the audience members to receive information passively, relieving them of the responsibility to become active participants in the presentation.[19]

No matter what type of presentation aid you are using, you have to be explicit about the point you are making. Consider the story of the football coach who was convinced that his team's poor physical condition was caused by alcohol abuse. The coach set up a demonstration for the team. He took two worms, and dropped one into a glass of water and the other into a glass of beer. The worm that was dropped into the water just swam lazily about, apparently enjoying itself. The worm that was dropped into the beer writhed in agony and died within a few seconds.

"There," said the coach. "Do you see what I'm trying to tell you?"

"We sure do," said the offensive tackle, one of the worst guzzlers on the team. "If we keep drinking, we won't get worms."

You can use the types of supporting material we described in still other interesting ways. However, this sweeping coverage should give you the idea that explanation is a creative process that requires time and effort. That effort can make the difference between being understood and not being understood.

Audience Analysis and Forms of Support

In Chapter 4 we discussed how audience analysis can help you choose a suitable topic for a speech. It is also important in choosing effective support.

Before you decide to use a particular form of support, remember to ask yourself if this material will make your point clearer, more interesting, more memorable, or more convincing *for this particular audience*. Look at factors such as audience purpose, attitudes, beliefs, and values; and if the answer to your question is not yes, find some other form of support.

For example, consider the following introduction to a speech on "The Loss of Childhood" given at a recent national tournament.[20] The speaker knew that her audience of college students and professors were intelligent, well-read, and concerned about social issues. She began with a quotation:

> "As a distinctive childhood culture wastes away, we watch with fascination and dismay." This insight of Neil Postman, author of *Disappearance of Childhood,* raised a poignant point. Childhood in America is vanishing. Gradually, subtly. And to many, almost imperceptibly . . .

Was this enough supporting material to involve this particular audience? These were men and women who believed in thinking about a topic in depth, and to think about something in depth you have to focus on your specific object of inquiry. The speaker would have to add a definition of precisely what she meant by "the loss of childhood":

> What do I mean when I talk about the loss of childhood? I don't mean the physical growth of a child into an adult, but I am talking about pressure. The pressure placed by adults in a child's life to grow up fast.

Now she had clarified what she meant, but when she thought about her audience some more, she recognized that they would be most concerned about a problem of genuine social importance. So she added the following:

> As Postman stated it, "The language, games, tastes, sexuality, and clothing of our children and adults are becoming indistinguishable." During a recent ABC News report, it was stated that "one of the major reasons children are turning to alcohol, drugs, early sexual activity, and suicide is to alleviate the pressures to grow up fast."

Sample Speech

The following speech was given before a congressional subcommittee looking into the problem of television violence.[21] The speech relies heavily upon statistics and testimony as supporting material. Notice also how these forms combine with other forms of support.

Violence on TV

The Effect on Children
Dr. Thomas Elmendorf
American Medical Association

Quantification (of
experience)

1 Mr. Chairman and members of the subcommittee, I am Dr. Thomas Elmendorf. I have been in general practice in California for 28 years and in emergency medicine for the last two in Sacramento, California. I appear here today as a past president of the California Medical Association and as a CMA delegate to the American Medical Association. The medical associations that I represent and I are deeply concerned about the effects of television on the youth of today.

Analogy (comparing
TV viewing time to
being "at the
movies")

2   Suppose you sent your child off to the movies for three hours next Sunday. And three hours on Monday and the same number of hours Tuesday, Wednesday, Thursday, Friday, and Saturday. That is essentially what is happening to the average child in America today, except it is not the screen in the movie house down the street he sits in front of, it is instead the television set right in your own home.

Statistics/Comparison

3   According to the Nielsen Index figures for TV viewing, it is estimated that by the time a child graduates from high school he has had 11,000 hours of schooling, as opposed to 15,000 hours of television. I would like to repeat that. By the time a child is 18 years old, he has spent more hours in front of the television set than he has in school. Over TV he will have witnessed by that

Statistics/Description/Examples

time some 18,000 murders and countless highly detailed incidents of robbery, arson, bombings, shooting, beatings, forgery, smuggling, and torture — averaging approximately one per minute in the standard television cartoon for children under the age of ten. In general, seventy-five percent of all network dramatic programs contain violence with over seven violent episodes per program hour.

Statistics

4   Concurrent with this massive daily dose of violence over our television screens has been a dramatic rise in violence in our society. In 1973, 18,000 young Americans from 15 to 24 years of age died in motor-vehicle accidents, with one of every six of these fatalities estimated to be due to suicide. In 1973, more than 5000 were murdered, and an additional 4000 committed suicide. The death rate for this age group was 19 percent higher in 1973 than in 1960, due entirely to deaths by violence.

Example/Statistics

5   The largest rise in deaths by homicide during the past two decades was at the ages of one to four. More than a million American children suffer physical abuse or neglect each year, and at least one in five dies from mistreatment. It is a social problem of epidemic proportions.

Statistics/Analogies
(comparing U.S. to
Scandinavia,
Manhattan to U.K.)

6   In fact, murder is the fastest growing cause of death in the United States. The annual rate of increase exceeded 100 percent between 1960 and 1974. Our homicide rate is 10 times greater than in the Scandinavian countries. More murders are committed yearly in Manhattan, with a population of

Forms of Support

one-and-a-half-million, than in the entire United Kingdom, with a population of 60-million.

Statistics/Examples 7   The age group most involved, with the greatest number of both victims and arrests, is 20 to 24. In 1972, 17 percent of all homicide victims and 24 percent of all arrests were in this age group. Teenagers from 15 to 19 account for another nine percent of all murder victims and nearly 19 percent of the arrests. In commenting about such crimes by youths, one author said,

Quotation (by anonymous author, for memorable wording) "It is as though our society has bred a new genetic strain, the child-murderer, who feels no remorse and is scarcely conscious of his acts."

8   What is to blame for these heinous statistics? What are the chances that this trend of rising violence can be controlled and reversed? The probabilities are small unless something is done about the moral and socioeconomic environment in which our young people are growing up today in America. One thing is certain. For a considerable proportion of American children and youth, the "culture of violence" is now both a major health threat and a way of life.

9   We of the medical profession believe that one of the factors behind this

Comparison (TV = school) violence is televised violence. Television has become a school of violence and a college for crime.

Testimony (of Surgeon General) 10   Let us take a look at some of the evidence. The Surgeon General of the United States has said, based on a six-volume study of the problem, that "there is a causative relationship between televised violence and subsequent antisocial behavior, and that the evidence is strong enough that it requires some action on the part of responsible authorities, the TV industry, the government, the citizens."

11   This report was a twin to the Surgeon General's report on smoking. This

Comparison (of TV to cigarettes, another health hazard) report on TV violence, in effect, implied, "Warning: The Surgeon General Has Determined That Viewing of TV Violence Is Dangerous to Your Health."

12   Much of the report has been clouded in dispute, so that its full impact has not reached society as effectively as it could. Let me point out just one of the disputes. The committee responsible for summing up the evidence gathered said that the 23 studies of the report, done by renowned scientists,

Testimony provide "suggestive evidence in favor of the interpretation that viewing violence on television is conducive to an increase in aggressive behavior, although it must be emphasized that the causal sequence is very likely applicable only to some children who are predisposed in this direction." This has led critics to downgrade the report and say that violence on TV really only affects those already aggressive individuals, anyway. I would like to say to that, so what? If it makes aggression-prone people more aggressive, that is enough to make me say something should be done about violence on TV. But what is even more alarming is what the Surgeon General said about those predisposed to violence. He said that television can *cause* the predisposition. This point has been overlooked. So, televised violence can increase a child's aggressive behavior, especially if he has a predisposition for aggression. And, in addition to this, the predisposition itself can be caused by the viewing of TV.

Forms of Support

Testimony

13   Dr. Robert M. Liebert, associate professor of psychology at the State University of New York at Stony Brook, concluded in an overview of several studies of the report that "at least under some circumstances, exposure to television aggression can lead children to accept what they have seen as a partial guide for their own actions. As a result, the present entertainment offerings of the television medium may be contributing, in some measure, to the aggressive behavior of many normal children. Such an effect has been shown in a wide variety of situations."

14   And earlier in the report he said, "Experimental studies preponderantly support the hypothesis that there is a directional, causal link between exposure to television violence and an observer's subsequent aggressive behavior."

Description

Defining the effects of TV violence

Testimony

15   Let us go beyond the report to other findings. Dr. Albert Bandura of Stanford University set out to determine what happens to a child who watches as aggressive personalities on television slug, stomp, shoot, and stab one another. His research team reached two conclusions about aggression on TV: (1) that it tends to reduce the child's inhibitions against acting in a violent, aggressive manner, and (2) that children will copy what they see. Dr. Bandura points out that a child won't necessarily run out and attack the first person he sees after watching violence on the screen, but that, if provoked later on, evidence suggests that then he may very well put what he has learned into action. The reason that children do not indiscriminately copy their TV characters is that parents suppress any such learning that they don't consider desirable — that is, the children get punished — and children rarely have access to weapons necessary for showing off what they have learned.

Description/Examples (weapons)

"If," says Dr. Bandura, "they were provided with switchblade knives, blackjacks, explosives, six-shooters, and nooses, it is safe to predict that the incidence of tragic imitative aggression connected with television viewing would rise sharply."

Description (how TV teaches that "violence works")

16   One of the lessons of television is that violence works. If you have a problem with someone, the school of TV says to slap him in the face, stab him in the back. By aggressive acts, the bad guy, for example, may gain control of grazing land, gold mines, nightclubs, and perhaps the whole town. Not until the very end is he usually punished. And, as in the case of *The Godfather*, parts one and two, punishment may never really occur. Because most of the program has shown how well violence has paid off, punishment at the end tends not to have much of an inhibitory effect.

Testimony

17   "From these findings," Dr. Bandura says, "we can conclude that if children see the bad guy punished, they are *not* likely to imitate spontaneously his behavior. But they do acquire — and retain — concrete information about how to behave aggressively, and punishment of the bad guy does not make them forget what they have learned. They may put into practice this knowledge on future occasions if they are given adequate instigation, access to the necessary weapons, and the prospect of sufficiently attractive rewards for the successful execution of the behavior."

Description

18   Other studies have shown that viewing violence blunts a child's sensitivity to it. They become jaded to violence on the screen. They condition themselves to avoid being upset by the gougings, smashings, and stompings they see on TV. If they *did* get involved, their emotions could be shattered.

Testimony/Example

Testimony/Scientific study used as example

19   What about the long-term effects of violence on TV? Researcher D. J. Hicks found that even eight months after viewing a violent episode only once, almost half of all the children could act out again what they had seen so long ago. In 1955, Dr. Leonard Eron, head of research for the Rip Van Winkle Foundation, looked into the long-range correlations between a child's favorite television program, the program's violence content, and the aggressiveness of the child as reported by his classmates. The project, which covered a span of about 10 years, from age eight to 18, was later picked up by the Surgeon General's study on TV violence. The investigators found a strong correlation between the early viewing of television violence and aggressive behavior in the teenage years. In fact, according to the study, a child's television habits at age eight were more likely to be a predictor of his aggressiveness at eighteen than either his family's socioeconomic status, his relationships with his parents, his IQ, or any other single factor in his environment. The report concluded that a preference for violent television at a young age leads to the building of aggressive habits.

Testimony/Quotation

20   As equally alarming as these studies are the findings of researcher George Gerbner, dean of the Annenberg School of Communications at the University of Pennsylvania. He said, ''Anyone who watches evening network TV receives a heavy diet of violence. More than half of all characters on prime-time TV are involved in some violence, about one-tenth in killing.'' Because of this, TV breeds suspicion and fear. The report said, ''People who watch a lot of TV see the real world as more dangerous and frightening than those who watch very little. Heavy viewers are less trustful of their fellow citizens.''

21   To cope with this fear the heavy watcher also gets a thick skin. He becomes conditioned to being a victim. He becomes apathetic to violence.

Testimony

Gerbner concludes with the observation that ''acceptance of violence and passivity in the face of injustice may be consequences of far greater social concern than occasional displays of individual aggression.''

Comparison

22   So, we have a two-edged sword. Television violence tends to make some people more violent, and others it makes more willing to accept violence as a way of life.

Statistics

23   All in all, 146 articles in behavioral science journals and related reports, representing 50 studies involving 10,000 children and adolescents from every conceivable background, all showed that viewing violence produces increased aggressive behavior in the young.

24   The accumulation of evidence suggests, as you have heard, that children will copy TV violence, that they often do *not* do so because of parental control and lack of access to weapons, that TV teaches a child that often violence succeeds and that problems can be solved by violence, that viewing

TV violence blunts sensitivity to violence in the real world, that children remember specific acts of TV violence, and that preferring violent television at an early age leads to more aggressive teenage behavior.

25   What happens when these children grow up? There should be further studies on this. In-depth studies. What happens when these children grow up and no longer are under parental control, when they are conditioned into thinking that violence works, and when they have a diminished sensitivity to violence? What happens to these children when they grow up and *do* have access to weapons? What happens when they grow up in a world apathetic to violence?

26   Is it any coincidence, then, that our real world is looking more and more like the violent world of television? Sadistic, ingenious murders, hijackings, kidnappings, ransoms — news reports are sounding like TV plots. Many of us are questioning whether this resemblance is more than coincidental. In fact, a surprising number of bizarre crimes have been committed by young people who admit they were influenced by television.

Description

27   There is no doubting the power of TV. Possibly no other innovation of the twentieth century has so affected our daily lives. More than cars, planes, radios, movies, and appliances, TV is the most likely to alter our living patterns. Studies have shown that TV has reduced the amount of time we spend visiting and entertaining friends. We read fewer books and see fewer movies. Leisure time for such things as sports and hobbies has been reduced. We go to bed later because of TV, and we spend less time on household care, play, and conversation. It has changed our meal time, and most of us use it as an ''electronic babysitter.''

**Description (how
TV has changed our
living habits)**

28   The response of the television industry has been generally to uphold the need for violence because violence is what keeps the Nielsen ratings up. They say themselves that the network is run by salesmen, and that violence sells. . . .

29   Violence may make money for television, but it should not be made at the expense of our children. And I am not so sure that only violence makes money. The National Citizens Committee for Broadcasting recently released a report saying that according to their ratings the 10 least violent programs are successful network offerings with high ratings.

Testimony

30   Based on the evidence that has been developed, the American Medical Association recently authorized a remedial course of action. The AMA will publish a booklet that will emphasize parental responsibility for their children's viewing and will indicate what to look for in terms of suitable programming.

**Description (AMA's
course of action)**

31   AMA will explore with the National Association of Broadcasters the possibility of convening periodic joint conferences on the impact of TV on children. It will support full funding of research by the National Institute of Mental Health on the influence of television. AMA will urge television stations, in deciding on program content and scheduling, to use violence indexes, which are being prepared by various groups.

32   We of the medical profession agree with Dr. Liebert when he said that

**Forms of
Support**

Testimony/Quotation

"the most potent, the smoothest way to change television is through even a small minority of citizens who give the impression that they are going to react negatively to content."

33   That is why the American Medical Association at its recent annual meeting, acting on a resolution introduced by the California delegation, has declared violence on TV an environmental health risk and has asked doctors, their families, and their patients to actively oppose programs containing violence, as well as products and services of the sponsors of such programs.

Description (of parent's course of action)

34   In other words, if you, as a parent, see something on TV that you feel is too violent for your child to watch, turn the TV off or change the channel, and don't buy the products of the firms that support the program through their advertising.

35   As a representative of the California Medical Association, I want to thank you for allowing me to explain our position, and why we have taken this stand.

Summary

This chapter dealt with supporting material. The functions of supporting material include to clarify, to make interesting, to make memorable, and to prove. We explored the following types of support:

1. *Definitions* identify things in a brief, concise statement. Definitions of key terms can be particularly helpful. Definitions are of two types: traditional and operational.
2. *Descriptions* create detailed "word pictures" that enable an audience to visualize what you are talking about. Descriptions help an audience imagine something that they could otherwise experience only through their physical senses.
3. *Analogies* are extended comparisons that enable you to compare an unknown concept with something more familiar to your audience.
4. *Anecdotes,* or stories based on personal experience, help you develop ideas in a way that is lively and personal.
5. *Examples* allow you to demonstrate an abstract idea with a specific case. Examples can be either real or hypothetical. Scientific studies are often used as examples.
6. *Quantification* allows you to use numbers to develop an idea. *Statistics,* which are numbers that are organized to show trends, allow you to summarize something that is true for a large number of cases.
7. *Quotations* are used for memorable wording and for testimony from a well-known or authoritative source.
8. *Visual aids* allow you to take advantage of the audience's sense of sight, as well as their sense of hearing, during a speech.

Any piece of support might combine two or more of these forms. Supporting material works not only because it expands on your ideas, but also because it provides a different perspective from which an audience can view your ideas. The final test for effectiveness of support is audience analysis.

Questions/Assignments

1. Do you agree that many people suffer from "communication paranoia"? If so, on what issues have you experienced this problem, either in yourself or in others?

2. Consider all the forms of supporting material discussed in this chapter. Imagine you are listening to a speech on a topic about which you know very little. Which techniques do you think would be most effective? Explain your answer.

3. To illustrate the point that "meanings are in people and not in words," try using a fairly common word, but attaching an unfamiliar definition to it, preferably the fourth or fifth definition listed in the dictionary. Did your listeners understand your usage? If not, how did they react when you explained it? Did they think you used the word "correctly"?

4. Dictionaries often change more slowly than the meanings attached to words. List four or five fairly common words that have recently acquired new or different meanings (words like "pot," "heavy," and "wicked"). Does the dictionary you usually use include these new definitions?

5. The introduction to the Elmendorf speech employs no anecdotes or visual aids. Can you think of any ways in which he could have used these two forms of support?

Notes

1. C. Vick and R. Wood, "Similarity of Past Experience and the Communication of Meaning," *Speech Monographs* 36, 1969, pp. 159–162.

2. Those interested in this heady topic can consult Wilder Penfield, *A Critical Study of Human Consciousness and the Human Brain* (Princeton, N.J.: Princeton University, 1976).

3. This estimate is based on a quote from Ralph W. Gerard, "What Is Memory?," in Robert A. Daniel, ed., *Contemporary Readings in General Psychology* (Boston: Houghton Mifflin, 1959), p. 95. The actual quote was: "Some tests of perception suggest that each tenth of a second is a single frame of experience for the human brain. In that tenth of a second it can receive perhaps a thousand units of information. . . ." Cited in William D. Brooks, *Speech Communication,* 2d ed. (Dubuque: Wm. C. Brown, 1974), p. 33.

4. *Ibid.*

5. Recall that studies, cited in Chapter 2, indicate that our attitudes and prior experiences influence how we perceive what we see or hear. These studies are discussed in A. Hastorf, D. Schneider, and J. Polefka, *Person Perception* (Reading, Mass.: Addison-Wesley, 1970), pp. 3–10.

6. "End of an ERA?" *Time,* November 17, 1975, p. 65.

7. This slogan was the war cry of a movement called General Semantics that was once widespread and that still influences the thinking of communication theorists. The bible of the General Semantics movement was Alfred Korzybski's *Science and Sanity* (Lancaster, Pa.: Science Press, 1933). Unfortunately, that work is practically unreadable. If you are interested, a better treatment is in Wendell Johnson's masterwork, *People in Quandaries: The Semantics of Personal Adjustment* (New York: Harper & Row, 1946), or, more recently, Neil Postman's *Crazy Talk, Stupid Talk* (New York: Delacorte, 1976).

8. The potential problems with dictionary definitions, from a *communication* point of view, are discussed more extensively in I. A. Richards, *The Philosophy of Rhetoric* (London: Oxford University, 1936).

9. Martin Luther King, Jr., "I Have a Dream," speech at civil rights rally, Washington, D.C., August 28, 1963. See James C. McCroskey, *An Introduction to Rhetorical Communication* (Englewood Cliffs, N.J.: Prentice-Hall, 1968), pp. 248–249, for transcript.

10. Fred Macmullen, quoted in "The Shadows of Boxing," by Keith Murphy, *Winning Orations, 1984* (Interstate Oratorical Association, 1984), pp. 33–34.

11. Carl Sagan, *The Dragons of Eden: Speculations on the Evolution of Human Intelligence* (New York: Ballantine, 1978), pp. 13–17.

12. Bob Burgess, "Hiking/Biking," *Santa Barbara News Press,* February 25, 1978.

13. Edmund Fuller, *2500 Anecdotes for All Occasions* (New York: Avenel Books, 1970), p. 275.

14. Edward M. Kennedy, speech before Democratic National Convention, New York City, August 12, 1980. See *The New York Times,* August 13, 1980, p. B2, for transcript.

15. G. C. Wiegand, "Inflation," *Vital Speeches of the Day* 43, June 15, 1978.

16. Bert E. Bradley, *Fundamentals of Speech Communication: The Credibility of Ideas* (Dubuque: Wm. C. Brown, 1974), p. 157.

17. John F. Wilson and Carroll C. Arnold, *Public Speaking as a Liberal Art* (Boston: Allyn & Bacon, 1964), p. 160.

18. *A Gift of Laughter: The Autobiography of Alan Sherman* (New York: Atheneum, 1965), pp. 63–64.

19. A good discussion of the effects of presenting material through various media is provided in Joseph T. Klapper, *The Effects of Mass Communication* (New York: The Free Press, 1960).

20. Theresa Clinkenbeard, "The Loss of Childhood," *Winning Orations, 1984* (Interstate Oratorical Association, 1984), p. 4.

21. Thomas Elmendorf, speech before the House Subcommittee on Communications, Los Angeles, Calif., August 17, 1976. Reprinted by permission of *Vital Speeches of the Day* 43, October 1, 1976.

8

LANGUAGE

Language: An Introduction

Up to this point, we have been covering the general aspects of message preparation. This chapter discusses perhaps the most important *specific* aspect of message preparation: our use, and occasional abuse, of language.

The English language is amazingly complex. No matter what type of presentation you are using, you should take time to decide how to put your ideas into words. Even in a spur-of-the-moment, impromptu speech, you have time to consider more than one way of expressing your ideas. Language choices can be made even more carefully while preparing a planned speech. You make them while determining your main points, while roughing out the speech, and while practicing the speech. You need not memorize exact wording: simply making your language choices in advance will lead to a clearer presentation. We make two kinds of language choices: vocabulary (the words we use) and syntax (the way we put those words together).

Vocabulary

The words we use have two distinct levels of meaning: connotation and denotation. *Denotation* is the literal meaning of the word (the meaning found in the dictionary), and *connotation* is what the word suggests to the listener. "Fat," "stout," and "portly" all denote superfluous body tissue; yet the connotations of these words differ markedly. A "stout" person, for most audiences, would be strong and healthy. A "portly" person would probably be less strong but more dignified. The difference between connotation and denotation makes it necessary to plan carefully the words you use in a message. There are three basic guidelines for effective vocabulary: *appropriateness, vividness,* and *clarity.*

Appropriateness

The words you use must be appropriate to you, to your audience, and to your message. Four types of words are infamous for their frequent inappropriateness: *obscenity, slang, sexist language,* and *jargon.*

Obscenity

Obscene language is generally of a religious, sexual, or excretory nature. Society enforces strong sanctions against all three types of obscenity. Religious obscenity was banned from Judeo-Christian cultures with the Third Commandment: "Thou shalt not take the name of the Lord thy God in vain." Other religious cultures have similar taboos. Sexual obscenity is considered taboo in our culture because of the beliefs of our Puritan forebears, who believed that such words were "designed to incite to lust and depravity."[1] According to Harold Vetter in his book *Language Behavior and Communication,* all societies need a short, concise term for copulation, and yet nowhere is a society as threatened by the term as in the United States.[2] The intensity of our sexual taboos has lessened over the years, however. A list of words banned from U.S. movies in the 1930s included "eunuch," "courtesan," "harlot," "tart," "trollop," "wench," "whore," "sex," and "sexual."[3] Excretory obscenity is taboo in our culture because it evokes images of excretions, which most people consider unpleasant.

Obscenity is commonly used in protest communication. Jerry Rubin, a protest radical of the 1960s, explained why:

> Nobody really communicates with words any more. Words have lost their emotional impact, intimacy, ability to shock and make love. Language prevents communication. "Cars love Shell." How can I say, "I love you," after hearing "Cars love Shell"? Does anyone understand what I mean?[4]

Rubin believed that obscene language was needed to arouse emotion. He took this theory to the 1968 National Democratic Convention with him, and the Chicago police supplied proof of the emotional power of obscene words. The proof was supplied with such direct methods of feedback as billy clubs and Mace. There is a lesson to be learned in that: not to use obscenity unless you *want* the result that it is likely to provoke in your audience.[5]

Slang

Slang words are those that are not yet an accepted part of the language. "Bus," "cab," "hoax," and "mob" were all slang terms at one time, but they later became standard. "Ripped off" (meaning "stolen" or "victimized"), "uptight" (meaning "anxious"), and "laid back" (meaning "calm") are current slang terms.

Slang is more appropriate in a spoken message than in a written message, but it is troublesome even when spoken. Slang should not be used unless all members of the audience find it acceptable. Otherwise, it should be replaced with a more standard usage. You could say "They were very conceited" instead of "They were on a real ego trip," and "It was boring" instead of "It was a drag."

Sexist Language

Sexist language is made up of terms that stereotype people according to their sex. There are three types of sexist language to watch out for. The first is derogatory slang, such as "doll," "gal," "broad," and "chick" as substitutes for "woman." That these words *sound* old-fashioned is a good sign that sexist language styles are changing. The second type of sexist language is the use of occupation terms that include the word "man" when a woman also might have the job. Such terms include "salesman," "spokesman," "congressman," and "sanitation man." These terms can just as easily be changed to "sales representative," "spokesperson," "congressional representative," and "sanitation worker." The third type of sexist language is the use of "he" as an indefinite pronoun. This is the most difficult type of sexist language to work with because it is, by tradition, grammatically correct. In spite of its grammatical correctness, however, this usage perpetuates sexual stereotypes. It is usually awkward to attempt to say "he or she" wherever one of these phrases occurs. When possible, therefore, it is advisable to use the plural form:

Instead of, "A child who excels should be told *he* has done well," say, "Children who excel should be told *they* have done well."

Instead of, "A secretary has to be careful of the way *she* dresses," say, "Secretaries have to be careful of the way *they* dress."

Instead of "A doctor can be proud of *his* accomplishments," say, "Doctors can be proud of *their* accomplishments."

Jargon

Jargon includes words of a specialized nature that are used only by specific groups of people. Educators, for example, talk of "empirically validated learning" and "multi-mode curricula," and rather than saying that a child needs improvement, they say that "academic achievement is not commensurate with abilities." Doctors and military strategists are famous for their use of jargon, also. A heart attack is a "cardiovascular accident" for doctors, while air raids are "routine limited duration protective reactions" to the military. Business people, religious groups, sports enthusiasts, lawyers, and many other groups have semi-private vocabularies. *Words from these vocabularies are appropriate only when they are addressed to those who use them regularly.*

The rule works in reverse, too. If you can use a limited amount of an audience's jargon to communicate ideas that they are not familiar with, you could be one step ahead in the make-yourself-clear game. You could explain gourmet cooking to a group of computer experts by referring to the input-output of recipe ingredients or by stressing the GIGO principle (garbage in, garbage out) in selecting ingredients.

It is important to recognize that making language appropriate does *not* mean making it dry and lifeless. That is where the idea of vividness comes in.

Vividness

A vivid vocabulary gains your audience's attention because of the images the words evoke. Images are worth thousands of words; because of that, they help hold down the unnecessary verbiage. Vivid language tends to be *original, action-oriented,* and *sensuous.*

Originality

That first factor, originality, is a problem college students face in both written and spoken communication. An instructor at Mount Holyoke College claims that as a student she began seven years of English courses with some variation of the following theme:

How I Spent My Summer Vacation
When school let out I was happy as a lark. It was hot as hell and all I wanted to do was be as cool as a cucumber at the lake. I was brought back to reality with the profound realization that I was going to have to get a summer job. My parents said I was too old to be happy and carefree.

I got a job at an appliance store where I met some people as nutty as fruitcakes. . . . I got sick and tired of having dirty old men tell me I was as pretty as a picture. . . . They were on real ego trips.

The worst part of the whole summer was one day at work when I became as white as a sheet and my eyes overflowed with tears and then I slumped over with fatigue. I had to take a rest after that. Staying in bed was a real drag.

Soon though I was rosy with happiness and pretty as a peach. And I learned something over the summer that will start me on the yellow brick road to the end of my rainbow. Life is no bowl of cherries. The best things in life are those that come by starting out at the bottom of the ladder.[6]

Looking back on her years as a student, the author of this familiar-sounding passage remarks that the "How I Spent My Summer Vacation" assignment was usually "an exam on how many clichés we had remembered from the year before."[7] Granted, her example is overdone; but it is still a useful reminder of how boring some expressions are if we have heard them so many times that they no longer evoke an interesting image.

Some expressions are clichés because they have been around for so long:

a lame excuse
avoid it like the plague
better late than never
in no uncertain terms
in this day and age
last but not least
too good to be true
fighting city hall
sad but true

Others are of a more recent vintage:

neat (as in, "that's neat")
really (as a continual response)
awesome
totally (as in, "totally awesome, really")
cosmic
to the max
for sure (especially when pronounced, "fer shure")

Expressions can become clichés quickly if they are overused. A recent advertising slogan, "Where's the Beef?," was so overused that it became a cliché practically overnight.

You do not have to have the vocabulary of a genius to put words together in an interesting, original manner. You just have to be honest. You have to conjure up the image that *you* want to relate, and use *your own words* to describe that image.

Here is how Harry J. Gray, the Chairman and Chief Executive Officer of United Technologies Corporation, spoke about his childhood in a speech before a group of college students at the University of Illinois, Chicago Campus:

I was born in Georgia. But I grew up in the suburbs of Chicago. I entered the University of Illinois in 1936. Just being able to go to college was an achievement in those days. I had lots of ambition—but little money. So I worked my way through college. I washed dishes, waited on tables, and worked during school vacations.

In the summer of 1936 I unloaded fruit crates for 10 dollars a week. Of course, a dollar was worth something in those days. You could buy a loaf of bread for 9 cents. When you went to buy some meat, the friendly butcher would throw in a portion of liver for the cat — which the cat never got. Nowadays, if you go to an expensive restaurant in Chicago, a portion of liver costs $18. When I was in college, there wasn't a man alive who could *lift* $18 worth of liver![8]

There are no clichés or worn-out figures of speech in Gray's speech — just honest, straightforward language that describes his childhood in his own words. You can feel the personality behind those words.

Action Orientation

Notice all the action that takes place in the passage above: working at the various jobs, going to the butcher, receiving free liver, the image of a man attempting to lift huge amounts of liver. . . . Nothing just sits around in action-oriented language. Gray was talking about life, about things that actually happened. His speech continued as follows:

I had to drop out one year — my junior year — because I didn't have enough money. Anyone who grew up in the Depression knows what I mean. But now I look back on those days with nostalgia and fondness. The years I spent at the University of Illinois were some of the most memorable and emotionally rewarding of my life.

After graduation I felt prepared to take on the world. And that's what a lot of us did. It was 1941. We volunteered for the Army. I am particularly reminded of those days now because next month marks the 40th anniversary of the D-Day landings. I landed in Normandy and made 26 combat river crossings.[9]

One way to include action in your speech is to tell about what someone did — either yourself or someone else. You can also use personification (that is, give human characteristics to inanimate objects or concepts) to make language about ideas action-oriented. For example, Susan B. Anthony, the nineteenth-century feminist, gave a famous speech on why women should be allowed to vote. In it, she protested:

This oligarchy of sex, which makes father, brothers, husband, sons, the oligarchs over the mother and sisters, the wife and daughters of every household, which ordains all men sovereigns, all women subjects, carries dissension, discord, and rebellion into every home of the nation.[10]

In that passage, we can almost see the oligarchy of sex "carrying" dissension into our homes.

Sensuousness

Because we perceive reality through our senses, one method of evoking images is to use words that refer to things we can see, hear, smell, touch, or taste. Objects have size, color, shape, and position that can be seen. The size has dimension, the color has brightness, the shape has contours, and the position has some relationship in space to other objects. These qualities evoke images based on the sense of sight. You can evoke images based on hearing by telling of the tone, rhythm, and melody of a sound. Sounds *do* things. They chime, chatter, clang, clatter, clink, crackle, crash, and creak. We can use words to duplicate sounds by using onomatopoeia. For example, you can describe the "blip" of a radar screen or the "hiss" of a distant waterfall. Words that evoke images of smell will tell us about the sharpness or intensity of an odor. Odors can be "moldy" or "musky." They can also be "balmy" or "woodsy." Words that evoke images of taste could describe the sweetness, sourness, bitterness, or saltiness of a flavor. Words that evoke images of touch could refer to pressure, texture, or warmth of contact. A touch could be "slimy" or "stinging." It could also be "satiny" or "smooth."

Appropriateness and vividness, then, are important considerations in language use. Our final consideration, clarity, is most important of all.

Clarity

Clarity — the quality of being clear, without cloudiness — is saying what you mean with the greatest chance of being understood. Many language theorists suggest that clarity is becoming increasingly difficult in today's world. Peter Farb, in his book *Word Play: What Happens When People Talk* describes present-day language trends this way:

> An entire generation has grown up that distrusts language's ability to express a true picture of reality and that relies upon the empty intercalations of *like, you know, I mean.* The world has grown inarticulate at the very time that an unprecedented number of words flood the media. The output has burgeoned, but speakers have retreated into worn paths and stock phrases.[11]

Saying what you mean requires careful word choice. When planning a speech you have to become a wordsmith, an artisan just like a silversmith or a watchsmith. Just like any other person involved in a craft, as a wordsmith you have to use the tools that are available to you. If you are the type of wordsmith who likes simple, all-purpose tools, you might like to use a good standard dictionary — preferably a full-sized, current college edition. Dictionaries can be used for more than spelling and denotative meaning; they also supply word derivations, pronunciation guides, synonyms, antonyms, and word variations. All these things help you produce nuances of meaning.

If you are the type of wordsmith who likes specialized tools, you might like to use a thesaurus. A thesaurus is a dictionary of synonyms and antonyms. If you were planning a speech on "Poverty in America," you might find that the idea of "poverty" was repeated so many times, with different shades of meaning, that you needed more than one word to describe it. If you looked up "poverty" in one thesaurus you would find this:

POVERTY

Nouns—**1,** poverty, inpecuniousness, indigence, penury, pauperism, destitution, want; need, neediness; lack, necessity, privation, distress, difficulties; bad, poor *or* needy circumstances; reduced *or* straitened circumstances; slender means, straits; hand-to-mouth existence; beggary; mendicancy, loss of fortune, bankruptcy, insolvency (see DEBT).

2, poor man, pauper, mendicant, beggar, starveling.

Verbs—**1,** be poor, want, lack, starve, live from hand to mouth, have seen better days, go down in the world, go to the dogs, go to wrack and ruin; not have a penny to one's name; beg one's bread; tighten one's belt. *Slang,* go broke.

2, render poor, impoverish, reduce to poverty; pauperize, fleece, ruin, strip.

Adjectives—poor, indigent; poverty-stricken; poor as a church mouse; poor as Job's turkey; penniless, impecunious; hard up; out at elbows *or* heels; seedy, shabby; beggarly, beggared; destitute, bereft, in want, needy, necessitous, distressed, pinched, straitened; unable to keep the wolf from the door, unable to make both ends meet; embarrassed, involved; insolvent, bankrupt, on one's uppers, on the rocks. *Colloq.,* in the hole, broke, stony, looking for a handout.

Antonym, see MONEY[12]

Each of these terms for "poverty" will have a fine shade of connotation. Some of them might also be hopelessly out of date. Most college audiences, for example, would not understand expressions like "poor as Job's turkey" or "stony"; but the thesaurus is a handy tool for finding an appropriate synonym to use for a specific reason. The thesaurus is particularly handy when you have the word "on the tip of your tongue" but you cannot quite think of it. If you were looking for a more formal term for "poor person," and you knew there was such a term, but for some reason you had a mental block and could not think of it, the thesaurus would give you "pauper." If you were looking for a descriptive expression for "a life of poverty," the thesaurus would give you "hand-to-mouth existence."

A word of warning is appropriate here: Some students tend to go "thesaurus crazy," and try to use as many different words for the same thing as they can. They especially like obscure, little-known words like "medicancy" and "necessitous." Fanciness is definitely the *wrong* use for a thesaurus, and you should guard against it.

Whether you are using a thesaurus or a standard dictionary, there are two characteristics of clarity that, if you recognize them, will help you make the best word choice. These characteristics are *specificity* and *concreteness.*

Specificity

A specific word is one that restricts the meaning that can be assigned to it. "Specific" is therefore the opposite of "general." General words name groups of things; specific words name the individual things that make up that group. The term "transportation" is general. "Automobile," "sports car," and "Porsche 911-S Targa" are increasingly specific terms. Someone who says, "I had an automobile accident the other day" is likely to evoke less sympathy from a sports car enthusiast than one who says, "I demolished my 911-S Targa the other day."

One of the reasons some people distrust politicans is that politicians often do not speak in specifics because of the broad audience they attempt to please. Candidate X favors "law and order." What does that mean? Does the candidate favor registration of firearms, enforcement of busing for integration, or the suspension of the Fourteenth Amendment? (That is the one that guarantees "due process of law.") Advertisers also shy away from specific language. They use slogans, such as "Things go better with Coke." But what "things" are they referring to? And how do they "go better" with Coke?

Susan B. Anthony used highly specific language in her 1872 speech on woman's suffrage. She had just been arrested for voting in a presidential election:

FRIENDS AND FELLOW CITIZENS: — I stand before you tonight under indictment for the alleged crime of having voted at the last presidential election, without having a lawful right to vote. It shall be my work this evening to prove to you that in thus voting, I not only committed no crime, but, instead, simply exercised my *citizen's rights,* guaranteed to me and all United States citizens by the National Constitution, beyond the power of any State to deny.

The preamble of the Federal Constitution says:

"We, the people of the United States, in order to form a more perfect union, establish justice, insure *domestic* tranquillity, provide for the common defense, promote the general welfare, and secure the blessings of liberty to ourselves and our posterity, do ordain and establish this Constitution for the United States of America."

It was we, the people; not we, the white male citizens; nor yet we, the male citizens; but we, the whole people, who formed the Union. And we formed it, not to give the blessings of liberty, but to secure them; not to the half of ourselves and the half of our posterity, but to the whole people — women as well as men. And it is a downright mockery to talk to women of their enjoyment of the blessings of liberty while they are denied the use of the only means of securing them provided by this democratic-republican government — the ballot.[13]

One way to be specific in your language is to rely on statements of fact rather than inferences or value judgments. A *fact* is something that can be verified through objective measurement (the center of Hoop U's basketball team is 7 feet 6 inches tall), observation (it has been raining for more than an hour), or historical documentation (Richard Nixon resigned in 1974). An *inference* refers to something that cannot be measured objectively, such as someone's emotions (Lucy hates Charlie Brown). A *value judgment* is a statement of opinion (the center of Hoop U's basketball team is a bum) that may or may not have any basis in fact.

Facts are more specific than inferences or value judgments. You might be able to say, as a statement of fact, that the center of Hoop U's basketball team is 7 feet 6 inches tall. That is something you can measure objectively, given a ruler and a stepladder. If you added something to that statement that could not be measured objectively, you would be making an inference, as in "The center of Hoop U's team hates our center." Because we cannot get inside someone else's brain, human emotions are something that we have to infer. After all, the center of Hoop U's team might act as if he hated our center, but he might actually love him, deep down inside. To be specific in that case, you might use a quotation: "The center of Hoop U's basketball team said recently that he hates our center's guts." That is a specific statement of fact.

When you make a value judgment, you also add something to the facts of the case. If you said "The center of Hoop U's basketball team is a bum," you would be telling more about your own personal tastes and preferences than you would about Hoop U's center. Generally speaking, the more value statements you use, the more facts you need to back them up. For the example above, you might need to define the term "bum" or describe the particular behaviors that make the basketball player, in your estimation, a bum.

Notice the different levels of specificity in the following:

value judgment: The Rolling Stones are fine musicians.
inference: Our bandleader thinks the Rolling Stones are fine musicians.
statement of fact: At rehearsal last night, the bandleader stated that, in his opinion, the Rolling Stones are fine musicians.

Specificity (or "accuracy" or "precision") in word choice is one characteristic of clarity. Another is concreteness.

Concreteness

Concrete words refer to things in actual physical reality, things that we can perceive with our senses. "Concrete" is therefore the opposite of "abstract." Abstract words refer to concepts that we cannot see, hear, taste, touch, or feel. "Freedom," "democracy," "capitalism," and "communism" are typical abstract concepts, whereas "hot fudge sundaes," "skinny bodies," and "the smell of rotten garbage" are more concrete.

Concrete words help us visualize abstract concepts. When one modern philosopher spoke about how productive John Dewey had been in his lifetime, he said, "Indeed he stopped thinking only when his heart stopped beating at 93. His reflection had produced a pile of books and articles twelve feet high."[14] The image of that pile of scholarship is far more concrete than one that would be created by saying "an enormous number of books and articles." Susan B. Anthony used concrete language in her speech on woman's suffrage. In it, she stated that she *voted* and was *arrested*. Consider how much clearer this wording is than an abstract wording such as "I performed a democratic duty in the interest of liberty and was persecuted for it."

Ronald Reagan is a successful politician at least partially because he is good at using concrete language to discuss abstract issues. For example, in one of his first presidential debates he said:

> We talk about unemployment lines. If all the unemployed today were in a single line, allowing two feet for each one of them, that line would reach from New York City to Los Angeles, California.[15]

An understanding of levels of abstraction helps us understand concreteness.

Levels of Abstraction

Words are symbols. A symbol is something that stands for or represents something else. Words merely represent reality. They are labels. Some of those labels refer to things we can perceive. We cannot, however, perceive everything. No one has eyes in the back of the head. What we do perceive is distorted; we all perceive according to our prior experience. To make matters worse, we each assign different labels to what we perceive. The buzzing confusion of "reality" is like a garbage dump, at which we are all pickers. Some of us pick out some things; some of us pick out others. Even if by some stroke of luck two of us picked out the same thing, one of us might call it "a piece of trash" and the other might call it "a charming antique."

Words are labels, and labels are generalizations for the way one person perceives reality. Because no two people perceive reality in exactly the same way, you should be careful about labeling *your* reality. One heartbreaking story of the effects of improper labeling goes like this:

> There once was a brilliant but poverty-stricken entomologist who spent years breeding an uncommonly intelligent breed of housefly. One day, through a loophole in the laws of genetics, there appeared in his collection a young fly who could actually talk. Elated, the entomologist set about teaching the fly to sing, tell jokes, and play a few simple tunes on a small rubber band. When the fly had been sufficiently primed for a career in show business, the entomologist set off to find an agent. Since he would soon be wealthy, he decided to celebrate at a tavern along the way. He sat down at the bar and proudly displayed the fly to the bartender.
>
> "See that fly?" he asked.
>
> "Yup," said the bartender, slapping his hand on the bar and squashing the fly. "What'll ya have?"

It is an old story, but do not let that obscure the point. The label "fly" meant something entirely different to the entomologist than it did to the bartender. They were, as we say in the language business, operating on two different levels of abstraction. Levels of abstraction for the word "cow" are illustrated in Figure 8–1.[16]

This figure shows how confusing levels of abstraction can be. If you wanted to tell someone that you milked a cow, it would be just as confusing to say "I milked the atoms yesterday" as it would be to say "I milked

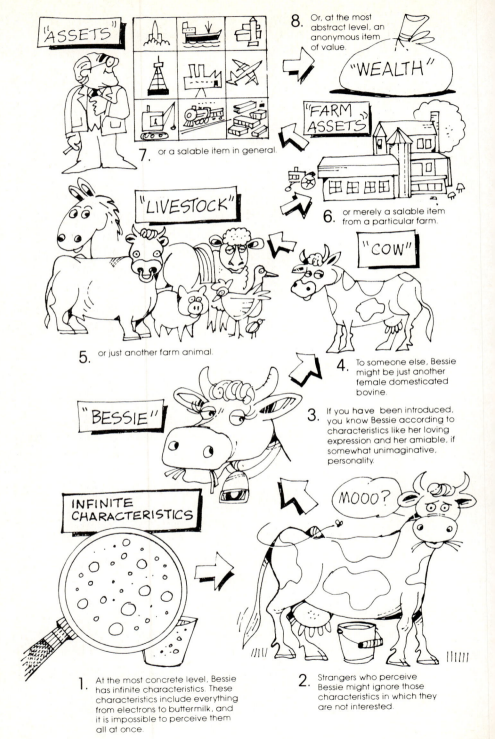

"ASSETS"

8. Or, at the most abstract level, an anonymous item of value.

"WEALTH"

7. or a salable item in general.

"FARM ASSETS"

6. or merely a salable item from a particular farm.

"LIVESTOCK"

"COW"

5. or just another farm animal.

4. To someone else, Bessie might be just another female domesticated bovine.

"BESSIE"

3. If you have been introduced, you know Bessie according to characteristics like her loving expression and her amiable, if somewhat unimaginative, personality.

INFINITE CHARACTERISTICS

MOOO?

1. At the most concrete level, Bessie has infinite characteristics. These characteristics include everything from electrons to buttermilk, and it is impossible to perceive them all at once.

2. Strangers who perceive Bessie might ignore those characteristics in which they are not interested.

Figure 8–1

the wealth." The key here is recognizing the level of abstraction that you are dealing with and choosing words that are appropriate to that level.

An example might clarify this piece of advice. When one student returned from a weekend communication training session, she presented a speech on what she had learned.

> I learned how to be really real. I learned that each of us is the only one who can give each of us what we really need. I learned that the only way to self-actualization, self-realization, and true human dignity is through being really real. I learned that what is, is.

The class favored her with the polite, easygoing attention that one would give to a song sung in an unknown language. The class members believed that what she said was true, but they did not understand what she was talking about. They still did not know what she had done over the weekend or what she had learned by doing it. Her audience had no way of knowing what she meant by expressions like "really real," "what we really need," or "what is, is." For her second try, she decided to talk about an actual exercise that she had been involved in, and what that exercise had accomplished. Her second try went something like this:

> Last weekend I attended a communication training session. In one exercise we all dressed in swimsuits and painted each other's bodies. It was a great feeling. We felt really close. We learned how to be really real. We learned that what is, is. We learned—

"Wait a second," one of her classmates pleaded. "You're making it sound like an orgy that turned into a religious experience. What exactly went *on* up there?"

The speaker's problem was her use of abstract terms. *She* knew what she was talking about, but she used terms that were much too abstract to describe her experiences for her audience. To help solve the problem, she made up the following abstraction ladder by substituting for the various levels of "cow" the levels of "a group of people body painting."

6. A group of people being really real.
5. A group of people controlling barriers to everyday communication.
4. A group of people recognizing and controlling communication barriers in a group exercise.
3. A group of people body painting.
2. A group of people with various characteristics.
1. A group of people with infinite characteristics.

Then, using the levels of abstraction that were appropriate for her audience, she formulated a clear message. Her next speech went something like this:

> Last weekend, as part of a 48-hour communication training session, I was involved in a group exercise that was designed to break down our barriers to effective communication. We often worry too much about what we look like to interact honestly and openly in a group of people. We worry more

about our clothes and grooming than about our personalities. In this exercise we wore only bathing suits and we were painted — from head to toe — by the other people in our group. Who could worry about *looks* in a situation like that? The exercises helped us recognize the kind of barriers we put up in everyday communication. We hope recognition of these barriers will help us control them.[17]

Vocabulary, then, must be appropriate, vivid, and clear. The next language consideration is syntax.

Syntax

Syntax refers to the way we put our sentences together. Two of the most important considerations for effective syntax are *directness* and *variety*.

Directness

There are two ways to express ideas: in a direct style or in a complex, intricate style. The most effective style for a public speaker is usually the direct style. There are three rules to keep in mind if directness is your goal: use a *simple construction,* use an *active voice,* and use a *simple tense.*

Usually if a sentence is not constructed simply, it is because it contains too much. Generally, you can either throw away superfluous words or break a long, complex sentence into shorter, simpler ones. Some complex sentences contain two or more thoughts sitting too closely together:

The registration of firearms is being considered by some members of Congress because they are owned by criminals.

This statement is confusing because it sounds as though the members of Congress are owned by criminals, which is another issue entirely.[18] The issue of gun control is better expressed by breaking this sentence up into two simpler ones:

Unregistered firearms are often owned by criminals. Because of this, some members of Congress are considering legislation that would require firearms to be registered.

Sometimes, all you need to do to simplify a sentence is to throw away words that you do not need. One way to check for excess wording is to see how long it takes you to get to the point you want to make:

I'm not completely sure about all sides of the issue, but I think in the final analysis the registration of firearms is a procedure that we might want to support.

That is superfluous wording. Your audience will not be interested in the mental processes that brought you up to the point you are making.

They just want to hear the point:

The registration of firearms should be supported by us.

This statement can be made even more direct by using the active rather than the passive voice. The active voice has the subject of the sentence perform action rather than be acted upon:

We should support the registration of firearms.

Also, you should use the simplest possible verb tense: Stick to the present, past, and future tenses if at all possible, and stay away from the present perfect, past perfect, and future perfect. Compare the following verb tenses in active and passive voices. The simple tenses in the active voice are generally the most direct:

	Tense	*Active Voice*	*Passive Voice*
Simple Tenses	present	I ask	I am asked
	past	I asked	I was asked
	future	I will ask	I will be asked
Not-So-Simple Tenses	present perfect	I have asked	I have been asked
	past perfect	I had asked	I had been asked
	future perfect	I will have asked	I will have been asked

Of course, in speaking you can afford to be more verbose than in writing—but use your verbosity to expand your ideas with anecdotes, examples, and other forms of support. When it comes time to make a point—especially one that you want your audience to understand and remember—say it as simply and directly as possible.

Harry Gray, the Chairman of United Technologies, continued his speech to the Chicago students in this way:

A lot of things have changed since those days of the Great Depression and the Second World War. It's not just that the price of bread costs more than 9 cents a loaf! Our country and the rest of the world have changed dramatically and in fundamental ways. We have just to look around us. The world is completely different.

Yet, if we look beyond the externals to the essentials, I think we find that the really important things have *not* changed. I refer to the traditional values—the simple, basic truths—all of us believe in and try to live by. . . . Other things may change, but our national virtues remain constant.[19]

Thus, after telling his long, interesting anecdote about the way things used to be, Gray makes a simple, direct statement of his main idea: "Other things may change, but our national virtues remain constant."

Keeping your sentences simple will help you to keep them direct, and keeping them direct will help you to keep them clear. Of course, you should also want to make your syntax interesting. That is where variety comes in.

Variety

Variety is interesting. It keeps people waiting to see what will happen next. It also helps to emphasize ideas. Variety in syntax is accomplished by using sentences of different *length, type,* and *structure.*

Sentence Length

If your sentences are all the same length, they will have a tendency to lull your audience to sleep. Your audience will be less interested in what comes next because they will already have a subconscious feel for how long each sentence will be. Even, steady rhythms are too smooth, too reassuring. Keep them guessing. Throw in some shorter sentences now and then. Do it for emphasis. It helps.

Sentence Type

Have you ever noticed that an occasional question seems to spice up a speech? A *rhetorical question* does not require a direct response from your audience—it simply gives them something to think about. Questions should not be just "thrown into" the speech, though. They should be planted carefully, with enough room between to allow each one to germinate. You should answer a rhetorical question once you ask it, or at least give your audience enough information so they can answer it for themselves.

You can also use an occasional imperative sentence to keep your syntax interesting: "Take the initiative!" for example, rather than "We should take the initiative."

Sentence Structure

Finally, you can vary the structure of your sentences occasionally to give them a snappy, memorable sound. Chapter 6 mentioned that a conclusion should state the main idea of the speech in a convincing and memorable way. There will be other places besides the conclusion for memorable wording, though, so it would be a good idea to look at some of the methods for achieving it. One method, for example, is *parallel sentence structure.* Parallel sentence structure allows one idea to balance with another, such as John F. Kennedy's "Ask not what your country can do for you, ask what you can do for your country."[20] With a little less care J.F.K. might have said, "You should ask what services you can perform for the United States, rather than looking to the government to help you." That would have been far less snappy and memorable.

You could also vary your sentence structure so you put two or three words together with the same first letter or sound. This *alliteration* is a device for which former Vice-President Spiro Agnew was famous. He used to talk about "middle-aged malcontents" and "nattering nabobs of negativism." Such phrases were memorable. Susan B. Anthony used alliteration when she said, "Are women persons? I *hardly* believe any of our opponents will *have* the *hardihood* to say they are not."

Assonance, the repetition of similar vowel sounds, is more difficult to do well. In fact, assonance is often accomplished accidentally, and it winds up sounding silly. William W. Watt, in *An American Rhetoric,* complains about "tone-deaf experts in several fields" who insist on using phrases like "the evaluation of the examination with relation to integration in education."[21] The repetition of all those "ations" gives the phrase the pleasant, empty cadence of a nursery rhyme. No word or phrase is stressed for importance because they all fall in with the pattern of the tune.

Of course, some expressions are not memorable because of a device like parallelism, assonance, or alliteration. They are memorable simply because the speaker has experimented with different ways of saying something and then said it the way it sounded best. Do the following expressions ring a bell?

"You wouldn't be Dr. Livingstone by any chance, would you?"
"Don't fire until they get right up next to you."
"Old soldiers don't die, they just leave."
"Why, I'd sooner die than not have liberty."

Consider how the first sentence of Lincoln's "Gettysburg Address" might have sounded if someone else had written it:

As Lincoln Wrote It
Fourscore and seven years ago our fathers brought forth on this continent a new nation, conceived in liberty, and dedicated to the proposition that all men are created equal.

As Someone Else Might Have
Eighty-seven years ago, the founders of this country established a system of government based on the idea that everyone should be free and equal.

The second version is not terrible; it is merely adequate. Lincoln's version, on the other hand, has an almost biblical sound, as illustrated by both "four score and seven" and "fathers" rather than "forefathers."

Varying the length, type, and structure of your sentence syntax will make your message sound more interesting and your points more emphatic. Direct syntax and clear, vivid, appropriate vocabulary should allow you to *design* an effective message. These rules work for all types of messages that use language, written or spoken. However, there are some important differences between written and spoken language.

Written and Spoken Style

Effective spoken language is generally less formal. It contains more sentence fragments, more colloquial language, more contractions, and more interjections such as "well," "oh," and "now" than written language.[22] Spoken language is generally more personal, too. More references are made to yourself ("I," "me," "mine") and to your specific audience. There are subtle stylistic differences, too. As Shana Alexander points out,

"The very weakness of writing, which is adjectives, is the strength of speaking."[23]

Spoken language is also more redundant. The structured introduction, body, and conclusion of a speech might seem unnecessarily repetitive if the same message were written out. You are required to repeat yourself in a speech, because your audience cannot go back to look over your words. Therefore *restatement* is a valuable tool for a speaker.

There are two types of restatement: repetition and paraphrasing. *Repetition* is repeating a key idea word for word. By repeating, you not only stress that particular idea, you also give your audience some extra time to mull it over and, perhaps, find a new perspective on it for themselves. Sometimes you can emphasize particular words in repeating. If you were speaking on "The Need for Permanent Peace in the Middle East" you might introduce one of your main points like this:

> World peace is dependent upon peace in the Middle East. Allow me to repeat that. *World peace* is dependent upon peace in the Middle East.

Paraphrasing is repeating an idea in different words. If you wanted to stress the idea in the example above by paraphrase, you might follow it up like this:

> That is not an overstatement. Every military power in the world now has a stake in the Middle East, so there is no hope for global peace until the Arabs and the Israelis mend their differences.

One way to repeat through paraphrasing is first to ask a rhetorical question and then to answer it. That way, the audience takes an active part in the message by formulating a mental response. You then reaffirm (or, if necessary, "correct") that mental response for them. For example:

> Is peace in the Middle East important to us? Think about it. There is no hope for world peace without peace between the Israelis and the Arab nations.

Restatement is especially effective when you want to stress the importance of a concept.

Written and spoken language may differ in degree of restatement and in other ways, but they call for the same clarity, vividness, and appropriateness of vocabulary, and directness and variety of syntax.

Guidelines for Language Improvement

"You are what you speak" might be the war cry of the time-honored school of self-improvement that teaches that if you improve your ability with language, you improve your chances for success, however you define it. Here are the traditional guidelines for language improvement:

1. Read and Listen. We improve our language skills most efficiently by taking an interest in thoughtful writing and speech. As we read and listen, we learn new words through their context, and we learn new and graceful constructions through our observations of how professionals use them. Read and listen to the best and the most challenging material you can. This guideline is most helpful when combined with the next one.

2. Get into the Dictionary Habit. When you see or hear a word you are unsure about, look it up. Check the meaning, the derivation, the pronunciation, and the root of the word. The root is especially important. It will help you remember the word, and it will also give you a better understanding of words you already know that contain that root. In fact, the root might acquaint you with a whole new family of words you do not know yet.

For example, you might look up *vertigo,* and find that it means "dizziness, a feeling that everything is turning." The Latin root for the word is *vert-,* Latin for "turn." You therefore have a clue to the meaning of all the words in the "vert-" family, including (but not limited to) the following:

extrovert: a person whose attention turns outward to others.
introvert: a person whose attention turns inward, away from others.
revert: to turn back to a former habit, belief, and so on.
divert: to turn aside.
vertex: turning point.
convert: to turn something into another form or use.
invert: to turn upside down.

Many professional writers and speakers have read the entire dictionary page by page, taking note of any words they were unfamiliar with. You can take up this exercise and put it down as the spirit moves you. Even if you only read a few pages a week, eventually you will get through the entire dictionary.

3. Experiment with Language. Use new vocabulary and new constructions in conversation and in writing, especially when you are in an environment in which someone will correct you if you are wrong. William Safire tells the following anecdote about how former Governor Jerry Brown of California follows this advice:

> The Governor, who likes to use unfamiliar words to clothe fresh ideas, was talking about space-age projects in California "as a synecdoche for the world's future space interest." He used the word "synecdoche" correctly, as a part to be taken for a whole — as one speaks of "head" for cattle. But he pronounced it wrong. He said "SY-neck-doash," when the Greek-rooted word should be pronounced "sin-EK-doe-key," roughly rhyming with "Schenectady" . . . Later in the interview, I asked a question using the word as if repeating his own use, but pronouncing it correctly. . . . "If the pen is mightier than the sword — to use a couple of synecdoches, Governor, as you did before . . ." I dribbled off onto another subject, but the Governor stopped me: "Is that how you pronounce it? I'd seen the word in print, but I never heard anyone pronounce it before."[24]

Safire goes on to admit that "not all speakers are so willing to learn," but the implication of his anecdote is clear. It pays to be willing to use language incorrectly once, so you can use it correctly the next time. This is how one speaker told of his experimentation with language in college:

> I remember my own college years as a long series of trials and errors in language use. I remember the day I learned that you don't pronounce the "c" in "indictment," after I had pronounced it incorrectly at a political rally. I remember a kindly professor explaining to me that I had used the word "placenta" when I meant "placebo." And I remember another professor pointing out that "forte," when it means a person's strong point, has only one syllable, and that the first consonant in "chasm" is pronounced as a "k" rather than a "ch." In fact, this trial-and-error learning of my native tongue goes on to this day.

Thus as you observe clarity, vividness, and appropriateness in others' language, your own language improves. Observe the way these traits are put to work in the sample speech that follows.

Sample Speech

Excellence in language does not always call attention to itself. The following speech contains no flowery figures of speech or prosaic *bon mots,* but it does take a difficult concept (the theory of relativity) and present it in a clear and interesting way.

The speech was presented by Sammy Hill, a senior at the University of North Carolina. With it, Sammy won first place in informative speaking at the American Forensic Association National Tournament in 1984.

Relativity

Sammy Hill
University of North Carolina

> There once was a lady named Bright
> Who could travel faster than light.
> She went out one day,
> In a relative way,
> And came back the previous night.

1 This now-famous limerick captures one of many ramifications of Albert Einstein's theory of relativity. Whenever someone mentions the theory of relativity, we automatically conjure up images of a gray-haired Albert Einstein, hard at work in his study, pencil in hand. But the theory that Einstein developed, from an overall perspective, can be summarized by an analogy created by the celebrated French mathematician Henri Poincaré. Poincaré argued as follows: Suppose one night while you're sleeping, everything in the universe increased in size by 1000-fold — everything — you, your house, your car, light waves, radio waves, everything. Would you be able to prove that there had been an increase? "No," said Poincaré, because to say that something is bigger is to say that it is bigger than something else, and in the case of the universe, there is nothing else. That is, size is a relative concept because it is measured relative to something else.

2 The reason that the theory of relativity is looked upon as being incomprehensible is not because its results are difficult to understand, but because they're difficult to believe. The reason that results are difficult to believe is because we see Newtonian physics at work in the world around us. What we must realize is that Einsteinian physics is what makes this world go around.

3 To better understand this concept of "relativity," let's first see how Einstein developed his theory, then let's look at the implications inherent in that theory.

4 Einstein wrote in his autobiographical notes that the catalyst for his research was a paradox that he spotted at the ripe old age of 16 years. He asked himself, "What would happen if I could ride on a beam of light?" The answer to that question, and subsequent others, led to the development of the Special Theory of Relativity. In this theory Einstein brought together several notions and concepts, the first of which was the notion of the reduction in size of moving bodies. If A and B are moving in opposite directions, and A can measure the length of B, then B appears to A to have shrunk. For example, if you and I were both ten feet tall while standing still, and we are now separating at a rate of 93,000 miles per second, you would appear to me to be only 8.5 feet tall, and the inverse is true as well; I would appear to you to be only 8.5 feet tall. This perceived reduction in size of moving bodies is referred to as the Fitzgerald/Lorentz contraction.

5   A second concept relied upon by Einstein is that of mass increasing with velocity. The faster an object moves, the heavier it becomes. If an ace tennis player is able to serve a tennis ball and accelerate that ball to the speed of light, the ball would gain weight. As the ball moves faster and faster, it becomes heavier and heavier. It becomes heavier than a herd of elephants, heavier than the NYC skyline, heavier than the entire earth, and as the ball reaches the speed of light, its weight becomes infinite. Consider this concept of man increasing with velocity the next time you see an overweight jogger. According to the Special Theory of Relativity, the faster he runs, the more he weighs! Consider: if a 300-pound man could jog at 15 mph (a highly unlikely phenomenon if you know much about jogging), his weight would increase by one millionth of one millionth of an ounce. Of course the effect would be greater if he could run faster. But take heart, joggers, remember the Fitzgerald/Lorentz contraction says that even though he's gaining weight, he's decreasing in size. (That's the goal of most joggers, anyway, isn't it?)

6   A third relationship predicted by Einstein's theory suggests that there exists a maximum possible velocity. There must exist a certain speed beyond which nothing can go. We saw in the Fitzgerald/Lorentz contraction that the faster a object moves the smaller it becomes; as an object moves faster and faster, its length becomes smaller and smaller, and as it reaches the speed of light its length becomes 0 and it disappears from our perceptions altogether. We saw in the tennis ball example that the faster the ball moved, the more its mass increased. As the ball's speed reached the speed of light, its weight became infinite. So we can only conclude that the maximum possible velocity for any moving object is 186,000 miles per second, the speed of light. Nothing can go faster, for not only does its length become zero, but its weight becomes infinite. I'm willing to wager that nothing is heavier or smaller than infinity.

7   What all these equations point to is an equivalence of mass and energy. Simply put, a tiny amount of matter can produce enormous amounts of energy. This was proved in August of 1945 when a bomb called "Little Boy" was dropped on the Japanese city of Hiroshima. Einstein summarized this equation by writing $E = mc^2$. E stands for energy, m for mass, and c for the speed of light. If we plug in the mass of one pound of coal into $E = mc^2$, the resultant energy is 30 quadrillion foot-pounds of force. That's 3 with 16 0's after it, or equivalent to the amount of energy produced by all the power plants in the U.S. for one month. We've seen how Einstein developed his theory and how it might be used, but why is $E = mc^2$ the literally earth-shattering theory that it is? Let's look at its implications.

8   One of the most popular features of Albert Einstein's theory of relativity is that it explains our existence in the universe — the Big Bang theory. Rather than deal with our cosmological origins I'll deal with something only slightly less auspicious — the concept of time. Time is truly a curious implication in the theory in that Einstein predicted that a moving clock would run more slowly than a stationary one. This was proven experimentally by a British scientist, Dr. H. Hay, who visualized our world squashed flat in the form of a disk with the equator in the perimeter of the disk and the North Pole

at the center. By placing a clock at the center and one at the perimeter Dr. Hay proved Einstein correct. This holds true for any disk on any turntable. So, the next time you play your favorite album, keep in mind that the center of the album is aging more quickly than its perimeter. Furthermore, the concept that time and distance are relative values and not absolute ones leads to what is known as the Twin Paradox. If a man standing on a launch pad could see a clock in a rocket moving at the speed of light, then the clock would appear to be moving very slowly indeed. What is more, if the observer on the launch pad had an identical twin as an astronaut in the rocket, upon the astronaut's return, there would be a physically measurable age difference in the two men. I.e., ultra-high speed travel is the fountain of youth that Ponce de León searched for so earnestly hundreds of years ago.

9   One of the most baffling consequences of the theory of relativity is the prediction of the existence of black holes, the corpses of what were once massive stars that can no longer be seen because their gravitational forces are so intense as to capture light. During the stable lifetime of a star there exists an equilibrium of pressures between gravity pushing inward on the star and heat and radiation emanating outward from the star as it burns its core. As the core is completely consumed, the star begins collapsing inwardly upon itself. It finally condenses itself to a tiny volume of immense density and gravity. By definition, our most powerful telescopes cannot make a black hole visible, but their existence in the universe can be detected by their effect on neighboring stars. With their insatiable gravitational appetites, they be-have like giant interstellar vacuum cleaners. Any particle hapless enough to be caught in this gravitational force is pulled endlessly inward toward the black hole, burning and emitting heat and radiation. This heat and radiation can be measured by astronomers here on earth.

10   We've seen how Einstein developed his theory and some of its implica-tions, but what is the true essence of relativity? Simply this:

11   Relativity is the realization of a world situated beyond our sensations and perceptions, yet possessing its own superior reality. We cannot *know* what that world is like, we can only compare what it looks like to each and every one of us. Relativity is the understanding of the world not as events, but as relations.

Analysis of the Speech

Sammy Hill's vocabulary is appropriate to his college audience — both students and faculty — throughout his speech. Obviously, no obscenity or slang was called for, and the absence of jargon with a topic like this is very important. Sammy avoids clichés that might have gotten in the way of clear thought, and he strives for original wording that expresses the concept as he sees it. ("Relativity is the understanding of the world not as events, but as relations.")

His language is action-oriented. ("If an ace tennis player is able to serve a tennis ball and accelerate that ball to the speed of light . . ." "Any particle hapless enough to be caught in this gravitational force is pulled endlessly inward toward the black hole, burning and emitting heat and radiation.") Every chance he gets, Sammy evokes his listener's senses: ("a gray-haired Albert Einstein, hard at work in his study, pencil in hand."). He uses specific language (". . . a bomb called 'Little Boy' was dropped on the Japanese city of Hiroshima") when it is called for and highly abstract language ("possessing its own superior reality") when that is more appropriate. He reduces abstract concepts to concrete images. (Thirty quadrillion foot-pounds of force is "3 with 16 0's after it, or equivalent to the amount of energy produced by all the power plants in the U.S. for one month"; black holes behave "like giant interstellar vacuum cleaners.")

When Sammy has an important point to make, he says it directly. ("The faster an object moves, the heavier it becomes." ". . . A tiny amount of matter can produce enormous amounts of energy.") Finally, throughout his speech, he uses a variety of sentence types. ("'No,' said Poincaré . . ." "That's the goal of most joggers, . . . isn't it?")

Summary

The analysis of language presented in this chaper centers on *vocabulary* (the words we use) and *syntax* (the way we put those words together). Three aspects of vocabulary were discussed. *Clarity,* saying what you mean, includes *specificity* (using words that restrict meaning) and *concreteness* (using words that refer to things that we can perceive through the senses). *Vividness* includes *originality* (avoiding clichés), *action orientation,* and *sensuousness* (using words that evoke images). The discussion of appropriateness warns against the use of obscenity, slang, and sexist language, and warns that jargon should be used only with groups that are familiar with it.

Two aspects of syntax were discussed. *Directness* is accomplished through the use of simple, active sentence constructions, and *variety* results from the manipulation of sentence length, type, and structure. A consideration of these characteristics of language should help you make effective language choices. Three guidelines for language improvement were suggested: (1) reading and listening, (2) using the dictionary, and (3) experimenting with language.

Questions/Assignments

1. For practice at selecting your vocabulary carefully, write two descriptions of the *same* event, object, or person. Keep the *facts* exactly the same in each version, but change (where necessary) the *wording* to convey a positive attitude in the first case and a negative viewpoint in the second. For example, the first time you might refer to "a plump, relaxed, easygoing maintenance man," and in the second version you could write about "a fat, lazy janitor."

2. Select one main point from one of your previous speeches, or from a speech you have found in a source such as *Vital Speeches.* Reword the point in three different ways. Which one is the clearest wording? Why?
3. Do you agree that a lack of originality is one of the biggest problems college students encounter in their communication? If you agree, what are some of the overworked phrases or words that annoy you? If you disagree, what arguments can you raise against this statement?
4. Evaluate the sample speech at the end of this chapter according to the criteria for effective vocabulary and syntax. After doing so, do you agree or disagree with the criteria? Explain your answer, using examples from the speech.
5. Can you think of any situations in which obscenity might be effective? If so, why do you think such language might work in these instances?

Notes

1. *Webster's New Collegiate Dictionary,* 1973.
2. Harold Vetter, *Language Behavior and Communication* (Itasca, Ill.: Peacock, 1969), p. 170.
3. *Ibid.*
4. Jerry Rubin, *Do It* (New York: Simon and Schuster, 1970), p. 99.
5. The more general concept, known as "language intensity," includes "sex metaphors," such as "getting screwed." The experimental evidence suggests that such language usage hampers a message's effectiveness, and the speaker's credibility, if the audience initially holds attitudes strongly opposed to those of the source. See J. W. Bowers, "Language Intensity, Social Introversion, and Attitude Change," *Speech Monographs* 30, 1963, pp. 345–352; M. Burgoon and L. King, "The Mediation of Resistance to Persuasion Strategies by Language Variables and Active-Passive Participation," *Human Communication Research* 1, 1974, pp. 30–41; and M. Burgoon, S. B. Jones, and D. Stewart, "Toward a Message-Centered Theory of Persuasion: Three Empirical Investigations of Language Intensity," *Human Communication Research* 1, 1973, pp. 240–256.
6. Cindy Limauro, "The Student's Epidemic," *College English* 37, April 1976, p. 813. © 1976 by the National Council of Teachers of English. Reprinted by permission of the publisher.
7. *Ibid.*
8. Harry J. Gray, "The Essential American Virtues," *Vital Speeches of the Day,* June 15, 1984, p. 526.
9. *Ibid.*
10. Susan B. Anthony, "On Woman's Right to Suffrage" (1872), from Lewis Copeland and Lawrence Lamm, eds., *The World's Great Speeches* (New York: Dover, 1958), pp. 321–322.
11. Peter Farb, *Word Play: What Happens When People Talk* (New York: Knopf, 1974), p. 193.
12. From Albert Morehead, *The New American Roget's College Thesaurus in Dictionary Form.* (New York: Signet, 1962), p. 271. Reprinted by arrangement with The New American Library, Inc., New York, N.Y.

13. Susan B. Anthony, *op. cit.*

14. Brand Blanshard, "Think!," *Vital Speeches of the Day,* July 15, 1984, p. 594.

15. From the closing statement of the final Carter/Reagan debate. See *The New York Times,* October 29, 1980, p. A29.

16. Adapted from a diagram in S. I. Hayakawa, *Language in Thought and Action,* 2d ed. (New York: Harcourt Brace Jovanovich, 1964), which was adapted from a diagram in Alfred Korzybski, *Science and Sanity* (Lancaster, Pa: Science Press, 1933).

17. A true classroom experience in which not even the footnoted name of the student, Margo Bradden, has been changed to protect her innocence.

18. The sentence is an example of a dangling construction. For a description of common grammatical mistakes, see William W. Watt, *An American Rhetoric* (New York: Holt, Rinehart and Winston, 1964), or any other writing text in that section of the library shelves.

19. Harry J. Gray, *op. cit.*

20. From John F. Kennedy's Inaugural Address, delivered January 20, 1961.

21. William W. Watt, *An American Rhetoric* (New York: Holt, Rinehart and Winston, 1964), p. 224.

22. Studies pertaining to the differences between written and spoken language are reviewed in John F. Wilson and Carroll C. Arnold, *Dimensions of Public Communication* (Boston: Allyn & Bacon, 1976), pp. 195–198.

23. Shana Alexander, "Unaccustomed As I Am," *Life,* May 19, 1967.

24. William Safire, "The Wiseguy Problem," *New York Times Magazine,* March 25, 1979, p. 12.

9

Delivery

Delivery: An Introduction

"So far, so good," you may be thinking to yourself. You have developed a purpose; you have chosen and researched a topic that suits your own interests, your audience, and the occasion. You feel confident about your ability to organize your ideas in a logical, effective way, and you have built up a healthy reserve of supporting material.

Then, when you think about the act of standing before a group, your self-confidence begins to erode. How will you act? Should you be formal or casual? Should you memorize your remarks, read from a script, or use notes? How loudly should you speak, and how quickly? What about your nerves? The prospect of talking to an audience probably seems much more threatening than expressing yourself in a blue book or even mixing chemicals in a laboratory.

It is difficult to talk about the problems of presenting a speech, because everyone's speeches (and everyone's delivery) are unique. In fact, if you have ever sought out advice on how to give a speech, you probably ran up against the same contradictions that journalist Shana Alexander heard when she was preparing to make a speech at a banquet:

> Friends rallied round with all sorts of advice, mostly contradictory. Don't be afraid to write it out. Read it. Memorize it. Put it on cards. Speak it off the

cuff. Start funny. Start dull—an early joke lets them off the hook of curiosity. Turn from side to side so they can all see you. Find one nice face in the audience and tell it all to him. Get a new dress. Get a little drunk. By the afternoon of the speech, trying to follow all the advice at once, I sat stupefied with terror in my room in the hotel where the banquet was to be held. . . .[1]

As Alexander points out, too much advice can be stifling. A speaker concentrating on all the classic bits of advice becomes like the centipede who, when asked how it operated all its legs, thought about it and found that it could not. Besides, as Wilson and Arnold point out, "No one has ever found prescriptions for delivery in speech which work for everyone and which are appropriate for all speaking situations—even public ones."[2]

Because the act of speaking before a group of listeners may be a new one for you, we will look at the process now. The purpose of this chapter is to make you feel more confident about yourself as a speaker and to give you a clearer idea of how to behave before an audience.[3]

Speaking with Confidence

The terror that strikes into the hearts of so many beginning speakers is called communication apprehension or speech anxiety by communication scholars, but it is more commonly known to those who experience it as stage fright.

Facilitative and Debilitative Stage Fright

Although stage fright is a serious problem for many speakers, it can be overcome. Interestingly enough, the first step in feeling less apprehensive about speaking is to realize that a certain amount of nervousness is not only natural but facilitative. That is, it can help improve your performance. Just as excitement helps athletes or musicians to perform at the top of their potential, speakers think more rapidly and express themselves more energetically when their level of tension is moderate.

It is only when the level of anxiety is intense that it becomes debilitative, inhibiting effective self-expression. Intense fear causes trouble in two ways. First, the strong emotion keeps you from thinking clearly. Second, intense fear leads to an urge to do something, anything, to make the problem go away. This urge to escape often causes a speaker to speed up delivery, which results in a rapid, almost machine-gun style. As you can imagine, this boost in speaking rate leads to even more mistakes, which only adds to the speaker's anxiety. Thus, a relatively small amount of nervousness can begin to feed on itself until it grows into a serious problem.

Sources of Debilitative Stage Fright

Before we describe how to manage debilitative stage fright, it might be helpful to look at some reasons why people are afflicted with the problem.[4]

Previous Experience. One reason people feel apprehensive about speech-giving is because of unpleasant past experiences. A traumatic failure at an earlier speech or low self-esteem from critical parents during childhood are common examples. You might object to the idea that past experiences cause stage fright. After all, not everyone who has bungled a speech or had critical parents is debilitated in the future. To understand why some people are affected more strongly than others by past experiences, we need to consider another cause of speech anxiety.

Irrational Thinking. Cognitive psychologists argue that it is not *events* that cause people to feel nervous, but rather the beliefs they have about those events.[5] Certain irrational beliefs leave people feeling unnecessarily apprehensive. Psychologist Albert Ellis lists several such beliefs, which we will call "fallacies" because of their illogical nature.[6]

1. **The Fallacy of Catastrophic Failure.** Some people operate on the assumption that if something bad can happen, it probably will. Their thoughts before and during a speech resemble these:

   "As soon as I stand up to speak, I'll forget everything I wanted to say."
   "Everyone will think my ideas are stupid."
   "Somebody will probably laugh at me."

   Although it is naive to imagine that all your speeches will be totally successful, it is equally wrong to assume they will all fail miserably. One way to escape from the fallacy of catastrophic failure is to take a more realistic look at the situation. Would your audience really hoot you off the stage? Will they really think your ideas are stupid? Even if you did forget your remarks for a moment, would the results be a genuine disaster?[7]

2. **The Fallacy of Perfection.** Other speakers expect themselves to behave flawlessly. Whereas such a standard of perfection might serve as a target and a source of inspiration (rather like making a hole-in-one for a golfer), it is totally unrealistic to expect that you will write and deliver a perfect speech — especially as a beginner.

3. **The Fallacy of Approval.** Another mistaken belief is the idea that it is vital — not just desirable — to gain the approval of everyone in the audience. It is rare that even the best speakers please everyone, especially on topics that are at all controversial. To paraphrase Abraham Lincoln, you cannot please all the people al! the time . . . and it is irrational to expect you will.

4. **The Fallacy of Overgeneralization.** This fallacy might also be labeled the fallacy of exaggeration, for it occurs when a person blows one poor experience out of proportion. Consider these examples:

> "I'm so stupid! I mispronounced that word."
> "I completely blew it—I forgot one of my supporting points."
> "My hands were shaking. The audience must have thought I was a complete idiot."

A second type of exaggeration occurs when a speaker treats occasional lapses as if they were the rule rather than the exception. This sort of mistake usually involves extreme labels such as "always" and "never."

> "I *always* forget what I want to say."
> "I can *never* come up with a good topic."
> "I can't do *anything* right."

Overcoming Stage Fright

There are four fairly simple ways to overcome debilitative stage fright. The first, as suggested earlier, is to be rational about the beliefs that cause your stage fright. The other three are to be receiver-oriented, positive, and prepared.

Be Rational. Listen to your thought processes, your internal voice, and try to figure out if the basis for your stage fright is rational. Then dispute any irrational beliefs. Use the list of fallacies to discover which of your internal statements are based on mistaken thinking.

Be Receiver-Oriented. Concentrate on your audience rather than on yourself. Worry about whether they are interested, about whether they understand and about whether or not you are maintaining contact with them.

Be Positive. It is important to build and maintain a positive attitude toward your audience, your speech, and yourself as a speaker. Some communication consultants suggest that public speakers should concentrate on three statements immediately before speaking. The three statements are:

> "I'm glad I'm here."
> "I know my topic."
> "I care about you" ("you" of course being the audience).

Keeping these ideas in mind can help you maintain a positive attitude.

Be Prepared. If you are fully prepared, your speech will represent less of a threat. Devote enough time to each step of message preparation so you can feel secure. Be especially sure to leave enough time to *practice* your presentation. And when it comes time to give your presentation, keep in mind that nervousness is normal. Expect it, and remember that its symptoms — even shaky knees and trembling hands — are more obvious to you than they are to the audience. Beginning public speakers, when congratulated for their poise during a speech, are apt to make such remarks as "Are you kidding? I was *dying* up there."

These four guidelines will enable most speakers to control their stage fright to the point where it will be facilitative rather than debilitative. Speakers who find these methods inadequate have two other options: They might enlist the help of a professional counselor (these services are often provided free by colleges), or they could research a more extensive procedure for themselves, such as systematic desensitization. Ron Adler's book *Confidence in Communication: A Guide to Assertive and Social Skills*[8] outlines several procedures for managing communication anxiety.

Improving the way you feel as a speaker plays an important role in your effectiveness. Now we will turn to another vital part of your delivery: how you look and sound as a speaker. The first thing to consider in this area is the style of delivery you choose.

Types of Delivery

There are four basic types of delivery — extemporaneous, impromptu, manuscript, and memorized. Each type creates a different impression and is appropriate under different conditions. Any speech may incorporate more than one of these types of delivery. For purposes of discussion, however, it is best to consider them separately.

Extemporaneous Speeches

An extemporaneous speech is planned in advance but presented in a direct, spontaneous manner. This style of speaking is generally accepted to be the most effective, especially for a college class. In a classroom you generally speak before a small audience (five to fifty people) made up of people with diverse backgrounds. Spontaneity is essential with this type of audience, but so is careful message planning. Extemporaneous speaking allows you to benefit from both careful planning and spontaneous delivery. A speech presented extemporaneously will be focused, organized, and planned out in advance, but the exact wording of the entire speech will not be memorized or otherwise predetermined. Because you speak from only brief, unobtrusive notes, you are able to move and maintain eye contact with your audience.

Extemporaneous speaking is not only the most effective type of delivery for a classroom speech, but it is also the most common type of delivery in the "outside" world. Most of those involved in communication-oriented careers find that the majority of their public speaking is done before audiences that, in terms of size and diversity of interests, resemble those found in a college classroom. Professional public speakers recognize the advisability of both careful planning and spontaneity with such an audience.

The extemporaneous speech does have some disadvantages. It is difficult to keep exact time limits, to be exact in wording, or to be grammatically perfect with an extemporaneous speech. Therefore, if you are speaking as part of a radio or television broadcast or if your speech will be reproduced "for the record," you might want to use a manuscript or to memorize your speech. Also, an extemporaneous speech requires time to prepare. If you do not have the time, an impromptu speech might be more appropriate.

Impromptu Speeches

You give an impromptu speech off the top of your head, without preparation. An impromptu speech is often given in an emergency, such as when a scheduled speaker becomes ill and you are suddenly called upon:

> Grunt Johnson couldn't make it this evening, folks, but I notice in our audience another Sioux U student leader who I am sure would be glad to say a few words . . .

Impromptu speeches are sometimes given when speakers forget they are scheduled for extemporaneous speeches. In fact, a certain amount of confusion exists between the terms *extemporaneous* and *impromptu.*

The problem with an impromptu speech is that it is given on the spur of the moment and, as Monroe and Ehninger have pointed out, "Too often the 'moment' arrives without the necessary informed and inspired 'spur.' "[9] There are, however, advantages to impromptu speaking. For one thing, an impromptu speech is by definition spontaneous. It is the delivery style necessary for informal talks, group discussions, and comments on others' speeches. It also can be an effective training aid; it can teach you to think on your feet and organize your thoughts quickly. To take full advantage of an impromptu speaking opportunity, remember the following points:

Think Quickly. Take advantage of the time between being called on to speak and actually speaking. Review your personal experiences and use them. Do not be afraid to be original; you do not have to remember what every other expert says about your topic — what do *you* say about it? If nothing else, consider the questions "Who? What? When? Where? How?" and formulate a plan to answer one or more of them. Even if you have only a minute, you can still scribble a few brief notes to protect against mental blocks.

Be Observant. Observe what is going on around you and respond to it. If there were other speakers, you might agree or disagree with what they said. You can comment on the audience and the occasion, too, as well as on your topic.

Be Positive. Keep a positive attitude. Remember that audience expectations are low. They know you have not prepared in advance, and they do not expect you to be Patrick Henry.

Be Brief. Finally, and most important, keep your comments brief. Especially, do not prolong your conclusion. If you have said everything you want to say or everything you can remember, wrap it up as neatly as possible and sit down. If you forgot something, it probably was not important anyway. If it was, the audience will ask you about it afterward.

Manuscript Speeches

Manuscript speeches are necessary when you are speaking "for the record," as at legal proceedings or scientific conventions. The greatest disadvantage of a manuscript speech is the lack of spontaneity. Manuscript readers have even been known to read their directions by mistake: "And so, let me say in conclusion, look at the audience with great sincerity . . . oops!" Needless to say, this can lead to extreme embarrassment.

Manuscript speeches are difficult and cumbersome, but they are sometimes necessary. If you find occasion to use one, here are some guidelines:

1. When writing the speech, recognize the differences between written essays and speeches. Speeches are usually less formal, more repetitive, and more personal than written messages.[10]
2. Use short paragraphs. They are easier to return to after establishing eye contact with your audience.
3. Type the manuscript triple-spaced, in all caps, with a dark ribbon. Underline the words you want to emphasize. (See Figure 9–1.)
4. Use stiff paper, so it will not fold up or fly away during the speech. Type on only one side, and number the pages as visibly as possible.
5. Rehearse until you can "read" whole lines without looking at the manuscript.
6. Take your time, vary your speed, and try to concentrate on ideas rather than words.

Manuscript speeches that are prepared for radio and television speaking have additional requirements, which will be discussed in Chapter 13.

```
        TO SUMMARIZE, WE ARE IN THE EARLY STAGE OF DEVELOPMENTS IN

   THE SCIENCE AND TECHNOLOGY OF INFORMATION PROCESSING THAT WILL

   TRULY REVOLUTIONIZE OUR SOCIETY.  ADVANCES ARE OCCURRING AT SUCH

   A FAST PACE THAT RECENT EXPERIENCE IS NOT ALWAYS A GOOD GUIDE TO

   THE FUTURE.  IN THE PAST 30 YEARS, COMPUTER COMPUTATIONS HAVE

   GONE FROM A FEW INSTRUCTIONS PER SECOND AT A COST OF SEVERAL

   DOLLARS TO MILLIONS OF INSTRUCTIONS PER SECOND AT A COST OF LESS

   THAN 1 CENT.  BUT SUCH DRAMATIC INDICATORS OF PROGRESS DO NOT

   MEASURE THE FULL IMPACT OF WHAT IS TAKING PLACE OR WHAT IS LIKELY

   TO OCCUR IN THE NEXT 30 YEARS.  THERE CAN BE LITTLE DOUBT THAT

   THESE CHANGES WILL ALTER THE WAY PEOPLE LIVE AND EARN A LIVING,

   AND THE WAY THEY PERCEIVE THEMSELVES AND RELATE TO ONE ANOTHER.
```

Figure 9-1   Sample page from a manuscript speech

Memorized Speeches

Memorized speeches are the most difficult and often the least effective. They usually seem excessively formal. They tend to make you think of words rather than ideas. However, like manuscript speeches, they are sometimes necessary. They are used in oratory contests and on very formal occasions such as eulogies or church rituals. They are used as training devices for memory. They are also used in some political situations. For example, in the 1984 presidential debates, Walter Mondale and Ronald Reagan were allowed to make prepared speeches, but they were not allowed to use notes. They had to memorize precise, "for-the-record" wording.

There is only one guideline for a memorized speech: practice. The speech will not be effective until you have practiced it so you can present it with what actors and term-paper recyclers call "the illusion of the first time."

You will want to choose the appropriate delivery style for the type of speech you are giving. To assure that you are on your way to an effective delivery, practice in front of a small sample audience — perhaps one or two friends — and have them comment on it.

Guidelines for Delivery

The best way to consider guidelines for delivery is through an examination of the nonverbal aspects of presenting a speech. Nonverbal messages can change the meaning assigned to the spoken word and in some cases contradict that meaning entirely. In fact, if the audience wants to interpret how you *feel* about something, they are likely to trust your nonverbal communication more than the words you speak. If you tell an audience, "It's good to be here today," but you stand before them slouched over with your hands in your pockets and an expression on you face as if you were about to be shot, they are likely to discount what you say. This disbelief might cause your audience to react negatively to your speech, and their negative reaction might make you even more nervous. This cycle of speaker and audience reinforcing each other's feelings can work *for* you, though, if you approach a subject with genuine enthusiasm. One way that you manifest enthusiasm is through the visual aspects of your delivery.

Visual Aspects of Delivery

Visual aspects of delivery include appearance, movement, posture, facial expressions, and eye contact.

Appearance. Appearance is not a presentation variable as much as a preparation variable. Some communication consultants suggest new clothes, new glasses, and new hairstyles for their clients. In case you consider any of these, be forewarned that you should be attractive to your audience, but not flashy. Research suggests that audiences like speakers who are similar to them, but they prefer the similarity to be shown conservatively. For example, studies run in 1972, when long hair on males was becoming popular, showed that even long-haired listeners considered long-haired speakers less credible than shorter-haired speakers.[11]

Movement. Movement is an important visual aspect of delivery. The way you walk to the front of your audience, for example, will express your confidence and enthusiasm. Once you begin speaking, nervous energy can cause your body to shake and twitch, distressing both you and your audience. One way to control involuntary movement is to move voluntarily when you feel the need to move. Do not feel that you have to stand in one spot or that all your gestures need to be carefully planned. Simply get involved in your message, and let your involvement create the motivation for your movement. That way, when you move, you will emphasize what you are saying in the same way you would emphasize it if you were talking to a group of friends. If you move voluntarily, you will use up the same energy that would otherwise cause you to move involuntarily.

Movement can help you maintain contact with *all* members of your audience. Those closest to you will feel the greatest contact with you, whereas the people who are less interested will have a tendency to sit farther away to begin with. This tendency creates an "action zone" of audience members sitting in the front and center of the room. Movement enables you to extend this action zone, to include in it people who would otherwise remain uninvolved. Without overdoing it, you should feel free to move toward, away, or from side to side in front of your audience.

Remember: Move with the understanding that it will add to the meaning of the words you use. It is difficult to bang your fist on a podium or to take a step without conveying emphasis. Make the emphasis natural by allowing your message to create your motivation to move.

Posture. Generally speaking, good posture means standing with your spine relatively straight, your shoulders relatively squared off, and your feet angled out to keep your body from falling over sideways. In other words, rather than standing at military attention, you should be comfortably erect.

Of course, you should not get *too* comfortable. There are effective speakers who sprawl on table tops and slouch against blackboards, but their effectiveness is usually in spite of their posture rather than because of it. Sometimes speakers are so awesome in stature or reputation that they need an informal posture to encourage their audience to relax. In that case, sloppy posture is more or less justified; but because awesomeness is not usually a problem for beginning speakers, good posture should be the rule.

Good posture can help you control nervousness by allowing your breathing apparatus to work properly; when your brain receives enough oxygen, it is easier for you to think clearly and dispel irrational fears. Good posture will also help you get a positive audience reaction because standing up straight makes you more visible. It also increases your audience contact, because the audience members will feel that you are interested enough in them to stand formally, yet relaxed enough to be at ease with them.

Facial Expressions. The expression on your face can be more meaningful to an audience than the words you say. Try it yourself with a mirror. Say, "College is neat," with a smirk, with a warm smile, deadpan, and then with a scowl. It just does not mean the same thing. When speaking, keep in mind that your face might be saying something in front of your back. Remember also that it is just about impossible to control facial expressions from the outside. Like your movement, your facial expressions will reflect your involvement with your message. Do not try to fake it. Just get involved in your message, and your face will take care of itself.

Eye Contact.   Eye contact is the most important nonverbal facet of delivery. Eye contact not only increases your direct contact with your audience, it also should increase their interest in you by making you more attractive. Eyes are beautiful things; much more beautiful than eyelids, foreheads, or scalps.

Furthermore, contrary to popular opinion, eye contact can be used to help you control your nervousness. Direct eye contact is a form of reality testing. The most frightening aspect of speaking is the unknown. How will the audience react? What will they think? Direct eye contact allows you to test your perception of your audience as you speak. Usually, especially in a college class, you will find that your audience is more "with" you than you think. In their first speeches, most speakers are terrified of the audience members who slither down in their chairs, doodle, and generally seem bored. These audience members upset new speakers so thoroughly that the speakers usually try *not* to look at them. Avoidance makes matters worse. By deliberately establishing eye contact with them, speakers find that those audience members often *are* interested; they just are not showing interest because they do not think anyone is looking. Once the bored-looking audience members realize that someone is actually noticing them, they make their attention more obvious by sitting up and looking back. The more eye contact they receive, the more interested they appear.

To maintain eye contact you might try to meet the eyes of each member of your audience, squarely, at least once during any presentation. Once you have made definite contact, move on to another audience member. You can learn to scan quickly, so you can visually latch onto every member of a good-sized class in a relatively short time.

The characteristics of appearance, movement, posture, facial expression, and eye contact are visual, nonverbal facets of delivery. Now consider the auditory, nonverbal messages that you might send during a presentation.

Auditory Aspects of Delivery

The way you use your voice says a great deal about you: most notably about your sincerity and enthusiasm. In addition, using your voice well can help you control your nervousness. It is another cycle: controlling your vocal characteristics will decrease your nervousness, which will enable you to control your voice even more. This cycle can also work in the opposite direction. If your voice is out of control, your nerves will probably be in the same state. Controlling your voice is mostly a matter of recognizing and using appropriate *volume, rate, pitch,* and *articulation.*

Volume. Volume—the loudness of your voice—is determined by the amount of air you push past the vocal folds in your throat. The key to controlling volume, then, is controlling the amount of air you use. The key to determining the *right* volume is audience contact. Your delivery should be loud enough so that your audience can hear everything you say but not so loud that they feel you are talking to someone in the next room.

Too much volume is seldom the problem for beginning speakers. Usually they either speak too softly or fade off at the end of a thought. Sometimes, when they lose faith in an idea in midsentence, they compromise by mumbling the end of the sentence so it is not quite coherent. That is an unfortunate compromise, rather like changing your mind in the middle of a broad jump.

One contemporary speaker who has been criticized for inappropriate volume is Senator Edward M. Kennedy. A researcher pointed out that ". . . Kennedy tended to shout when an audience was small or uninterested or when he sensed he was losing them. Thus, his volume was often inappropriate to the time and place."[12] *Newsweek*'s John Walcott observed, "When he had an unresponsive audience—300 Iowa farmers who were not jumping up on their chairs—he tended to shout more and it became more and more incongruous."[13]

Rate. Rate is your speed in speaking. Normal speaking speed is around 150 words per minute. If you talk at a slower rate than that, you may tend to lull your audience to sleep. Faster speaking rates are typically associated with speaker competence,[14] but if you talk too rapidly, you will tend to be unintelligible. Once again, your involvement in your message is the key to achieving an effective rate.

Pitch. Pitch—the highness or lowness of your voice—is controlled by the frequency at which your vocal folds vibrate as you push air through them. Because taut vocal folds vibrate at a greater frequency, pitch is influenced by muscular tension. This connection explains why nervous speakers have a tendency occasionally to "squeak." Pitch will tend to follow rate and volume. As you speed up or become louder, your pitch will have a tendency to rise. If your range in pitch is too narrow, your voice will have a singsong quality. If it is too wide, you may sound overly dramatic. You should control your pitch so your listeners believe you are talking *with* them rather than performing in front of them. Once again, your involvement in your message should take care of this matter naturally for you.

When considering volume, rate, and pitch, keep *emphasis* in mind. You have to use a variety of vocal characteristics to maintain audience interest, but remember that a change in volume, pitch, or rate will result in emphasis. If you pause or speed up, your rate will suggest emphasis. Words you whisper or scream will be emphasized by their volume. One student provided an example of how volume can be used to emphasize an idea. He was speaking on how possessions like cars communicate things about their owners. "For example," he said, with normal volume, "a Lincoln Continental says, 'I've got money!' But a Rolls- Royce says, *I'VE GOT MONEY!*'" He blared out those last three words with such force the podium shook.

Articulation. The final auditory nonverbal behavior, articulation, is the most important. For our purposes here, articulation means saying all the parts of all the necessary words and nothing else.

It is not our purpose to condemn regional or ethnic dialects within this discussion. Native New Yorkers can continue to have their "hot dawgs" with their "cawfee," and Southerners can drawl as much as they-all please. You *should* know, however, that a considerable amount of research suggests that regional dialects can cause negative impressions.[15] On the other hand, an honest regional accent can work in your favor. For example, when Paul Volcker was president of the Federal Reserve Bank of New York, he used his accent to his benefit when he began a speech this way:

> Fellow New Yorkers: I am emboldened to use that simple salutation tonight for more than one reason. At the most personal level, I was reminded the other day where my own roots lay. I heard a tape recording of some remarks I had made. After spending three-quarters of the past 16 years in Washington, I confess to being startled by what I heard — the full, rounded tones of a home-grown New York accent.[16]

The purpose of this discussion is to suggest *careful,* not standardized, articulation. Incorrect articulation is nothing more than careless articulation. It usually results in (1) leaving off parts of words (deletion), (2) replacing part of a word (substitution), (3) adding parts to words (addition), or (4) overlapping two or more words (slurring).

Deletion   The most common mistake in articulation is deletion, or leaving off part of a word. As you are thinking the complete word, it is often difficult to recognize that you are only saying part of it. The most common deletions occur at the end of words, especially "-ing" words. "Going," "doing," and "stopping" become "goin'," "doin'," and "stoppin'." Parts of words can be left off in the middle, too, as in "natully" for "naturally" and "reg'lar" for "regular."

Substitution   Substitution takes place when you replace part of a word with an incorrect sound. The ending "-th" is often replaced at the end of a word with a single "t," as when "with" becomes "wit." (This tendency is especially prevalent in many parts of the northeastern United States.) The "th-" sound is also a problem at the beginning of words; "this," "that," and "those" have a tendency to become "dis," "dat," and "dose."

Addition   The opposite articulation problem is adding extra parts to words that are already perfectly adequate, such as "incen*ta*tive" for "incentive," "ath*a*lete" for "athlete," and "orien*ta*ted" for "oriented." Sometimes this type of addition is caused by incorrect word choice, such as "irregardless" (which is not a word) for "regardless."

Another type of addition is the use of "tag questions," such as "you know?" or "you see?" or "right?" To have every other sentence punctuated with one of these barely audible superfluous phrases can be maddening.

Probably the worst type of addition, or at least the most common, is the use of "uh" and "anda" between words. "Anda" is often stuck between two words when "and" is not even needed. If you find yourself doing that, just pause or swallow instead.

Slurring   Slurring is caused, in effect, by trying to say two or more words at once — or at least overlapping the end of one word with the beginning of the next. Word pairs ending with "of" are the worst offenders in this category. "Sort of" becomes "sorta," "kind of" becomes "kinda," and "because of" becomes "becausa." Word combinations ending with "to" are often slurred, as when "want to" becomes "wanna." Sometimes even more than two words are blended together, as when "that is the way" becomes "thatsaway." Careful articulation means using your lips, teeth, tongue, and jaw to bite off your words, cleanly and separately, one at a time.

The general rule for articulation in extemporaneous speaking is to be both natural and clear. Be yourself, but be an understandable, intelligent-sounding version of yourself. The best way to achieve this goal is to accept your instructor's evaluation of whether you add, substitute, drop, or slur word sounds. Then you can, as Shakespeare had King Lear suggest, "Mend your speech a little, lest you may mar your fortune."

Summary

This chapter dealt with the problems inherent in the actual delivery of your speech. The most serious of these problems is debilitative (as opposed to facilitative) stage fright. Sources of debilitative stage fright include irrational thinking, which might include: the fallacy of perfection (a good speaker never does anything wrong), the fallacy of absolute approval (*everyone* has to like you), the fallacy of overgeneralization (you *always* mess up speeches), the fallacy of helplessness (there is nothing you can do about it), and the fallacy of catastrophic failure (all is lost if this speech bombs).

There are several methods of overcoming speech anxiety. The first is to refute the irrational fallacies just listed. The others include being receiver-oriented, positive, and prepared.

There are four types of delivery: extemporaneous, impromptu, manuscript, and memorized. In each type, the speaker must be concerned with both visual and auditory aspects of the presentation. Visual aspects include appearance, movement, posture, facial expressions, and eye contact. Auditory aspects include volume, rate, pitch, and articulation. The four most common articulation problems are deletion, substitution, addition, and slurring of word sounds.

Questions/Assignments

1. Name a speaker whose delivery you find effective. What specific aspects of the delivery are most impressive?
2. What are your own delivery problems? What can you do to correct them?
3. What *type* of delivery will you use for your next speech? Why? Under what circumstances might you give the same speech with a different type of delivery? Why?
4. Many experts insist that the time to "worry about yourself" is before your presentation and that once you are actually speaking, you should worry about your audience. How might such an attitude help a speaker to control nervousness? Do you agree or disagree with this advice? Why?
5. It is stated in the chapter that an audience is more likely to "trust your nonverbal communication . . . than the words you say." From *your experience,* hearing and seeing public speakers, do you agree or disagree? Be prepared to defend your answer.

Notes

1. Shana Alexander, "Unaccustomed As I Am," *Life,* May 19, 1967.
2. John Wilson and Carroll Arnold, *Dimensions of Public Communication* (Boston: Allyn & Bacon, 1976), pp. 201–202.
3. We will not, at this point, get into the age-old argument of the relative importance of substance (what you say) and style (how you say it). Suffice it to say that this question is as old as the study of public speaking. See, for example, Barbara Warnick, "The Quarrel Between the Ancients and the Moderns," *Communication Monographs* 49, December 1982, pp. 263–276. One recent study pointed out that media commentators viewed substance as *less* important than delivery, appearance, and manner in the 1980 presidential debates. See Goodwin F. Berquist and James L. Goldin, "Media Rhetoric, Criticism, and the Public Perception of the 1980 Presidential Debates," *Quarterly Journal of Speech* 67, May 1981, pp. 125–137.
4. A substantial body of research literature on communication apprehension and anxiety has accumulated. See James C. McCroskey, "Oral Communication Apprehension: A Summary of Recent Theory and Research," *Human Communication Research* 4, 1977, pp. 78–96. Or see James C. McCroskey, "Oral Communication Apprehension: A Reconceptualization," in Michael Burgoon, ed., *Communication Yearbook 6* (Beverly Hills, Ca.: Sage, 1982), pp. 136–170.

5. See John O. Greene and Glenn G. Sparks, "Explication and Test of a Cognitive Model of Communication Apprehension: A New Look at an Old Construct," *Human Communication Research* 9, Summer 1983, pp. 349–366. See also Ralph R. Behnke and Michael J. Beatty, "A Cognitive–Physiological Model of Speech Anxiety," *Communication Monographs* 48, June 1981, pp. 158–163.

6. Adapted from Albert Ellis, *A New Guide to Rational Living* (North Hollywood, Ca.: Wilshire Books, 1977).

7. Expectations are a significant predictor of communication apprehension. See, for example, John O. Greene and Glenn G. Sparks, "The Role of Outcome Expectations in the Experience of a State of Communication Apprehension," *Communication Quarterly* 31, Summer 1983, pp. 212–219.

8. Ronald B. Adler, *Confidence in Communication: A Guide to Assertive and Social Skills* (New York: Holt, Rinehart and Winston, 1977).

9. Alan H. Monroe and Douglas Ehninger, *Principles and Types of Speech Communication,* 7th ed. (Glenview, Ill.: Scott, Foresman, 1974), p. 142.

10. For a recent synthesis of findings on these differences, see F. Niyi Akinnaso, "On the Differences Between Spoken and Written Language," *Language and Speech* 25, March–June 1982, pp. 97–125.

11. These studies are reviewed in Lawrence R. Rosenfeld and Jean M. Civikly, *With Words Unspoken* (New York: Holt, Rinehart and Winston, 1976), p. 62.

12. L. Patrick Devlin, "An Analysis of Kennedy's Communication in the 1980 Campaign," *Quarterly Journal of Speech* 68, November 1982, pp. 397–417.

13. *Ibid.*

14. A study demonstrating this stereotype is Richard L. Street, Jr., and Robert M. Brady, "Speech Rate Acceptance Ranges as a Function of Evaluative Domain, Listener Speech Rate, and Communication Context," *Speech Monographs* 49, December 1982, pp. 290–308.

15. See, for example, Anthony Mulac and Mary Jo Rudd, "Effects of Selected American Regional Dialects upon Regional Audience Members," *Communication Monographs* 44, 1977, pp. 184–195. Some research, however, suggests that nonstandard dialects do not have the detrimental effects on listeners that were once believed. See, for example, Fern L. Johnson and Richard Buttny, "White Listeners' Responses to 'Sounding Black' and 'Sounding White': The Effects of Message Content on Judgments about Language," *Communication Monographs* 49, March 1982, pp. 33–49.

16. Paul A. Volcker, "The Dilemmas of Monetary Policy," *Vital Speeches of the Day* 42, January 15, 1976.

PART THREE

Types of Speaking

10

Informative
Speaking

Informative Speaking: An Introduction

Informative speaking is especially important in the dawning "age of information," in which transmitting knowledge will account for most of the work we do and, in a large part, for the quality of our lives. Although much of the information of the future will be transmitted by machines — computers and electronic media — the spoken word will continue to be the best way to reach small audiences with messages tailored specifically for them. At least some of these messages will be designed to help people make sense of the glut of information that surrounds them.

Informative speaking seeks to increase the knowledge and understanding of an audience. This type of speaking goes on all around you: in your professors' lectures, in news reports on radio and TV, in a mechanic's explanation of how to keep your car from breaking down. All demonstrations and explanations are forms of informative speaking. You engage in this type of speaking often, whether you realize it or not. Sometimes it is formal, as when you are giving a report in class. At other times it is informal, as when you are telling a friend how to prepare your favorite dish. It is often this everyday, informal type of informative speaking that we find most frustrating. One of the objectives of this chapter is to bolster some skills that can help relieve that frustration. Another objective is to apply some general principles from earlier chapters to the specific task of informative speaking.

Techniques of Informative Speaking

Define a Specific Informative Purpose

As Chapter 4 explained, any speech must be based on a purpose statement that is audience-oriented, precise, and attainable. When you are preparing an informative speech, it is especially important to define in advance, for yourself, a clear informative purpose. The purpose statement for an informative speech will generally be worded to stress audience knowledge and/or ability:

> After listening to my speech the audience will be able to name three types of witchcraft practiced today.

> After listening to my speech the audience will be able to list the three main causes of World War II.

> After listening to my speech the audience will be able to recall the four major components of an internal combustion engine.

Notice that in each of these purpose statements a specific verb such as "to name," "to list," or "to recall" points out the kind of thing the audience will be able to do after hearing the speech. Other key verbs for informative purpose statements include:

analyze	contrast	explain	recognize
apply	describe	identify	summarize
compare	discuss	integrate	support

Setting a clear informative purpose will help keep you focused as you prepare and present your speech. Now that you have a purpose in speaking, you must give your audience a purpose in listening.

Create "Information Hunger"

In informative speaking, you must create a reason for your audience to want to listen to and learn from your speech. The most effective way to do that is to respond in some way to their needs — either general needs that all human beings feel or specific needs that are unique to your audience.

General Needs

To relate your speech to general human needs, you can use Maslow's analysis, discussed in Chapter 4, as a guide. You could tap *physiological needs* by relating your topic to your audience's survival or to the improvement of their living conditions. If you gave a speech on food (eating it, cooking it, or shopping for it), you would automatically be dealing with that basic need. If you gave a speech on water pollution, you could relate it to physiological needs by listing the pollutants in one of your local lakes and explaining what each one could do to a human body. In the same way, you could meet *safety needs* by relating your topic to your audience's security; you could touch upon *esteem needs* by showing your audience how to be respected — or simply by showing them that *you* respect them. You can appeal to *self-actualization needs,* those based on the need to accomplish as much as possible with our lives, by showing your audience some way to improve themselves.

One speaker tapped a variety of audience needs in his speech "Waking Up the Right Lobe":

> . . . My text is drawn from an exciting book by Julian Jaynes, called *The Origin of Consciousness in the Breakdown of the Bicameral Mind.* You must read it or else you will not be aware of some of the most exciting stuff that's going on in the scientific and academic search for how we came to be, who we are now, and what we are becoming.
>
> We don't have to generalize about these discoveries or speak in the abstract. You can apply these ideas right now, right here.
>
> . . . The ultimate goal is to be fully alive — to your family, your work, and to yourself — to use your full brain! You will never possess anything in your life that is more valuable to you or will give you more thrills and excitement and pleasure than your mind![1]

This speaker is creating information hunger mostly by touching upon self-actualization needs, but he also taps all of the other needs Maslow outlined. Being "fully alive" is a physiological need; "family" is a social need; and the world of "work" involves both security and esteem needs.

Specific Needs

Maslow's analysis of needs should be kept in mind for all audiences, for all human beings share them. Yet the closer you can come to the specific needs of your audience, the more information hunger you will generate. For example, sleeping problems are universal. Everyone has a physiological need for sleep; but you could adapt this problem for a particular audience:

> Tonight, 50 million American adults will crawl into bed, draw up the covers, lay their heads down on their pillows, and then, try as they might, they will not be able to find restful sleep. You may very well be one of them. In fact, many college students suffer from sleep disorders that are particularly harmful to their academic and social success. And the chances are very good that the disorder will hit the night before a big test, just when you need your sleep more than ever. In just one month, we will all be involved in final exams. How many of us will get lower grades than we might have, simply because we couldn't get to sleep the night before?

Emphasize Important Points

Along with defining a specific informative purpose and creating information hunger, you should stress the important points in your speech
through *repetition* and *"signposts."*

Repetition

Chapter 6 discusses ways that you can emphasize material through clear
organization: limiting your speech to three to five main points; dividing,
coordinating, and ordering those main points; using a strong introduction
that previews your ideas; using a conclusion that reviews them and makes
them memorable; and using lots of transitions, internal summaries, and
internal previews. Strong organization, in effect, provides your listeners
with a repetition of important points, and that repetition will help them
understand and remember those points.

As mentioned in Chapter 8, you can also be repetitive stylistically by
saying the same thing in more than one way, through paraphrasing:

> It is a known fact that jogging is good for your heart; medical research is
> unequivocal in supporting the fact that jogging builds up heart muscle by in-
> creasing the flow of blood that nourishes the muscular tissue of the heart itself.

This is the type of repetition that Candy Lightner used in her speech in
Chapter 1. She wanted to emphasize, without *sounding* redundant, the
number of people killed by drunk drivers; so she said:

> Each year in the U.S., about 25,000 people are killed in alcohol-related
> crashes. In the past 10 years more than 250,000 have been killed nationwide
> and millions have been injured—many crippled or impaired for life.

Twenty-five hundred a year is the same as 25,000 every 10 years, but
stated in this way the point does not sound redundant. Notice also that
Lightner adds new information to her repetition of this important point.
This expansion is another technique for making the second statement of a
point "fresh."

Redundancy is no crime when you are using it to emphasize important points; it is only a crime when (1) you are redundant with obvious,
trivial, or boring points, or (2) you run an important point into the ground.
There is no sure rule for making sure you have not overemphasized a
point. You just have to use your own best judgment to make sure that you
have stated the point enough that your audience "gets" it, without repeating it so often that they want to give it back.

Signposts

Another way to emphasize important material is by using "signposts" to
warn your audience that what you are about to say is important. You can
say, simply enough, "What I'm about to say is important"; or you can use
some variation of that statement: "But listen to this . . . ," or "The most

important thing to remember is . . . ," or "The three keys to this situation are . . . ," and so on.

Use Clear Informative Organization and Structure

The following principles of organization become especially important in the *introduction* of an informative speech:

1. Establish the importance of your topic to your audience.
2. Preview the thesis, the one central idea you want your audience to remember.
3. If possible, preview your main points.

This is the way Kim Perry, a student at the University of Northern Iowa, organized the introduction of her speech on "Effortless Exercise":

> It matters not whether one is young or old, male or female, black or white. The victim is obsessed with single-minded purpose, and will do almost anything to reach his goal. I know I've suffered from this affliction, and I'm sure that you have or know of someone who has, also.
>
> I'm talking about the new American obsession — becoming "fit and trim." Yes, it's great that we're more aware of the importance of exercise and fitness, but unfortunately, we're also seeking lazy alternatives for our overweight and out-of-shape bodies.
>
> Passive exercise is one of the fastest growing gimmicks offering quick fixes to our body bulges. The main promotion involving passive exercise is EMS, electrical muscle stimulators. . . . I'd like to explain what EMS is, the potential dangers associated with it, why little is currently being done, and what measures should be taken to forestall further problems.[2]

In the *body* of an informative speech, the following organizational principles take on special importance:

1. Use only three to five main points.
2. Limit your division of main points to three to five subpoints.
3. Use transitions, internal summaries, and internal previews.
4. Order your points in the way that they will be most easy to understand and remember.

This is the way Kim Perry organized the body of her speech on "Effortless Exercise":

I. Electrical Muscle Stimulators (EMS) are devices that contract muscles involuntarily by delivering an electrical current through electrodes attached to the skin.
    A. They can be used as physical therapy under proper medical supervision.
    B. Individuals are turning to EMS to replace exercise.

Internal preview:

    So what are the complications associated with EMS? At least three can be identified: no significant muscle improvement, no cardiovascular benefits, and health hazards caused by improper use.

II.   Electrical Muscle Stimulators are potentially dangerous.

    A.   The "muscle toning effects" from EMS devices are basically worthless.

Transition:

    Not only does EMS fail to strengthen muscles, it may also indirectly contribute to reduced cardiovascular fitness.

    B.   People are being lulled into a false sense of fitness, which could stop them from performing the muscle-strengthening types of exercise required in a balanced exercise routine.

Internal summary and preview:

    And aside from the fact that EMS does not really improve muscle strength or promote cardiovascular fitness, many hazards are associated with its misuse.

    C.   Improper use results in electrical shocks and burns.

Transition:

    So in consideration of the intended uses and actual abuses of EMS, why isn't something being done to stop these multimillion-dollar industries from flourishing, at the expense of our pocketbooks and our health?

III.   Why isn't more being done to control EMS?

    A.   The Food and Drug Administration (FDA) has limited authority.

        1.   FDA has the authority to seize but not to ban.

        2.   FDA funding is limited.

        3.   FDA authority is fraught with legal loopholes.

    B.   Uninformed consumers are lulled into accepting EMS devices.

        1.   Advertisements offer "money-back guarantees."

        2.   Consumers avoid expensive lawsuits.

        3.   Some consumers see an improvement because of a "placebo effect."

Internal summary and preview:

    Tens of thousands of untrained consumers are continually buying EMS devices. How can we stop this growing epidemic?

IV.   Measures should be taken to control EMS.

    A.   Sales to the general public should be forbidden.

    B.   Operation should be restricted to licensed practitioners.

Organizational principles are important in the *conclusion* of an informative speech, also:

1. Review your main points.
2. Remind your audience of the importance of your topic to them.
3. Provide your audience with a memory aid.

For example, here is the way Kim Perry concluded her speech on "Effortless Exercise":

> I hope you now have a clearer understanding of what EMS is, its definitive hazards, and steps which the FDA, the state legislators, and we can take to stop such hazards from arising. Most of you know the only way you can fit back into your size 9 dress or your favorite blue jeans is by proper diet and exercise. Yet it's clear that the problems we've seen to date are merely "early warning signals" and will multiply with the growth in use of EMS. So if you're tempted to be an armchair jogger, maybe it's time to get out of your chair and into your jogging suit, or even your swimsuit. Who knows, you may find it "stimulating!"[3]

Use Supporting Material Effectively

The fifth technique for effective informative speaking has to do with the supporting material discussed in Chapter 7. Three of the purposes of support (to clarify, to make interesting, and to make memorable) are essential to informative speaking. Therefore, you should be careful to support your thesis in every way possible.

Use *examples,* lots of them. Often, if you cannot think of an example to support your idea, then there is something wrong with the idea. It might be a little misstated or undeveloped. Either way it is going to be confusing to your audience. Susan Martinez, a student at Bethany College in West Virginia, used examples to good effect when she began her speech on the importance of learning a foreign language with three of them:

> —When General Motors advertised its "Body by Fisher" car in Belgium, the slogan was described in Flemish as "corpse by Fisher."

> —In Spanish-speaking countries, car buyers avoided the Chevrolet Nova because "No va" in Spanish means "It doesn't go."

> —And at the 1981 economic summit meeting held in Canada, President Reagan had to ask Canadian Prime Minister Pierre Trudeau for a translation when world leaders began chatting informally in French.[4]

Provide *detailed descriptions* to increase audience involvement in the information you are presenting. Here is the description Vic Vieth, a student at Winona State University in Minnesota, used to begin his speech on "Prisoners of Conscience":

> Tenzin Chodrak lived on nine ounces of grain a day as he was forced to work a rock-hard soil beneath a beating sun. In time, his hair fell out and his eyebrows fell off. Tortured by his hunger he ate rats and worms and, eventually, his leather jacket. Hector Martinez was blindfolded and then beaten. His head was repeatedly submerged in buckets of vomit and urine. His head was then placed inside a suffocating plastic bag and banged against a wall. Ashraf Mahmoudi, four months pregnant at the time, was seized on a street corner and then beaten with the rifle-butts of her captors.

She awoke in a prison cell bleeding from her abdomen. Yet her cries for assistance went mocked, and she lost her baby. . . .[5]

Define your key terms if there is any chance that the audience might be confused by them. Here is the way Vic Vieth defined his key term in "Prisoners of Conscience":

Prisoners of conscience, according to *Newsweek,* are simply those who have been jailed for their beliefs, those whose convictions often directly challenge their governments. Prisoners of conscience do not advocate violence and they have no hope of overthrowing their governments. Yet oftentimes they do speak out against tyranny.[6]

Use *analogies* to enable your audience to view your information from a different perspective. One student's speech on the false testing of medicines was built around the analogy of poison:

The falsifying of tests in laboratories does exist and the harm that can and does come of it has turned it into a deadly poison. There are antidotes but they're useless unless they're injected into the system. . . .[7]

Use *quantification and statistics* to make your information more authoritative and accurate. One student used quantification and statistics when explaining the dangers of boxing:

Since 1945, 339 professional fighters have died in the ring. 53 of those deaths since 1970. . . . This figure includes only professional fighters, so you must include injury and death among the estimated 10,000 10- to 15-year-old amateurs, the estimated 12,500 golden-glove boxers, and innumerable contestants in "tough-man" contests.[8]

Use *anecdotes* to make your information more interesting and memorable. Here is how one student used an anecdote in her speech about the importance of speech education in public schools:

As I was working my way through the public school system, I, like my peers, believed that I was receiving a fine education. I could read and write, and add and subtract — yes, all of the essentials were there. At least that's what I thought. And then, the boom lowered: "Attention class — your next assignment is to present an oral report of your paper in front of the class next week." My heart stopped. Panic began to rise up inside. Me? In front of thirty other fourth-graders giving a speech? For the next five days I lived in dreaded anticipation of the forthcoming event. When the day finally arrived, I stayed home. It seemed at the time to be the perfect solution to a very scary and very real problem. Up to that time, I had never been asked to say a word in front of anyone, and, more importantly, had never been taught anything about verbal communication skills.[9]

Any time you can make your ideas visual in an informative speech, do so. Sometimes one *visual aid* displays all of your main points, and therefore keeps your audience constantly attuned to your topic. The following map could be used in that way:

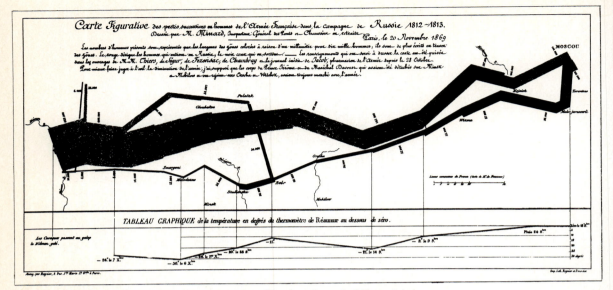

The map, drawn by the French engineer Charles Joseph Minard in 1869, portrays the losses suffered by Napoleon's army in the Russian campaign of 1812. Beginning at the left on the Polish-Russian border near the Niemen, the thick band at the top shows the size of the army (422,000 men) as it invaded Russia in June 1812. The width of the band indicates the size of the army at each position. In September, the army reached Moscow, which was by then sacked and deserted, with 100,000 men. The path of Napoleon's retreat from Moscow in the bitterly cold winter is depicted by the dark lower band, which is tied to a temperature scale (note how the path of retreating army and the temperature line move in parallel). The remains of the Grande Armée struggled out of Russia with only 10,000 men remaining. Minard displayed *six* dimensions of data on the two-dimensional surface of the paper. It may well be the best statistical graphic ever drawn. This "Carte Figurative" was meant as an anti-war poster.[10]

Demonstrations can be particularly effective in creating impact and understanding. One physics major wanted to give a speech with the following purpose:

> After listening to my speech, my audience will understand the total independence of contiguous motions that are directed along mutually perpendicular axes.

When he gave his speech, the class did not know what he was talking about; so he tried clarifying his purpose somewhat, and including a demonstration. This time, his purpose was:

After listening to my speech, my audience will understand that to predict trajectory, you have to take two different perpendicular motions into consideration.

Believe it or not, his speech fulfilled his purpose, because it included the following demonstration:

Apparatus: toy crossbow, teddy bear

Procedure: Hang teddy from coat rack. Secure crossbow and aim directly at teddy. Explain that both y motion and x motion must be taken into consideration to shoot teddy out of tree — place diagram on board. With help of volunteer, release arrow and teddy simultaneously. Because of interaction of x motion and y motion, arrow will drop at the same rate as teddy, and you will score a bull's-eye every time!

Diagram:

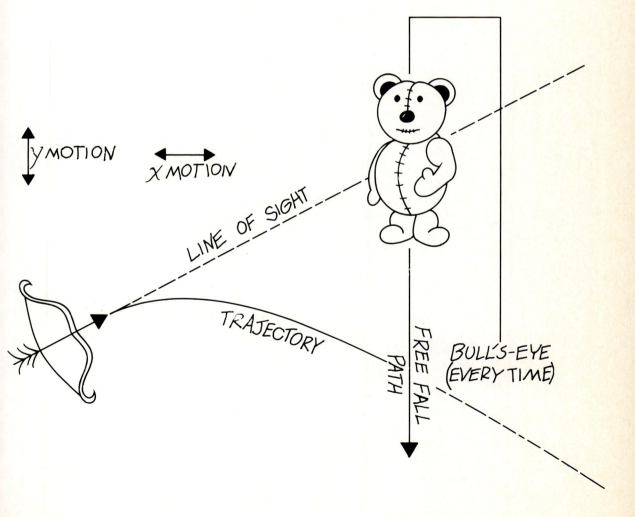

Use Clear Language

Another technique for effective informative speaking is to use clear language — which means using precise, vivid, simple wording.

Precise Vocabulary

If you have any doubt about the clarity of something you are saying, you should devise several different ways of saying it and choose the best way. Notice the way Porter Crow used precise language to explain the difference between the perceptions produced in the two lobes of the brain:

> What, then, are the differences in these perceptions, Right and Left? Now, please note, the following generalizations are reversed if you are left-handed! Isn't that rich?
>
> To begin, then: The Left Lobe is often viewed as more masculine. It's more logical, sequential, and orderly. It is most interested in problem-solving and that which is pragmatic — the "business" mind.
>
> Now, on the other hand — rather, on the other side — the Right Lobe is often perceived as more feminine. It's more inclined toward the whole picture, the spatial, the artistic, the musical. It's more intuitive and humanistic — the "home" mind.[11]

Vivid Language

You should make you language "come alive" through devices such as action-oriented vocabulary and varied sentence structure. Crow continued his description of the two lobes of the brain vividly:

> But! And this is where it all starts to get really exciting! More and more, we are recognizing these differences are not a matter of sex identification but a matter of training and culture. You all can use both sides of your brain more effectively and more creatively. Whichever lobe you are inclined to use, the other can be turned on! Never forget that! You have a whole brain, a whole mind! We are inclined to use only part of our greatest piece of equipment. It's like having a computer with two drives and using only one.[12]

Of course, the last part of that description is an analogy, giving us another example of how these principles combine in practice.

Simple Vocabulary

Using the right word, the most precise word, seldom means using a word that is difficult to find. In fact, just the opposite is true. Important ideas do not have to sound complicated. Consider the following passage:

> Objective considerations of contemporary phenomena compel the conclusion that success or failure in competitive activities exhibits no tendency to be commensurate with innate capacity, but that a considerable element of the unpredictable must invariably be taken into account.[13]

That is George Orwell's satirical idea of how a biblical passage would be written in twentieth-century jargon. The original verse, from the King James translation of Ecclesiastes, reads:

> . . . the race is not to the swift, nor the battle to the strong, neither yet bread to the wise, nor yet riches to men of understanding, nor yet favor to men of skill; but time and chance happeneth to them all.

Generate Audience Involvement

The final technique for effective informative speaking is to get your audience involved in your speech. Educational psychologists have long known that the best way to *teach* people something is to have them *do* it; social psychologists have added to this rule by proving, in many studies, that involvement in a message increases audience comprehension of, and agreement with, that message.

There are many ways to encourage audience involvement in your speech. One way is by following the rules for good delivery by maintaining enthusiasm, energy, eye contact, and so on. Other techniques include audience participation, the use of volunteers, and a question-and-answer period.

Audience Participation. One way to increase audience involvement is to have the audience members actually *do* something during your speech. For example, if you were giving a demonstration on isometric exercises (which don't require too much room for movement), you could have the entire audience stand up and do one or two sample exercises. (Exercise not only involves them psychologically, it also keeps them more alert physically by increasing the flow of blood and adrenalin in their systems.) If you were explaining how to fill out a federal income-tax long form, you could give each class member a sample form to fill out as you explain it. Outlines and checklists could be used in a similar manner for just about *any* speech.

Volunteers. If the action you are demonstrating is too expensive or intricate to allow all the class members to take part in it, you can select one or two volunteers from the audience to help you out. You will increase the psychological involvement of all the members, because they will tend to identify with the volunteers.

Question-and-Answer Period. One way to increase audience involvement that is nearly *always* appropriate if time allows is to answer questions at the end of your speech. You should encourage your audience to ask questions. Solicit questions and be patient waiting for the first one. Often no one wants to ask the first question. When the questions do start coming, remember the following three techniques: avoid defensive reactions, listen for substance, and answer constructively.

Avoid Defensive Reactions. Even if the questioner seems to be calling you a liar, or stupid, or biased, try to listen to the substance of the question and not to the possible personality attack. You can always get even sometime later; do not let one heckler detract from the contact that you have established with the rest of your audience.[14]

This type of question is common: "You said A, but isn't B actually the case?"

Two questions are here. On one level, the question is, "Isn't B actually the case?" This question is the one you should listen to. If you listen defensively, you will hear the question as, "Aren't you, in fact, a liar?" Responding to that question would be self-defeating.

This advice should not preclude a defense against a direct attack. If one of your listeners raises a hand and asks, "Aren't you in fact a dirty communist?" you don't have to respond, "Now that you mention it, my political leanings are somewhat to the left, and I don't bathe as often as I should. . . ." You are entitled, under those circumstances, to defend yourself. Remember that, unfair though it may be, the question refers to you and cannot be answered by referring to the questioner or by asking another question, such as "Aren't *you* in fact an idiot?" In other words, in answering questions defenses are sometimes justified, but offenses never are.

Listen for the *Substance* of a Question. Try to understand the basic, overall question that is being asked, rather than one or two insignificant details. Some people, when accused of killing two men, three women, four children, and a cow will produce the cow as proof of their innocence. Answer the general question. If you have just given a speech using scientific evidence, someone might ask, "Are the demonstrations that you cited actually valid?" and you might respond:

> I did not cite demonstrations. I cited experiments. In demonstrations, you know what the outcome will be in advance. In experiments, you seek answers to the unknown.

If you said that, not only would you have demonstrated that you missed the point of the question, you also would probably have offended the questioner. Instead, an appropriate response might be:

> Yes, I think they are valid. The experiments that I cited were as carefully controlled as possible. They were conducted by experienced researchers who were well respected in their fields. I believe that the probability that they are valid is extremely good.

Respond Constructively. Respond to the question by showing that you understand it, answering it as briefly as possible, and checking to make sure that your answer was understood.

A psychologist named Carkhuff has devised a method of training counselors to respond that you can use for questions after a speech. According to Carkhuff, responses can be separated into five levels according to their quality.[15] For our purposes, we will reduce Carkhuff's model to three general levels of response:

Level One: The speaker rejects the question, or answers the wrong question.

Level Two: The speaker shows that he has received and understood the question.

Level Three: The speaker recognizes the question, answers it as briefly as possible, and verifies comprehension.

A Level One response might be a rejection, such as "You are talking out of turn again," or "Please don't ask questions until I'm done talking," or "That is a ridiculous question and it doesn't deserve a response," or "Bailiff, throw that troublemaker out!" A Level One response need not be intentionally nasty. One of the worst, and most common, Level One responses is usually directed to someone of the opposite sex. It is usually an absent-minded response such as, "You have beautiful eyes."

A Level Two response would paraphrase the question: "If I understood your question, you are asking _____," or "Let me see if I understand your question. . . ." A Level Two response is important to recognize because it is the lowest possible level of *effective* response. In other words, even if your answer was then incorrect, at least the audience member would know that you were responding to the correct question.

A Level Three response accepts the question and shows that it is understood. It also answers the question briefly, without unnecessary verbiage, and seeks verification that the answer has been understood. For example: "As I understand your question, you want to know _____. Is that right? Well, I think _____. Does that answer your question?" This response would be far more effective than one that supplies too much information:

> I told you that already, in the beginning of my speech. Weren't you listening? In order to answer that, I have to start from the beginning. Now you'll remember that I began by saying, "Good afternoon, fellow classmates . . ."

Sample Speech

The following speech was given by Professor Jerry Tarver of the University of Richmond. Professor Tarver, discussing the use of language in speech writing, spoke before a group of professional speech writers in Hartford, Connecticut.[16]

Can't Nobody Here Use This Language?

Function and Quality in Choosing Words
Jerry Tarver
Professor, University of Richmond

Comments

Introduction: Reference to audience and conference coordinator increases audience interest.

1 I learned last May you have to be careful in speaking to a group of professional communicators. After I conducted a writer's workshop at the Toronto Conference of the International Association of Business Communicators, Janine Lichacz wrote asking me to speak here tonight and used the communication techniques I had recommended. She even included a footnote citing my lecture. I am susceptible to good communication — and to flattery — so I am pleased to be with you to discuss your topic for the evening, the use of language in the art of speech writing.

He begins to develop his first main point: the current state of language. (See outline on p. 230.)

2 I suppose we must begin by shaking our heads woefully over the sad state of language today, whether in formal speeches, casual conversation, or in writing. Most of us in this room no doubt agree with the generally negative tone of *Time Magazine*'s year-end assessment which claims "our language has been besieged by vulgarities." But to preserve our sanity as professionals in communication, most of us would probably join *Time* in optimistically expecting English somehow to survive and even to prosper.

Quotation as supporting material

3 On the negative side, if I may use a vulgarity to criticize vulgarity, I am often moved in my own profession to paraphrase Casey Stengel and ask, "Can't nobody here use this language?"

4 To generalize about the language ability of students, I would say far too many of them can't express themselves well, and they don't seem to care. The most significant hollow verbalization among students today is not "y'know." It is "needless to say."

Example used as supporting material

5 I have a respectful appreciation of the rules of the classical rhetoricians, and on occasion I have discussed in class the stylistic device of antithesis. One of my students, quite unconsciously I am sure, gave the technique a try in a speech on physical fitness and said, "A well-rounded body makes for a well-rounded mind." We've come a long way down from *mens sana in corpore sano*.

Example

6 Faculty members are often worse. Some time back I attended a conference on setting standards for language competence in Virginia's schools. In one presentation a professor from a distinguished university repeatedly used the expression "scribal language." I finally turned to someone to ask what the devil that meant and was told the term was a fancy synonym for "writing." I wrote a letter to the professor suggesting a requirement for a report on competence in language should be competence in language. He did not take it well.

Example

7 One of my colleagues wrote a lengthy document on the proper use of classrooms and stated forthrightly, "It is necessary to employ characteristics

Comments

of uniqueness where uniqueness is held to be important. The idea of flexibility should be placed in a balanced way with other particular instructional and
design needs to achieve a maximized learning atmosphere. In some instances, degrees of flexibility may have to give way to other equally creative
and significant dimensions of a classroom environment.''

8   I happen to know what that means, and I will be happy to provide a
translation at twenty cents a word. If you want the answer, send your dollar
to me at the University of Richmond.

Example 9   A certain church group which supports many colleges throughout the
South regularly sends me a publication which purports to be educational.
Leaders of this group use up a goodly portion of the alphabet with the
impressive degrees they attach to their names and employ this publication to
increase the size of the audience for their various pronouncements. The
quality of the writing is so gloriously and innocently bad that the entire
magazine could easily pass as a satire written by a clever member of a high
school debating team. One of the speeches from a couple of months ago
contained the striking statement, ''Drifting causes a loss of direction.'' That
was one of the major points in the speech, which incidentally was delivered
at the inauguration of a college president.

Quotation 10   On the positive side, *Time* finds our language ''enriched by vigorous
phrases and terms'' from such sources as CB radio and situation comedies.
The major bright spots I see are the writing in advertising and on the
bathroom wall. Let me quickly add that the *worst* writing also appears in
these two places. Some of the most crude and senseless tripe I have encountered has appeared in ads or graffiti. But when they are good, they are very,
very good. Both the ad writer and the graffiti artist must work within a small
compass. They must be concise. To the point. And each is moved, urgently
moved, to communicate. Unfortunately for the motivation of the advertiser, I
am one of those people who can enjoy the sizzle and forgo the steak. I don't
Examples   smoke cigars, and I don't even remember the brand involved, but who can
forget the classic commercial in which Edie Adams used to urge, ''Why don't
you pick one up and smoke it sometime?'' I admit I don't have a Texaco credit
card, but little I read of modern academic poetry moves me as much as the
soothing jingle, ''You can trust your car to the man who wears the star.''

Example/Anecdote 11   My favorite graffiti are the plaintive sort. A poor soul eloquently crying
out to be understood. In the men's room just down from my office, someone
in apparent anguish wrote with painstaking care in the grout between the
tiles, ''What in the hell am I doing here?'' Weeks passed before someone
undertook a reply. Whether done in a spirit of helpfulness or malice, I cannot
say, but finally in different handwriting, there appeared, ''If this is an existen-
tial question, contact Dr. Hall in the Philosophy Department. If this is a
theological question, contact Dr. Alley in the Religion Department. If this is a
biological question, take a look.''

12   Years ago I saw a quotation printed on a little gummed paper strip
which had been attached to the wall of a men's room off the New Jersey
Turnpike. It offered a simple biblical text and had apparently come to the

Example/Anecdote   attention of a tired truck driver. The quotation asked the question, "If God be for us, who can be against us?" No doubt in despair, the truck driver had replied underneath, "The dispatcher."

Stresses importance 13 of point to audience

How can we capture the vitality of the best of graffiti and advertising in our own writing and speaking? Perhaps some of you would agree with a sociologist friend of mine, Dr. James Sartain. Whenever Jim is offered a chance to improve his teaching, he says, "I already know how to teach better than I do." I suspect this is true for most of us. So, we may not be discovering tonight as much as reminding.

Analogy— 14 comparing grammar with manual skill—used as supporting material

But there could be some ground for controversy. Let me first of all attempt to play down the current emphasis on correctness. Grammar — much like spelling — is one of the manual skills of expression. Almost any fool can learn to make a subject agree with a verb according to the standard rules of English.

15   I think the pseudo-objectivity of correctness attracts many followers. But grammatical systems are, after all, themselves arbitrary. We could change the rules if we wanted to. Our failure to alter our grammar to include a sexless pronoun can hardly be blamed on the sanctity of the rules. If you

Example   wish to attack the sentence, "He done done it," you can't attack it by claiming it does not follow a rigid set of rules. It just doesn't follow the system most widely taught.

16   I'm not suggesting you break rules at random. Just don't be too proud

Examples/Quota- of yourself for not using "very unique" or "hopefully, it will rain." And tion   remember George Orwell's advice that you should break any rule rather than "say anything outright barbarous."

17   I suggest to write and speak our best we need, first, a grasp of the function of language and, second, a sensitivity to the quality of our words.

Definition of key 18 term

My desk dictionary includes among its definitions of the word *function,* "The action for which a . . . thing is specially fitted or used or for which a thing exists." The concept of function reminds us that words act upon people.

Example   19   Let me give you an example of a piece of communication which illustrates function. You may recall in *Catch-22,* Lt. Milo Minderbinder at one point instituted an elaborate procedure for going through the chow line. It involved signing a loyalty oath, reciting the pledge of allegiance, and singing "The Star-Spangled Banner." But the entire system was destroyed one day when Major de Coverly returned from a trip and cut through the red tape with two words: "Gimme eat."

20   That simple, and quite ungrammatical, phrase shows language in action. Words at work. Expression that eliminates the unnecessary and gets down to cases.

21   A grasp of function causes a writer to think of results. Impact. Effect. Audience becomes important. Who will read or listen? Why? Function calls for the communicator to examine the reason for the existence of a given communication and to choose words that will be a means of expression and not an end.

Comments

Operational
definition of key
term

22   Next, as I said, we must be sensitive to quality. I know of no objective way to determine quality. But I agree with Robert Pirsig who insists in *Zen and the Art of Motorcycle Maintenance* that most people intuitively know quality in language when they encounter it.

23   Most of us have written material we knew was merely adequate. No errors. All the intended ideas in place. No complaints from the boss or the editor. But deep down inside we knew we had done a pedestrian job.

24   I use a chill bump test for quality. For poor writing or speaking I get one type of chill bumps. For good language, a better brand of chill bumps. For most of the mediocre stuff in between, no chill bumps at all.

Example/Quotation

Example/Quotation

25   Quality does not mean fancy. When General McAuliffe reportedly answered a Nazi surrender ultimatum with the word "Nuts," his language had no less quality than the declaration of the Indian Chief Joseph, "From where the sun now stands, I will fight no more forever." Either of my examples would probably not fare well in a classroom exercise in English composition. But anyone who objected to the use of such language in that situation would be guilty of ignoring the concept of function.

Transition: internal
preview of
following points

26   Only after we agree that we must be concerned about function and quality can we properly turn our attention to rules. I offer the following ten guidelines for the speech writer. Some of the guidelines apply primarily to the language of speeches; some apply to almost any kind of writing. I do not consider my list exhaustive, and I should point out that the items on it are not mutually exclusive.

He stresses the
importance of these
points by listing
them as numbered
"guidelines."

27 **Guideline Number One.**   Be simple. Tend toward conversational language. Earlier this month I conducted speaker training for a corporation which distributed a speech manuscript containing such expressions as "difficult to ascertain" and "management audits attest." There's nothing wrong with these phrases in print, but I wouldn't say ascertain or attest out loud in front of the Rotary Club. "Find out" and "show" would sound more natural.

28 **Guideline Number Two.**   Be expansive. Speeches use more words per square thought than well-written essays or reports. The next time you get a speech-writing assignment, see if you can't talk your boss into throwing out two-thirds of the content and expanding the remainder into a fully developed expression of a limited topic. I realize gobbledygook is wordy, but I assume none of us will be writing gobbledygook. And I don't know of anyone who

Example

has suggested that Martin Luther King's "I Have a Dream" speech suffered from excessive repetition.

29 **Guideline Number Three.**   Be concrete. Specific terms limit a listener's chances to misunderstand. Back in November, Combined Communications

Example

Corporation President Karl Eller gave a speech out in Phoenix in which he used a glass of milk to describe our free enterprise system. He said, "Some farmer bred and raised the cow. Some farmer owned and tended the land it grazed on. He bought special feed from someone. Some farmer milked the cow or cows and sold the milk to someone else who processed it, pasteurized it, and packaged it. He sold it to a wholesaler who sold it to a retailer. And all along the line the product was either made better or its distribution was simplified and narrowed, and a lot of people had jobs. Wealth was created." I've quoted less than a fifth of Eller's description. I'm convinced nobody left his speech confused.

Example/Quotation

30 **Guideline Number Four.** Be vivid. Appeal to the senses. President Carter's speech writers attempted to paint a word picture in the state of the union address when they wrote of the power of nuclear weapons "towering over all this volatile changing world, like a thundercloud in a summery sky." I am reminded of Mark Twain's distinction between lightning and the lightning bug. The Carter image fails to stir the imagination. But vivid language can be effective.

Example/Analogy

31 In demonstrating the point that his company's nuclear plants are safe, Ontario Hydro Board Chairman Robert Taylor told members of the Kiwanis Club of Ottawa, "You could sit naked, if you had a mind to, at the boundary fence around the Pickering nuclear station for a year, drink the water and eat the fish from nearby Lake Ontario, and you would pick up a total of five units of radiation. That's less than you would get from natural sources such as rocks, good air, and cosmic rays. A single chest X-ray would give you eight times that exposure."

Example/Anecdote/ Example

32 **Guideline Number Five.** Be personal. Use the personal pronoun. Don't be afraid of making a speaker sound egotistical. Ego springs from attitude, not language. A modest speaker can say "I know" and "I did" and "I was" with no problem. But I know a fellow who is so egotistical he can say "Good morning" and seem to take credit for it. Still, it's hard to imagine Caesar saying, "One comes, one sees, one conquers."

Examples

33 **Guideline Number Six.** Be smooth. Speech demands uncluttered rhythm. Avoid clauses which interrupt your idea. It's a bit awkward for a speaker to say, "William Safire, former Nixon speech writer," but "former Nixon speech writer William Safire" flows a bit better. If you must add a clause, make a big deal out of it. For example, you might say, "Jogging — which can have a fantastically positive effect on your sex life — may clear up minor sinus problems."

One of the few points not supported with an example. Clear as is.

34 Feel free to use contractions if they help the flow of the speech. In conversation the absence of contractions often becomes a device for emphasis. If you don't use contractions in speaking, you risk overemphasis.

35 In writing jokes into a speech, be sure to put the "they saids" *before* the quoted material, especially in punch lines. Observe the effect of reading: "'Why does a chicken cross the road?' she asked. 'To get to the other side,' he answered."

Example

Example

36 **Guideline Number Seven.** Be aggressive. Don't use the loaded language of your enemies. Let me get my prejudice clearly before you. As a consumer, I deeply resent the careless use of the term "consumer advocate." As a breather of air and drinker of water and observer of sunsets, I resent the

Comments

haphazard application of the term "environmentalist" to anyone who can gather six friends in a living room to organize a Snailshell Defiance. My sympathy goes out to the engineer who finds it all but impossible to explain how fish like warm water without describing the fish as victims of thermal pollution.

37   I do not assume that American business and industry always have in mind the best interests of consumers, the environment, and fish, but we need to avoid one-sided language if we are to have an honest discussion of the issues. I would prefer to keep away from loaded words or to qualify them with "so-called" or "self-styled."

38 **Guideline Number Eight.**   Be purposeful. Meaning is assigned to words by listeners; your intent is less important than your listener's perception. The controversy over sexism and racism in language can be settled if we re-

Examples

member words are symbols which listeners interpret. I will not use the phrase "girls in the office" because a significant number of people who hear me will react negatively. For the same reason, avoid "a black day" on the market, in favor of a bleak day or a bad day. We need not resort to awkward constructions. You might not want to say "unmanned boat," but this does not mean you must blunder along with "unpeopled boat." What about "a boat with no one aboard"?

39 **Guideline Number Nine.**   Be eloquent. Use an occasional rhetorical device to enhance your expression of an idea. Indulge at times in a little light

Example

alliteration. Balance a pair of phrases: "Ask not what the country can do for General Motors, ask what General Motors can do for the country."

40 **Guideline Number Ten.**   Be adaptable. Write to suit your speaker. A speech writer for Phillips Petroleum once described his role as being that of a

Description

clone. A writer must know the speaker's feelings and the speaker's style. And remember your speaker may need a tersely worded speech one week and a flowery one the next.

A short, concise conclusion

41   My guidelines are far easier to express than to execute. Writing a good speech requires talent, brains, and effort. If you write for others, add to the requirements a self-effacing attitude and a thick skin.

42   Our language will not be saved by the exhortations of evangelists in the Church of the Fundamental Grammar. It can be saved by writers and speakers

A final reference to audience

with a grasp of function and a sense of quality. We should be proud of your organization's contribution; it enrolls and nurtures communicators who use language well.

Analysis of the Speech

From the marginal comments you can see that Tarver followed many of the techniques mentioned in this chapter. For example, he seemed to have a clear-cut, specific, informative purpose:

> After listening to my speech, my audience members will be able to recall five or six of my ten guidelines for the speech writer.

If he had wanted his audience to remember more, or to have a copy of his guidelines for future reference, he might have handed out a list of guidelines or provided an outline as a visual aid.

Tarver taps general social and esteem needs by reminding his audience that "our language is being besieged by vulgarities." He taps self-actualization needs by showing his audience how to improve themselves. He taps their specific needs by telling them that good English preserves their "sanity as professionals."

He emphasizes his important points by using numbered guidelines as signposts. His use of language throughout is precise and simple; he defines his meaning of a key term, *function*. He uses supporting material —especially examples and quotations—to back up his ideas. Finally, he generates audience involvement by using several references to his audience during his speech and by soliciting questions afterward.

We should also notice the organization of this speech. It follows this outline:

I.   Introduction
II. Body
  A. The present state of language
    1. The negative side
      a. Students: "Needless to say"
      b. Faculty: "Scribal language"
    2. The positive side
      a. Graffiti
      b. Advertising
  B. First concerns
    1. Function: Words act upon people.
    2. Quality: We know it intuitively.
  C. The ten guidelines
    1. Be simple.
    2. Be expansive.
    3. Be concrete.
    4. Be vivid.
    5. Be personal.
    6. Be smooth.
    7. Be aggressive.
    8. Be purposeful.
    9. Be eloquent.
    10. Be adaptable.
III. Conclusion

This organizational plan is clear. It conforms to all the principles of informative organization except one: It contains too many subpoints under point IIC, "The ten guidelines." The rule does not properly apply to this point; to break it up into subpoints would create false divisions and interrupt the flow of the speech. Besides, this audience was made up of professional speech writers, so these guidelines were reminders rather than new material. Be willing to break any of these hard-and-fast rules creatively, if by doing so you make your speech more understandable, interesting, or appropriate to a particular audience.

Summary

This chapter suggested techniques for effective informative speaking. These suggestions include the use of a specific informative purpose, the creation of "information hunger" by tapping both general and specific audience needs, the emphasis of important points through repetition and "signposts," the use of clear informative organization and structure, the use of effective supporting material, the use of clear language (language that incorporates precise, vivid, simple vocabulary), and the involvement of the audience.

Questions/Assignments

1. For practice in defining informative speech purposes, reword the following statements so they specifically point out what the audience will be able to do after hearing the speech.
   a. My purpose is to tell my audience about Hitler's rise to power.
   b. I am going to talk about internal combustion engines.
   c. My speech is about the causes and cures of premature baldness.
2. Consider your classmates as an audience. How does Maslow's analysis of needs relate to these people? What other, more specific needs do they have? How could you relate the following speech topics to these needs?
   a. The Changing Climate of the United States
   b. Civil Rights
   c. Gun Control
   d. U.S. Foreign Policy
3. For practice in using clear language, select an article from any issue of a professional journal in your major field. Using the suggestions in this chapter, rewrite a paragraph from the article so that it will be clear and interesting to the layperson.
4. To analyze an informative speech, you go through it and point out where the speaker used effective techniques; if necessary, you point out places where effective techniques are still needed, making specific suggestions for improvement. To hone your skills in recognizing effective informative speaking, try one of the following analyses:
   a. Go over the analysis of the sample speech on pages 229–231. See which points you agree and/or disagree with, and tell why. What would you add to the analysis?
   b. Select an informative speech from *Vital Speeches of the Day, Representative American Speeches,* a newspaper, or any other source. Analyze this speech in terms of its effectiveness as an informative message. Use our analysis of the sample speech as a model.

c. Perform your analysis on your own informative speech, as delivered or to be delivered in class.

Notes

1. Porter Crow, "Waking Up the Right Lobe," *Vital Speeches of the Day,* July 15, 1984, pp. 600–601.

2. Kim Perry, "Effortless Exercise," *Winning Orations, 1984* (Interstate Oratorical Association, 1984), pp. 27–28.

3. *Ibid.,* p. 30.

4. Susan Martinez, "Sorry . . . We Only Speak English," *Winning Orations, 1983* (Interstate Oratorical Association, 1983), p. 82.

5. Vic Vieth, "Prisoners of Conscience," *Winning Orations, 1984* (Interstate Oratorical Association, 1984), p. 46.

6. *Ibid.,* pp. 46–47.

7. Veda M. Backman, "Science's Internal Poison," *Winning Orations, 1984* (Interstate Oratorical Association, 1984), p. 21.

8. Keith Murphy, "The Shadows of Boxing," *Winning Orations, 1984* (Interstate Oratorical Association, 1984), p. 34.

9. Marcie Groover, "Learning to Communicate: The Importance of Speech Education in Public Schools," *Winning Orations, 1984* (Interstate Oratorical Association, 1984), p. 7.

10. From Edward R. Tufte, *The Visual Display of Quantitative Information,* © 1984. Reprinted by permission of Graphics Press, Box 430, Cheshire, CT 06410.

11. Porter Crow, *op. cit.*

12. *Ibid.*

13. George Orwell, "Politics and the English Language," in *Shooting an Elephant and Other Essays* (New York: Harcourt Brace Jovanovich, 1945).

14. Hecklers can be helpful. See "A Politician's Guide to Success on the Stump: Hire a Heckler," *Psychology Today,* April 1971.

15. R. R. Carkhuff, *Helping and Human Relations,* Vol. 1 (New York: Holt, Rinehart and Winston, 1969).

16. Reprinted by permission of the author and *Vital Speeches of the Day,* May 1, 1979, pp. 420–423.

11

Persuasive Speaking

The Merits of Persuasion

Persuasion is the act of motivating someone, through communication, to change a particular belief, attitude, or behavior. Persuading is different from informing, therefore, in that you always take a side and defend it. If informing is like being in a classroom, then persuading is like being in a courtroom. In fact, whenever you persuade, your communication behavior will be similar to that of a defense attorney or a prosecutor. You will, in effect, be defending your own opinions or refuting someone else's.

You can appreciate the importance of this skill by imagining how your life would be without the ability to persuade others. Your choice would be limited either to accepting people as they were or to coercing them to acquiesce.

This last point is worth further comment, for persuasion is not the same thing as coercion. If you held a gun to someone's head and said, "Do this or I'll shoot," you would be acting coercively. Besides being illegal, this approach would be ineffective. Once you took the gun away, the person would probably stop following your demands.

The failure of coercion to achieve lasting results is apparent in less dramatic circumstances. Children whose parents are coercive often rebel as soon as they can; students who perform from fear of an instructor's threats rarely appreciate the subject matter; and employees who work for abusive and demanding employers are often unproductive and eager to switch jobs as soon as possible. Persuasion, on the other hand, makes a listener *want* to think or act differently.

Even when they understand the difference between persuasion and coercion, some students are still uncomfortable with the idea of persuasive speaking. They see it as the work of high-pressure hucksters: salespeople with their feet stuck in the door, unscrupulous politicians taking advantage of beleaguered taxpayers, and so on. Indeed, many of the principles we are about to discuss have been used by unethical speakers for unethical purposes, but that is not what all — or even most — persuasion is about. Ethical persuasion plays a necessary and worthwhile role in everyone's life.

Persuasion Can Be Worthwhile

It is through persuasion that we influence others' lives in worthwhile ways. The person who says, "I do not want to influence other people," is really saying, "I do not want to get involved with other people," and that is an abnegation of one's responsibilities as a human being. Look at the good you can accomplish through persuasion: you can convince a loved one to give up smoking or to give up some other destructive habit; you can get members of your community to conserve energy or to join together in some other beneficial action; you can persuade an employer to hire you for a job where your own talents, interests, and abilities will be put to their best use.

Persuasion Can Be Ethical

Persuasion is considered *ethical* if it conforms to accepted standards. What standards are accepted today? Whose opinion should you accept for what is good or bad? If your plan is selfish and not in the best interest of your audience — but you are honest about your motives — is that ethical? If your plan *is* in the best interest of your audience, yet you lie to them to get them to accept the plan, is *that* ethical?[1]

These questions are thorny. Eventually the answer will depend on a set of moral values you decide to live by. For our purposes, however, a simple general definition is sufficient: Ethical persuasion is communication that does not depend on false or misleading information to induce attitude change in an audience.

Not all persuasion is ethical, even by this simple standard. Some messages are unethical because they border on deception, such as "Enter the Burpo sweepstakes and win a million dollars a week for the rest of your life" or "You may have already won a small country in the Burpo sweepstakes." Those appeals make it sound as though just entering the sweepstakes makes you an automatic winner, when your chances are actually slim.

Other messages are unethical because they are absolutely false. They purposely seek to mislead the audience. An example of this type of message might be: "Congratulations! You have won a free one-year supply of Burpo, and all you need to pay is the cost of postage and handling!" This strategy is used in door-to-door magazine con games. After people sign for the "free magazines," they wind up paying more for the "postage and handling" than they would for a regular subscription.

Types of Persuasion

There are two convenient ways to categorize types of persuasion: according to *approach* and according to *desired outcome*.

Directness of Approach

We can categorize persuasion according to the directness of the approach employed by the speaker.

Direct Persuasion. Direct persuasion will not try to disguise the desired audience response in any way. "Use seat belts—save lives" is a direct persuasive approach. Direct persuasion is the best strategy to use with a friendly audience, especially when you are asking for a response that the audience is reasonably likely to give you:

> I'm here today to let you know why you should take part in the Red Cross blood drive. . . .

> Have you ever wished that students had more rights and power? They can, if they organize effectively. I'm here today to show you how to do just that. . . .

> I'm going to try to convince you today that Candy Tate is the best choice for city council and that she needs your vote. . . .

In a speech that uses a direct persuasive strategy, you announce the desired audience response right away in the introduction of the speech. Then that response can act as the focus of the speech.

Indirect Persuasion. Indirect persuasion disguises or deemphasizes the desired audience response in some way. The question "Is a season ticket to the symphony worth the money?" (when you intend to prove that it is) is based on indirect persuasion, as is any strategy that does not express the speaker's purpose at the outset.

Indirect persuasion is not necessarily unethical. Sometimes, in fact, it is necessary to gain acceptance of a completely legitimate message.

When the audience is hostile to either you or your topic, you might want to ease into your speech slowly.[2] You might take some time to make your audience feel good about you or the social action you are advocating. If you are speaking in favor of Candy Tate for city council, but Tate is in favor of a tax increase and your audience is not, you might talk for a while about the benefits of that increase. You might even want to change your desired audience response. Rather than trying to get them to rush out to vote for Tate, you might want them simply to read a recent newspaper article about her or attend a speech she will be giving. The one thing you cannot do in this instance is to begin by saying, "I'm not here to speak in support of Candy Tate"—that would be a false statement. It is more than indirect; it is unethical.

Desired Outcomes

We can also divide persuasion according to two major outcomes: *convincing* and *actuating.*

Convincing. When you set about to convince an audience, you want to change the way they think. There are two ways that you can do that; the first is to change their beliefs about the *truth* of a fact. If you wanted to convince the Sons of Columbus that the Vikings were the first Europeans to discover America, you would be using this type of persuasion.

The second way to change the way your audience thinks is to change their *evaluation* of something. If you try to convince your audience that a certain type of diet is good or that a certain government action is bad, you would be using this type of persuasion.

When we say that convincing an audience changes the way they think, we do not mean that you have to swing them from one belief or attitude to a completely different one. Sometimes an audience will already think the way you want them to, but they will not be firmly enough committed to that way of thinking. When that is the case, you *reinforce,* or strengthen, their opinions. For example, if your audience already believed that the federal budget should be balanced but did not consider the idea important, your job would be to reinforce their current beliefs. Reinforcing is still a type of change, however, because you are causing an audience to adhere more strongly to a belief or attitude.

Actuating. When you set about to actuate an audience, you want to move them to immediate action. Whereas a speech to convince might move an audience to action at some future, indefinite time, a speech to actuate asks for action right then, on the spot.

There are two types of action you can ask for—*adoption* or *discontinuance.* The former asks an audience to engage in a new behavior; the latter asks them to stop behaving in an established way. If you gave a speech for a political candidate and then asked for contributions to that candidate's campaign, you would be asking your audience to adopt a new behavior. If you gave a speech against smoking and then asked your audience to sign a pledge to quit or to throw away the cigarettes they were carrying, you would be asking them to discontinue an established behavior.

Examples of both types of persuasive speech—to convince and to actuate—can be found at the end of this chapter. With the concepts of ethics, approaches, and outcomes in mind, we can move on to basic persuasive strategy.

Persuasive Strategy

The basic message strategies are cumulative. When you seek to persuade, you are still interested in maintaining audience interest by relating to needs. Psychologist James V. McConnell sums it up this way:

> The best "persuader" appears to be whatever best satisfies the deep-felt needs of the audience.[3]

You are still concerned with explanation, too. In fact a speech to convince is like two different "informative" speeches. You have to explain the problem and you have to explain the solution to that problem. A speech to actuate, on the other hand, is like three informative speeches: you have to explain the problem, the solution, and the part your audience can play in that solution. Each one of these explanatory tasks requires the same kind of planning that a full "speech to inform" would require.[4]

Strategy to Convince

At the risk of oversimplification, let us focus upon the two-step strategy that underlies every speech to convince: explain the problem, then explain the solution.

Explaining the Problem

In order to convince someone that something needs to be changed, you have to convince that person that something is wrong; you have to establish the problem. One way to establish a problem is to answer three basic questions. First: *Is there a problem from the audience's point of view?* After all, what seems like a problem to you might not seem like a problem to other people. For example, your topic might be "Legalizing Prostitution." You might want to show that laws against prostitution are a problem. What would make those laws a problem for your audience? Does the absence of legal prostitution lead to profits for organized crime? Does it lead to disease, or sex crimes? What arguments could you use to show that a problem exists?

The second question you need to answer is: *How does this problem relate to the audience?* Here you get back to the idea of audience needs. Do the profits of organized crime represent a threat to your audience's safety and security? Could they become infected with a dreaded social disease? Are their children safe from perverts? In other words, you must prove the relationship of your problem to your audience.

The final question is: *Does this problem actually require a change?* For example, if your main argument is that organized criminals benefit from illegal prostitution, your audience might mentally refute that argument by reminding themselves that there are laws against organized crime; therefore, the real problem would be a lack of law enforcement. Also, some problems go away if you ignore them long enough. How can you prove that your problem does not fit into this category?

As you plan your explanation, figure out why your audience might think that your problem was *not* a problem for them. Then you can handle their reluctance. For example, suppose you are proposing a program in which students will do volunteer counseling and tutoring at a nearby prison. Your first step in planning your message would be to analyze why the students would *not* want to take advantage of such a project. You might come up with these reasons:

1. They are too busy with activities that are more important to them.
2. They believe that their participation in such a program would not make a difference.
3. They do not believe that the prisoners are their concern.

Now you have a guide for establishing the problem. You proceed to answer those arguments:

1. Show that the program *will* be a valuable experience for them. You could explain what they are likely to learn or the feeling of fulfillment they are likely to achieve or how good "Tutor, State U. Prison Project" will look on their résumés when it is time to look for a job.
2. Show that their participation *will* make a difference. You can cite prison programs at other universities to prove this point.
3. Show that the prisoners *should* be their concern. You might explain that the more prisoners who return to their community without being rehabilitated, the more dangerous those communities will be.

There are at least two requirements for the problem you establish: First, it must *relate directly to your audience.* If you live in New Jersey, the repeal of the Nebraska state income tax would be an inappropriate problem. Second, it must be a problem that *your audience can play some part in correcting.* The existence of cancer would be an inappropriate problem, but the lack of funds for cancer research would be appropriate, because your audience could contribute money or sign a petition supporting government funding.

You should take both of these requirements into consideration when establishing the problem. Then you will be ready to consider the solution.

Explaining the Solution

Your next step in getting your audience to change something is to convince them that a change is possible. You establish a solution, which is a plan proposed to correct a problem.

Once again you might answer three questions to establish your plan as the answer to the problem. First: *Will the plan work?* If your plan is to legalize prostitution so that prostitutes can be regulated and therefore protected against crime and disease, can you give evidence to suggest that our frequently inept bureaucracy is capable of such regulation?

A second question is: *Will the plan be practical?* Supposing the bureaucracy is capable of regulating legalized prostitution, what would be the cost of such regulation? If the cost were too great, then the plan would not be practical. How can you prove that your plan will not cost more than it is worth?

The final question is: *What advantages or disadvantages will result from your plan?* This question takes into account that there are costs and rewards besides economic ones. In changing laws against prostitution there could be costs to our religious beliefs, our national self-concept, and our ability to teach morality to our young. How could you prove that your plan would not create more problems than it would solve?

Strategy to Actuate

When your purpose is to actuate your audience to a specific course of action, you have to add one extra step to your persuasive strategy. You have to make your audience members realize that *they* can play a part in bringing about the desired change.

You convince your audience to take part in the solution by explaining the *desired audience response.* At this step, like the first two, you should answer three questions. First: *What part can the audience play in putting the plan into action?* It does not help much if your audience simply agrees with you but does not do anything to help bring about change. The most brilliant speech is not good enough if your audience leaves thinking, "That speaker was right. There's a real problem there. I wonder what's for dinner tonight."

The second question that you might ask is: *How do the audience members go about playing their part?* The behavior you ask your audience to adopt should be made as simple as possible for them. If you want them to vote in a referendum, tell them when to vote, where to go to vote, and how to go about registering, if necessary. Be specific in your request. Do not ask them to write their congressional representative. *You* write the letter to the congressional representative who is in charge of the subcom-

TABLE 11–1   Outline for Persuasion

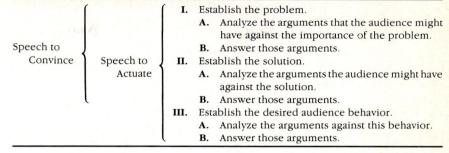

		I.	Establish the problem.
		A.	Analyze the arguments that the audience might have against the importance of the problem.
Speech to Convince	Speech to Actuate	**B.**	Answer those arguments.
		II.	Establish the solution.
		A.	Analyze the arguments the audience might have against the solution.
		B.	Answer those arguments.
		III.	Establish the desired audience behavior.
		A.	Analyze the arguments against this behavior.
		B.	Answer those arguments.

mittee that is investigating the problem and ask your audience members to sign it. Do not ask them to start a petition. *You* draw up the petition and have them sign it. Do not ask them to picket. Give them the placards and tell them what time to meet you at the picket site.

Finally you might answer the question: *What are the direct rewards of this response?* Your solution might be of importance to society, but this benefit is just one of the possible rewards that you can offer to your audience for responding the way you want them to. Try to offer some direct personal rewards also. Is there a chance that the congressional representative will answer them personally? Will the picket session be fun as well as meaningful? Will there be coffee and doughnuts and interesting people outside the polling place?

The study of persuasion is as complex as the study of human communication. In fact, some people believe the terms *persuasion* and *communication* are synonymous. To reduce persuasion to three steps is a tricky business. Table 11–1 sums up the process.

Types of Persuasive Appeals

A persuasive strategy is put into effect through the use of persuasive appeals. Persuasive appeals supply your audience with reasons to say yes to a plan. In other words, they make an audience *want* to adopt your plan.

The early Greeks first outlined a set of devices through which reasons could be given convincingly. Aristotle labeled them *ethos, logos,* and *pathos.*[5] These categories correspond roughly to appeals based on credibility, logic, and emotion.

Credibility-Based Appeals

An audience's evaluation of a speaker is based on their perception of many of the speaker's characteristics, but the two most important facets of credibility for our purposes are *authoritativeness* and *trustworthiness.*[6]

Authoritativeness, the most important determinant of credibility, refers to the speaker's competence to discuss the topic. Trustworthiness refers to the speaker's believability. The speaker's perceived honesty, integrity, and impartiality are all part of the audience's perception of that speaker's trustworthiness.

Credibility can be based on either the speaker's own reputation or on the testimony of an expert the speaker cites. If the speaker were an atomic physicist who had studied the safety of nuclear power plants for many years, an audience would probably consider that speaker a credible source on the topic of safety in nuclear power plants. Chances are that if the audience members were in favor of nuclear power and this speaker told them that nuclear power was unsafe, they would reconsider. If, on the other hand, the speaker was a student who had never even visited an atomic power plant, it would be easy for the audience members to discount the student's arguments. By quoting the expert or the results of a study the expert ran, that student could borrow some of that expert's credibility.

It is important to acquire expert testimony from highly credible sources and then carefully attribute that testimony to the proper source. The student with no background in nuclear power might still be able to decide on the basis of careful research that nuclear power plants are unsafe. That student might then say:

> Nuclear power plants are unsafe.

and expect the audience to believe it. Why should they take the student's word for it? To bolster credibility, the student might say:

> According to several books I have read, nuclear power plants are unsafe.

What are these books? They might be works of fiction or polemics by a writer no more authoritative than the speaker. Worse yet, these books might have been distributed by special-interest groups for propaganda purposes. The best move would be for the speaker to take an extra breath and give a concise, carefully worded statement of the credibility of the outside expert:

> According to Professor A. Thom Kerschmacher, winner of the Nobel Prize and highly respected for his work in nuclear safety, nuclear power plants are unsafe.

Establishing your own credibility requires a somewhat different procedure. If you are not already well known to your audience, you might have to answer the question, "Why should these people listen to me?" To answer this question you could make a statement about your experience concerning your topic or how important it is to you or the amount of research you have done on it.

Candy Lightner establishes her credibility in the speech in Chapter 1:

Following Cari's death I have learned a great deal about the seriousness and urgency of the drunk driving problem in this state. I had no choice — this was the second time my daughter was hit by a drunk driver. This time it cost her life.

. . . In the past three months I've learned a great deal about the drunk driving problem. . . . I have talked to numerous people in the field including judges, district attorneys, defense attorneys, directors of alcohol abuse programs, police officials, elected officials, concerned citizens, and victims. . . .

No matter how you establish your credibility, it is important that you believe in it yourself. You do not have to boast, but be wary of false modesty. As long as what you are saying about yourself is true and reasonable, do not be afraid to establish your qualifications solidly. For example, if you were giving a speech on a proposed tax cut in your community, you might begin this way:

You might say I'm an expert in the municipal services of this town. As a lifelong resident, I've been shaped by its schools and recreation programs, protected by its police and firefighters, served by its hospitals, roads, and sanitation crews. So when a massive tax cut was proposed, I did some in-depth investigation into the possible effects. I looked into our municipal expenses and into the expenses of similar communities where tax cuts have been mandated by law. . . .

If your audience accepts you and your sources of information as credible, they are likely to give your logical appeals a fair hearing.

Logical Appeals

Forms of Reasoning

In their purest form logical appeals supply an audience with a series of statements that lead to the conclusion the speaker is trying to establish. The most common forms of logical reasoning are *deduction* and *induction.*

Deduction. Deduction is reasoning from a generality to a specific; in other words, you present general evidence that leads to a specific conclusion. Deductive reasoning can be demonstrated in syllogisms, which are arguments made up of two premises (a major premise and a minor premise) and a conclusion. The classic syllogism is:

All men are mortal.
Socrates is a man.
Therefore, Socrates is mortal.

This is the way one student used deduction to argue one of her points in a speech on the problem of illiteracy:

We come into the picture as taxpayers, especially in welfare and unemployment costs. According to *U.S. News and World Report,* 75 percent of the unemployed lack the skills necessary in reading and communication. Welfare is the answer for those illiterates who can't work. This costs us $6 billion per year.[7]

This argument might be phrased in the following syllogism:

Unemployment costs us plenty.
Illiteracy causes unemployment.
Therefore, illiteracy costs us plenty.

If all logical appeals were expressed as complete syllogisms, people could examine the major and minor premises and decide if the conclusions drawn from those premises were valid. This method would make most arguments cumbersome, so we generally use *enthymemes* for logical appeals.[8] An enthymeme is a compressed version of a syllogism in which the underlying premises are concealed, as in:

Because Socrates is a man, he is mortal.

Enthymemes become dangerous when they disguise faulty premises. Some of the best examples of this type of enthymeme are provided in the form of arbitrary rules. For example, take the rule enforced by some college-town landlords: "Because Joe Schmidlap is a college student, he will have to pay a damage deposit before he can rent an apartment." This rule is based on an enthymeme that is based on the following syllogism:

All college students wreck apartments.
Joe Schmidlap is a college student.
Therefore, Joe Schmidlap will wreck this apartment.

The conclusion, "Joe Schmidlap will wreck this apartment," is based on an untrue, unstated premise: "All college students wreck apartments."

College students often run up against this type of reasoning from landlords and utility companies. Even if they can supply letters of reference from former landlords and receipts for utility bills paid on time, they are still told, "I'm sorry, we don't rent to college students. It's a rule we have," or "I'm sorry, we require a seventy-five-dollar deposit to turn on your electricity. It's a rule," or "There's no sense arguing. We don't need to give you a *reason.* It's a rule."

The frustration you feel when you are subjected to illogical rules is the same frustration that an audience feels when it is subjected to an argument that does not supply valid reasons. That is why we take this close look at deductive reasoning: to make sure that the reasons we use in deduction are valid, we examine the underlying premises of our argument.

Of course, formal logic does not explain all of human reasoning.[9] Humans are not inherently logical or illogical; they are instead "psychological," which means that their reasoning processes are far more complex than any set of rules, no matter how elaborate, could encompass. However, formal logic does have at least one specific use besides being a standard for testing arguments. People who reason fallaciously are generally able to recognize their reasoning as fallacious when confronted with their errors through formal proofs. Therefore, we use formal logic to point out errors in reasoning.[10]

Induction. Induction is reasoning from specific evidence to a general conclusion. In induction we observe that something is true for a specific sample. From this evidence we reason that it is *generally* true.

Induction would be the appropriate type of reasoning to use with a skeptical or hostile audience when you do not want to state an unpopular claim right away. If you are seeking to prove that your local government is generally corrupt, for example, you might build your case with specific examples: the mayor has been convicted of bribery, the building inspector has resigned after being charged with extortion, the fire chief has been indicted for running the station's Dalmation at the track, and the chief of police has admitted to keeping his infant nephew on the police department payroll. If you used these specific instances to conclude that most of your local officials are corrupt, you would be using induction.

The student speaking against illiteracy used induction to argue that it is a serious problem:

> Nonreading adults have innumerable problems because of their handi-
> cap. . . . Illiterates can't read maps or signs, bills or bank statements. They
> have problems telling the difference between, for example, dog food and
> beef stew because they can't read the labels. . . . In one case, an illiterate
> worker at a construction company was killed because he couldn't read a
> warning sign. . . . In another case, a 42-year-old mother from Syracuse who
> can't read or write unintentionally poisoned her young daughter because
> she confused pink dishwashing soap with Pepto-Bismol.[11]

Although induction and deduction are the most common types of logical reasoning, there are other forms. These forms include reasoning by sign, causal reasoning, and reasoning by analogy. Often these forms are combined with induction and deduction.

Reasoning by Sign. Sign reasoning is reasoning from specific evidence to a specific conclusion without explaining how the evidence and conclusion are related. The classic example of sign reasoning is, "It is snowing outside; therefore it must be winter." Sign reasoning is used when the argument will be easily accepted by the audience. For example, an audience would probably accept the claim that an increase in bank robberies is a sign that a community is becoming more dangerous to live in. We would not need to go into a long, logical explanation of our reasoning in that case, and the time we save could be used to develop more important aspects of the argument. For example, we might want to go on to claim a particular *cause* for the rash of bank robberies. That would require causal reasoning.

Causal Reasoning. Causal reasoning, like sign reasoning, is reasoning from one specific to another specific. However, in causal reasoning you go on to prove that something happened or will happen *because* of something else. If you claimed that the increase in bank robberies in your community was caused by a decrease in police manpower, you would be involved in causal reasoning. In fact, you would be using effect-to-cause reasoning, which is based on the organizational pattern of the same name discussed in Chapter 6. Effect-to-cause reasoning is used when you are talking about something that has already happened. If you were arguing about something that *will* happen (for example, the probability of future bank robberies because the police have cut the size of their force or the hours they patrol), you would be using cause-to-effect reasoning.

Reasoning by Analogy. Reasoning by analogy is reasoning from specific evidence to a specific conclusion by claiming that something is *like* something else. Although this type of reasoning could not be used for legal proof, it can help prove a point to an audience. For example, if you were arguing that the methods of law enforcement that curbed bank robbery in a nearby city would also work in your city, you would have to argue that your city is similar to that nearby city in all the respects that are important to your argument—number of banks, size of banks, size of police department, and so on. Thus, if you could argue that the two cities are alike except in one respect—for example, the size of their police forces—you could argue that this is what makes the difference in the incidence of bank robbery. If you did so, you would be arguing by analogy.

There are two types of analogy—*literal* and *figurative.* The analogy of the two cities is a literal analogy because it compares two things that are really (literally) alike. A figurative analogy compares two things that are essentially different. If you argued that bank robberies are like a disease that must be treated to keep it from spreading, you would be using a figurative analogy.

No matter which type of reasoning you are using (deduction, induction, sign, causation, or analogy), you can check the validity of your arguments by checking them against the basic logical fallacies.

Logical Fallacies

Scholars have devoted lives and volumes to the description of various types of logical fallacies.[12] The three most common types seem to be insufficient evidence, non sequitur, and evasion of argument. Most fallacies can be included under one of those categories.

Insufficient Evidence. The fallacy of insufficient evidence is sometimes difficult to recognize, especially when it is caused by *ignored causes* or *ignored effects.*

Examples of *ignored causes* run rampant through everyday conversations. Take a typical discussion about college sports:

> State U. beat State Tech.
> State Tech creamed State Teachers.
> Therefore, State U. will murder State Teachers.

This argument might ignore previously injured players who are now back in action, stars who are now injured, or a host of other variables.

Logical fallacies based on *ignored effects* are even worse:

> If other nations overcharge for oil that is needed for American consumers, an invasion of those countries is warranted.

That argument ignores undesirable effects of war, such as drafting college students who would rather be studying public speaking.

You might not recognize that an argument is based on insufficient evidence, because the argument *sounds* so reasonable. One cause of this deception is reasoning according to slogan, which occurs when we use some folksy, familiar expression as proof. Max Black provides two excellent examples:

> We hear all too often that "the exception proves the rule." Probably not one person in a thousand who dishes up this ancient morsel of wisdom realizes that "prove" is here used in its older sense of "probe" or "test." What was originally intended was that the exception tests the rule — shows whether the rule is correct or not. The contemporary interpretation, that a rule is confirmed by having an exception, is absurd. This tabloid formula has the advantage of allowing a person to glory in the fact that his general principle does *not* square with the facts.

> "It's all right in theory, but it won't do in practice," is another popular way of reveling in logical absurdity. The philosopher Schopenhauer said all that needs to be said about this sophism: "The assertion is based upon an impossibility: what is right in theory *must* work in practice; and if it does not, there is a mistake in theory; something has been overlooked and not allowed for; and consequently, what is wrong in practice is wrong in theory too."[13]

Non Sequiturs. Fallacies of insufficient evidence are caused by not telling enough. *Non sequitur fallacies* are those in which the conclusion does not relate to (literally, "does not follow from") the evidence. Unreasonable syllogisms such as those we described as being used by landlords and utility companies are non sequiturs based on faulty premises. Non sequiturs based on true premises can be just as dangerous. Take, for example, the non sequitur fallacy known as *post hoc,* which is short for *post hoc, ergo propter hoc.* Translated from the Latin, that phrase means "after this, therefore because of this." This fallacy occurs when it is assumed that an action was caused by something that happened before it. Post hoc arguments are often applied to politics:

> Obviously, Jimmy Carter caused the gas shortage of 1979. It happened, after all, during his administration.

Spurious research is often post hoc.

> Nearly all heroin users started with marijuana. Marijuana obviously leads to the use of harder drugs.

Nearly all marijuana users started with aspirin, too, but aspirin does not necessarily lead to the abuse of drugs.

Another type of non sequitur is an *unwarranted extrapolation,* which is a statement that suggests that because something happened before, it will happen again, or that because something is true for a part, it is true for a whole.

> State U. has massacred State Teachers every year for the past five years. They'll do it again this year.

> Ronald Reagan was a good actor. *Bonzo Goes to College* must be a good movie.

Then there is the *circular argument,* in which the evidence is dependent upon the truth of the argument:

> Of course the administration is concerned with student welfare. It says so right in the college catalog.

Evasion of Argument. In this final type of fallacy the speaker dodges the question at hand by arguing over some other, unrelated point. One such evasion is the *ad hominem* argument, which is the fallacy of attacking the person who brought up the issue rather than the issue itself:

> Of course, Louie thinks marijuana should be legalized. Louie is an idiot.

The most common type of evasion of argument is the *red herring.* This fallacy, which derives its name from the practice of dragging an odoriferous fish across a trail when running away from bloodhounds, consists of evading an issue by concentrating on another, more volatile one:

> Should cocaine be legalized? The real question here is, "Who would like to see us legalize cocaine?" And the obvious answer to that question is, *the Communists.* The threat of the Communist conspiracy is as real today as it was . . .

No argument is perfect. If all the evidence were available and it related perfectly to the argument, there probably would not *be* an argument in the first place. You should recognize the major fallacies, though, and watch for them in your own reasoning. If an audience is able to discount your arguments as illogical, you probably will not persuade them.

Emotional Appeals

An emotional appeal uses a feeling like love, hate, fear, guilt, anger, loneliness, envy, or pity to entice an audience to change its attitude. An emotional appeal is not necessarily unethical, although it does allow the most room for an unethical speaker to operate. It is not necessarily illogical either. Because emotional appeals are *psychological,* they can be particularly powerful.[14] Clarence Darrow once pointed out, "You don't have to give reasons to the jury. Make them *want* to acquit your client, and they'll find their own reasons."

It would be a good idea to accept half of Darrow's advice. Give your audience reasons, *and* make them want to accept your plan. Instead of just giving reasons from expert authorities why nuclear power plants are unsafe, you might also describe a nuclear holocaust or explain the details of radiation illness. On the other hand, if you were arguing in favor of nuclear power, you might describe what life would be like without any energy sources — slowly freezing to death. Let us take a look at four emotions on which emotional appeals are sometimes based: *fear, anger, pride,* and *pity.*

Fear. Appropriate fear appeals are sometimes effective persuaders. Modern advertising — especially the TV variety — commonly appeals to audience fears. In fact, television advertising has done more than its share of originating new fears. The fear of body odor, one of the classics of prime-time advertising, has recently been fragmented into more specific fears, like the fear of foot odor (one commercial featured a hapless father driving his entire family from the house by taking off his shoes), the fear of personal-hygiene odor, and the fear of soap odor. ("But I used a deodorant soap!" cries the sweet young thing in the kissing booth. "That's just it," explains the reticent young stranger in front of her. "You *smell* like a deodorant soap.")

Fear appeals can be detrimental if they go too far. In a classic study[15] high school students were presented several persuasive messages about toothbrushing. The high-fear appeal showed grotesque pictures of dental diseases, rotting gums, and black stumps of teeth. The moderate-fear appeal merely mentioned tooth decay in passing, but the researchers found it to be more effective. This study, like many that have come after it, suggests that if you tap audience fears, you should do so with moderation.

Anger. If an audience is angry (or can be *made* angry) about something, you should show them that you are angry about the same thing. This stance will do two things: (1) It will show that you are similar to them, increasing your persuasiveness. (This technique is known as "establishing common ground"; we will discuss it later.) (2) It will also allow you to offer your solution as a cure for whatever is causing the anger. For example, a bandwagon full of political hopefuls is telling people how angry they are about high taxes. Fear not, the audience is told. There is a way to change this situation: Vote for Candidate X.

Appeals based on anger can be successful, but in order to be ethical, you have to *feel* the anger honestly. According to our definition of ethics, you should not say you are angry if you are not.

Pride. The satisfaction audience members feel in their achievements or worth can be a rich vein to tap. Audience members might be proud of their work, their family, their community, their country, or any one of a thousand other things they identify with. If they are not proud to begin with, they can be made to feel proud by being reminded of the pride they *should* feel. A British professor who happened to be speaking before an American audience tapped their pride in this way:

> Let me start with a banal and embarrassing confession, such as is seldom nowadays made, either by Americans or by their allies. I love America. You are a truly amazing people: rich, ingenious, generous, entertaining, powerful, and deeply human. You are the leaders in every branch of science and technology, every field of scholarship and the arts. . . . There may still be Europeans who feel culturally superior, but I am certainly not one of them. I view the United States with admiration and gratitude for all it has done for mankind and is still doing. . . .[16]

Pity. Pity is the emotion that allows us to feel sorrow for the suffering of others. You can use pity as an emotional appeal by reminding your audience that someone, somewhere, is suffering. Pity is an especially potent emotion if the sufferer comes from a group toward which we already feel sympathetic, such as children or animals. One effective antiabortion message was delivered from the point of view of an unborn fetus, who claimed that it was able to feel pain from the beginning of its development. Therefore, to allow abortion to remain legal was to allow this fetus to suffer. The listeners were thus told that a *child* was suffering; and worse yet, that they were partially responsible.

The key to an emotional appeal is sincerity. Most audiences will be able to recognize false emotions and reject appeals based on them.

Emotional appeals, as well as logical reasoning and credibility, are important to keep in mind when planning a persuasive strategy. Although any one type of appeal might dominate a particular argument, different appeals can also be *combined* to good effect.

Techniques for Effective Persuasive Speaking

The preceding discussion suggested several techniques for effective persuasion. Let us focus on a few important techniques.

Analyze and Adapt to Your Audience

It is important to know as much as possible about your audience for a persuasive speech. For one thing, you should appeal to the values of your audience whenever possible, even if they are not *your* strongest values. This advice does not mean you should pretend to believe in something.

According to our definition of ethical persuasion, pretense is against the rules. It does mean, however, that you have to stress those values that are felt most forcefully by the members of your audience.[17]

Also, you should analyze your audience carefully to predict the type of response you will get. Sometimes you have to pick out one part of your audience — a "target" audience — and aim your speech mostly at them. Some of your audience members might be so opposed to what you are advocating that you have no hope of reaching them. Still others might already agree with you, so they do not need to be persuaded. A middle portion of your audience might be undecided or uncommitted, and they would be the most productive target for your appeals.

Of course, you need not ignore that portion of your audience that does not fit your target. For example, if you were giving a speech against smoking, your target audience might be the smokers in your class. Your main purpose would be to get them to quit; but at the same time, you could convince the nonsmokers not to start.

All of the methods of audience analysis described in Chapter 4 — surveys, observation, interviews, and research — are valuable in collecting information about your audience for a persuasive speech.

Set a Clear Persuasive Purpose

Remember that your objective in a persuasive speech is to move the audience to a specific, attainable attitude or behavior. In a speech to convince, the purpose statement will probably stress an attitude:

> After listening to my speech, my audience members will agree that steps should be taken to save whales from extinction.

In a speech to actuate, the purpose statement will stress a behavior:

> After listening to my speech, the audience members will sign my peitition to the United Nations.

As you learned in Chapter 3, your purpose statement should always be specific, attainable, and worded from the audience's point of view. "The purpose of my speech is to save the whales" is not a well thought out purpose statement.

Establish "Common Ground"

It helps to stress as many similarities as possible between yourself and your audience. This technique helps prove that you understand them; if not, why should they listen to you? Also, if you share a lot of common ground, it shows you agree on many things; therefore, it should be easy to settle one disagreement — the one related to the attitude or behavior you would like them to change.

The manager of public affairs for *Playboy* magazine gave a good demonstration of establishing common ground when he reminded a group of Southern Baptists that they shared some important values with him:

> I am sure we are all aware of the seeming incongruity of a representative of *Playboy* magazine speaking to an assemblage of representatives of the Southern Baptist Convention. I was intrigued by the invitation when it came last fall, though I was not surprised. I am grateful for your genuine and warm hospitality, and I am flattered (although again not surprised) by the implication that I would have something to say that could have meaning to you people. Both *Playboy* and the Baptists have indeed been considering many of the same issues and ethical problems; and even if we have not arrived at the same conclusions, I am impressed and gratified by your openness and willingness to listen to our views.[18]

Organize According to the Expected Response

It is much easier to get an audience to agree with you if they have already agreed with you on a previous point. Therefore, you should arrange your points in a persuasive speech so you develop a "yes" response. In effect, you get your audience into the habit of agreeing with you. For example, one of the sample speeches that follow is on the donation of body organs. The speaker begins by asking the audience if they would like to be able to get a kidney if they needed one. Then he asks them if they would like to have "a major role in curbing . . . tragic and needless dying. . . ." The presumed answer to both questions is yes. It is only when he has built a pattern of "yes" responses that the speaker asks his audience to sign organ donor cards.

Another example of a speaker who was careful to organize material according to expected audience response was the late Robert Kennedy. Kennedy, when speaking on civil rights before a group of South Africans who believed in racial discrimination, arranged his ideas so that he spoke first on values that he and his audience shared—values like independence and freedom.[19]

If an audience is already basically in agreement with you, you can organize your material to reinforce their attitudes quickly and then spend most of your time convincing them to take a specific course of action. If, on the other hand, they are hostile to your ideas, you have to spend more time getting the first "yes" out of them.

Use a Variety of Appeals and Supporting Materials

You should examine each of your points and ask, "Is there another appeal I could use here?" If you are using only a logical appeal, you could consider emotional appeals or credibility appeals also. The same test applies to supporting material—ask, "Is there any other support I could offer to help prove this point?"

Sample Speech to Convince

Our first sample speech was given by Roger Aden, a student at the University of Nebraska-Lincoln. With it, Roger won first place in the 1984 Interstate Oratorical Association annual tournament.[20] He was coached by Jack Kay. His purpose was to convince his audience that "atomic veterans" are being treated unfairly by the Veteran's Administration. Some comments on his persuasive strategy are in the margin.

The Forgotten Victims

Roger Aden
University of Nebraska-Lincoln

Strategy

Immediate preview. He uses the VA's own words as testimony against them. This technique recurs, to good effect, several times.

He begins development of the problem; he sets up the logic of his main argument and previews his main points.

1   The motto of the Veteran's Administration is simple — "to care for him who shall have borne the battle and for his widow and orphans." Certainly this is a very noble creed. Unfortunately, forcing the VA to carry through on this promise is another matter entirely.

2   Approximately 250,000 veterans from the different services can attest to the difficulty of this task. They participated in 235 atomic test explosions between the end of World War II and the signing of the Partial Test Ban Treaty in 1963. Like veterans of many other tests, they were told little about the possible dangers of their forced participation in the experiments. But unlike most veterans, atomic veterans have not received VA care for injuries resulting from their test participation. Atomic veterans suffer higher rates of radiation-caused diseases than the general public, yet the VA has refused to provide health care benefits for these men. In exploring the plight of this nation's atomic veterans, we must undertake an examination of the problems faced by these men, discover the three barriers between them and health care, and demand a solution to this problem.

Deductive reasoning serves to define and specify the problem.

3   Problems addressed today will be limited to the veterans themselves and not their relatives or people living near the atomic test sites. Those are civil questions for the courts to handle. We are dealing with the Veteran's Administration. By law the VA is required to provide health care and compensation to veterans for service-related disability and death. Veterans of our foreign wars have received care in VA hospitals. Vietnam veterans exposed to Agent Orange have collected relief. But *atomic veterans remain the forgotten victims* — victims of ionizing radiation and a careless VA. We need to discover the problems they encounter.

Testimony supports his basic premise.

4   In a study published in the Journal of the American Medical Association last August, Dr. Glyn Caldwell of the Center for Disease Control found that atomic veterans suffer leukemia at a rate three times the national average. A study conducted by the National Association of Atomic Veterans discovered

Strategy

that fully 70 percent of its membership was victimized by some form of cancer, heart disease, or degenerative muscle disease.

Example, with description and testimony.

5   John Smitherman was one of those men. He was a subject in two atomic test explosions in 1946 while serving in the navy. According to the *Atlanta Constitution* of May 23, 1983, doctors diagnosed his case as only a lymph system gone haywire. Both his legs were amputated. A chunk of flesh was removed from his back. His left hand swelled to the size of a cantaloupe. After going through this living hell, John Smitherman eventually died. Dr. Karl Morgan, Director of Health Physics at Oak Ridge National Laboratory, says there is no doubt that Smitherman's death resulted from his participation in atomic test explosions. Yet incredibly, the VA denied Smitherman's claim for health care benefits six times.

Statistics, testimony, and a transition to subpoints.

6   He is not alone. The VA reviewed the cases of nearly 2000 atomic veterans and found that about 40 percent were suffering various malignancies. But South Dakota Congressman Thomas Daschle reports that the VA has denied an astounding 98 percent of atomic veteran claims. Behind this twisted logic stand three barriers which are nearly insurmountable to atomic veterans seeking health care.

Each argument *against* health care for atomic veterans is analyzed and refuted; testimony and description are entered in evidence.

7   First, the VA claims that radiation doses received by atomic veterans weren't large enough to cause serious problems. But there is a fundamental flaw in that contention. Any radiation dose, no matter how minute, produces adverse health effects. In 1978, the Nuclear Regulatory Commission issued a document admitting that there is no known safe dose of ionizing radiation. In 1975, the American *Journal of Epidemiology* reported that physicians exposed to x-rays suffered higher rates of cancer and leukemia. When you consider the difference between an x-ray and a nuclear explosion, the absurdity of the VA's position becomes apparent, especially in light of the appalling safety procedures followed at the tests. In its September 26, 1982, edition, the *New York Times* printed a story about one serviceman who received an x-ray of sorts during a 1953 test explosion in the Nevada desert. Joseph Rovenski was told to cover his eyes with his hands when the bomb exploded. It didn't do much good. Rovenski said the blast was so bright he could see the bones through his hands.

A logical fallacy is pointed out to refute another argument; then comes more testimony and an analogy.

8   In two test explosions near Bikini Atoll in the South Pacific, the International Radiation Research and Training Institute found tolerance levels to be 5000 times the limit set by the Nuclear Regulatory Commission for nuclear power plant operators. John Smitherman participated in those tests. He was told it was safe to escape the South Pacific heat by cooling off in the Bikini Lagoon, even though dead fish were floating in the lagoon. Dr. Karl Morgan of Oak Ridge National Laboratory says Bikini Atoll is unsafe to inhabit today, but the VA maintains the island was perfectly safe over 30 years ago when the nuclear devices were first detonated. The logic of this statement is similar to me telling you that the sun doesn't set in the west.

Testimony backs up a deductive argument.

9   Besides ignoring the obvious, the VA also ignores federal law, the second barrier faced by atomic veterans. Public Law 97-72, signed in November, 1981, was intended to give any atomic veteran suffering any disability free health care at VA institutions, even if, according to the law, "there is

Strategy

insufficient evidence to conclude that such disability may be associated with exposure to radiation." But in drawing up the guidelines, the VA twisted the intent of Congress. Dr. D. Earl Brown, Associate Deputy Chief Medical Director of the VA, told a House subcommittee last May that any veteran with a history of radiation exposure will be treated, provided that "they have a condition for which there is no ready explanation." As VA officials see it, leukemia, cancers, and other well-known diseases suffered by atomic veterans have ready explanations which don't include radiation and don't qualify for health care. A partial explanation of the VA's actions can be found in an examination of the third barrier faced by atomic veterans — the attitude of the VA.

Another fallacy is pointed out; the VA's own words, once again, are used as testimony against it.

10   Put simply, the VA does not want to deal with this problem. VA spokesperson John Hickman says, "There's no way, medically or scientifically, that these veterans can prove a link between their cancers and the low level of radiation. Many have reached an age now where people tend to develop these problems." At times this blind attitude toward evidence reaches ridiculous proportions. The VA defended the Bikini Atoll tests saying they were one of the safest operations radiologically in the atmospheric nuclear testing program.

Emotion-laden language.

11   It would seem that the VA does not want to consider the possibility of dealing with 250,000 veterans who may be suffering fatal diseases because of their service. In holding this attitude, VA officials are sacrificing human lives at the expense of dollars. They are also committing one of the gravest injustices this nation has ever witnessed. Clearly, we have a problem begging for a solution.

The solution is previewed.

12   When considering a solution to this problem, we must keep in mind that the fatal diseases suffered by these men cannot be reversed. The solution, therefore, lies not in curing their ills, but in establishing a sense of justice. Health care will reduce the physical pain, plus give atomic veterans a feeling that their government cares. The morality of the situation can be restored with a three-step approach.

The three-part solution is developed.

13   First, an advisory committee must be established outside the VA composed of atomic veterans, representatives of the International Radiation Research and Training Institute, and officials of the VA's Department of Medicine and Surgery.

14   Second, this committee will be responsible for rewriting the VA guidelines for health care for atomic veterans in accordance with the intent of Public Law 97-72. Congress assumed that all atomic veterans suffering disabilities were harmed by radiation exposure. The guidelines should reflect that assumption.

15   Third, the committee will serve as an appeals board for VA decisions relating to the health care of atomic veterans now and in the future. If the VA refuses to recognize its responsibility to atomic veterans by denying them health care, the veterans can take their case to the committee.

Conclusion: He summarizes main points and supplies (cont. on p. 256)

16   Unfortunately, this three-step solution will probably not save the life of a single atomic veteran. The diseases they suffer cannot be corrected. But the injustice done them by the Veteran's Administration can be corrected. Shift-

Strategy

a memory aid in the form of a strongly worded statement.

ing the burden of proof to the VA and establishing an avenue of appeal will allow atomic veterans to receive the health care they deserve. That care may not save their lives, but it will preserve the justice and morality in a situation that has for far too long been unjust and immoral. Certainly, that is not too much to ask.

Roger spends most of his time establishing the problem; only when the problem is fully developed does he introduce the solution. He relies heavily on logical appeals bolstered by testimony. Compare both his strategy and his use of appeals with the second sample speech, below.

Sample Speech to Actuate

The following speech was given by Philip Doughtie, a student at the University of New Hampshire, Merrimack Valley Branch. His purpose was to persuade his classmates to sign and carry an organ donor card. Some comments on his persuasive strategy are noted in the margin.[21]

The Gift of Life

Philip Doughtie
University of New Hampshire, Merrimack Valley Branch

Strategy

His introduction suggests that this will be a direct persuasive strategy.

1 If any of you needed a kidney or other vital organ to live, would you be able to get one? Would you know where to begin searching for information which would lead to obtaining this needed organ?

He begins with a moderate fear appeal. He previews his thesis.

2 These are questions many of us have never even considered. Yet, each year, in America alone, many people die with kidney disease because donated kidneys are not available. Now wouldn't it be nice — no; *fantastic* — to have a major role in curbing some of this tragic and needless dying? You can do just that. I'd like to show you how, today.

His next statement suggests that both he and his information are credible.

3 In researching and preparing for this speech, I had the opportunity to conduct an interview with the state secretary for the Kidney Foundation, Mrs. Florence Murray, at her home. She related some basic background information about kidneys, kidney disease, and kidney donation, and I would like to relay this information to you.

He begins establishing the problem by explaining that the kidneys are essential organs.

4 Kidneys are vital to human life. They are the "twin organs" that perform the following vital life-maintaining functions:

1. They clean waste materials and excess fluids from the blood.
2. They filter the blood, retaining some compounds while excreting others.
3. They help regulate blood pressure and red blood cell count.

Strategy

5   The human body cannot function without kidneys, and kidney disease is the fourth leading health problem in this country today. Over 8,000,000 Americans suffer from some type of kidney disease. Approximately 60,000 people die of it each year. In addition, over 4000 children between the ages of 1 to 6 are stricken annually with "childhood nephrosis," which is simply medical jargon for kidney disease.

6   Perhaps your first question might be, "What is being done to combat this disease?" The National Kidney Foundation has many objectives, including the following:

1. It offers advice and assistance on important topics like kidney disease detection (warning signals), diagnosis (tests, X-rays, and so on), and drugs needed to treat this disease.
2. It provides assistance in obtaining artificial kidney machines, which are also called dialysis machines.
3. But most important, it coordinates the kidney donation and transplantation program, whereby donors may give one kidney while living or two kidneys posthumously in order to save another person's life.

7   Since the first kidney transplant back in 1954, over 5000 of these operations have been performed. Thanks to improved medical techniques, better blood testing, and new tissue-typing processes, doctors are now reducing the risk of organ rejection. If rejection does occur, the patient can go back on dialysis to await a second, third, or even a fourth transplant, until one is successful.

8   To accelerate organ donations, the Kidney Foundation is also responsible for the widespread distribution of these uniform donor cards.

9   These cards enable you to donate a vital organ after your death. In order to illustrate how this program works, let me use as an example one of our neighbors, whose life was recently saved by a transplant.

10   I refer to a 16-year-old New Hampshire boy, John Warner, Jr., whose body had already rejected his father's kidney transplant. Now a second transplant was essential to save the boy, whose parents could not afford the costly dialysis machine — $150 per treatment, three treatments per week. Luckily, on December 9th of this year, a matching tissue donor posthumously gave his kidney to Johnny and the transplantation was performed and determined a success. The original transplant from his father came three years earlier and the boy had waited since then for a matching kidney. Now, thanks to this wonderful donation, no further wait was necessary. Instances like these really touch us when we stop to realize that the next victim could be someone close to us.

11   I had the opportunity to speak with Dr. John Steinmuller, a well-known New Hampshire nephrologist and head of the "organ-retrieval team" whose job it is to go out and retrieve the organs that donors have pledged.

12   Dr. Steinmuller told me that skeptics always have excuses for not giving a vital organ, and he asked me to say a few words about some of those excuses:

Strategy

He answers some
potential argu-
ments.

1. The first excuse is usually a lack of knowledge about the donation procedures. People do not know where to go or whom to contact. This is a problem I hope to solve for you in just a minute.
2. Apathy and lack of time. Some people are indifferent to the needs of others — they just do not care or they claim to be too busy to waste time on such endeavors. Actually, there is little or no time involved, and I know from personal experience that you are not apathetic people.
3. Inconvenience. Some people fear a delay in funeral and burial arrangements. However, since the operation has to be performed immediately after death, no delay is ever caused in funeral arrangements.
4. Usefulness. Some people assume that their gift will not be used. So far, however, the overwhelming problem has been a lack of donors — not recipients.

He provides his
own arguments in
favor of the action
he wants them to
take.

13   Consider now two reasons why each of us should give of ourselves in this worthwhile way:

1. The gift of life itself. The act of giving this organ will very probably save someone's life in the future. Isn't that a nice thought — to think that you had a part in saving another human's life?
2. Personal pride and satisfaction. How can anyone be more proud or satisfied with himself than when he has contributed to an effort which saves lives? No emotions can compare with those associated with a generous donation for the sake of others.

He answers a final
argument.

14   Perhaps one last question in your mind might be: If I sign up at this time, can I change my mind later? The answer to this question is yes. Since the only way authorities will know you are a donor is by the donor card in your possession, you could simply tear up the card at any time and no one will be the wiser.

He asks for a
specific response,
and he makes it as
easy as possible.

15   Now that all of you are more informed about this vital and worthy program, I would like to conclude my speech by setting the example — signing the first donor card myself. Then, I will circulate the other cards to each of you.

16   Please search your innermost being and conclude that such a gift would be an unselfish and generous sacrifice on your part, and then sign the donor card. Thank you very much.

This speaker used many persuasive techniques in ways that are relatively easy to point out. Your own speech might not be as direct, and it might not follow persuasive strategy in quite so lockstep a fashion. However, your speech will almost certainly be improved by a consideration of the techniques discussed in this chapter.

Summary

Persuasion — the act of moving someone, through communication, toward some particular belief, attitude, or behavior — can be both worthwhile and ethical. It is different from coercion in that it makes an audience *want* to do what you want them to do.

Persuasion can be categorized according to its approach (direct or indirect) or its outcome (convincing or actuating). A typical strategy for a speech to convince requires you to establish a problem and a solution. For a speech to actuate, you also have to establish a desired audience response. For each of these components you need to analyze the arguments your audience will have against accepting what you say, and then answer those arguments.

A persuasive strategy is put into effect through the use of persuasive appeals, which include credibility appeals (based on the authoritativeness and trustworthiness of the source of information), logical appeals (based on reasoning), and emotional appeals (based on emotions like fear, anger, pride, or pity). Logical appeals must be checked for fallacies such as insufficient evidence, non sequiturs, or evasions of argument.

Techniques for effective persuasive speaking include the formulation of a clear persuasive purpose, establishing common ground, organizing material according to an expected ''yes'' response, and using a variety of appeals and supporting material.

Questions/Assignments

1. Examine several advertisements from television, magazines, newspapers, billboards, and so on. Which type of persuasive strategy is used most often, direct or indirect? Do you think the strategies are used effectively? Why or why not?
2. The chapter points out that one common shortcoming in the use of logical appeals is ''disguised faulty premises.'' In your experiences with landlords, banks, loan companies, registrars, deans, and other people, what ''disguised faulty premises'' and ''illogical rules'' have you encountered? Explain why you think the logic is faulty.
3. Consider the topic you have selected for your next speech. List four or five emotional appeals that you could employ. Which of these appeals are unethical, and why? Which appeals might be successful when you speak to your classmates? Why?
4. From your experiences hearing or reading persuasive messages about social or political issues, how well do you think the advice for planning a strategy to convince is followed? If you think such advice is *not* heeded, what steps or components of the process are most often ignored or slighted?
5. Study the sample speech to actuate. Has the speaker explained the problem, the solution, and the audience's role in the solution adequately? Can you suggest any changes that might have improved his presentation?

Notes

1. For an incisive look into the problem of deception, see Robert Hopper and Robert H. Bell, ''Broadening the Deception Construct,'' *Quarterly Journal of*

Speech 67:3, August 1984, pp. 288–302. These authors found six different types of deception: fictions, playings, lies, crimes, masks, and unlies. Another recent analysis is Michael Osborne, "The Abuses of Argument," *Southern Speech Communication Journal* 49:1, Fall 1983, pp. 1–11. Osborne lists six major abuses.

2. Some research findings suggest that audiences may perceive a direct strategy as a threat to their "freedom" to form their own opinions. This perception hampers persuasion. See J. W. Brehm, *A Theory of Psychological Reactance* (New York: Academic Press, 1966). There also exists considerable evidence to suggest that announcing an intent to persuade in the introduction can reduce a message's effectiveness. Sample studies on this matter include J. Allyn and L. Festinger, "The Effectiveness of Unanticipated Persuasive Communications," *Journal of Abnormal and Social Psychology* 62, 1961, pp. 35–40; C. A. Kiesler and S. B. Kiesler, "Role of Forewarning in Persuasive Communications," *Journal of Abnormal and Social Psychology* 18, 1971, pp. 210–221.

3. James V. McConnell, *Understanding Human Behavior* (New York: Holt, Rinehart and Winston, 1974), p. 820.

4. For an examination of how persuasive strategy related to the inaugurations of two presidents, see Bert E. Bradley, "Jefferson and Reagan: The Rhetoric of Two Inaugurals," *Southern Speech Communication Journal* 48, Winter 1983, pp. 119–136.

5. Aristotle, *The Rhetoric,* trans. W. Rhys Roberts (New York: Modern Library, 1954).

6. Other possible credibility factors have been pointed out by various researchers, including composure, sociability, and extraversion. These factors tend to act as intensifiers of authoritativeness and trustworthiness.

7. Joan Braaten, "It's English," *Winning Orations, 1984* (Interstate Oratorical Association, 1984), p. 64.

8. Aristotle once stated, "Everyone who persuades by proof in fact uses either enthymemes or examples. There is no other way." (*The Rhetoric, op. cit.,* 1.2, 1356b 5–7). An excellent modern look at the enthymeme and the nature of argument is Thomas M. Conley, "The Enthymeme in Perspective," *Quarterly Journal of Speech* 70:2, May 1984, p. 168.

9. An explanation of two theories of why reasoning breaks down is provided in Sally Jackson, "Two Methods of Syllogistic Reasoning: An Empirical Comparison," *Communication Monographs* 49, September 1982.

10. P. C. Wason and P. N. Johnson-Laird, *Psychology of Reasoning: Structure and Content* (Cambridge, Mass.: Harvard University, 1972), p. 2.

11. Joan Braaten, *op. cit.*

12. See, for example, Vincent E. Barry, *Practical Logic* (New York: Holt, Rinehart and Winston, 1976).

13. Max Black, "Fallacies," in Jerry M. Anderson and Paul J. Dovre (eds.), *Readings in Argumentation* (Boston: Allyn & Bacon, 1968), pp. 301–311.

14. Emotional proof is sometimes necessary because people will cling to unwarranted, untrue beliefs even if those beliefs have been disproved empirically. See, for example, Mary John Smith, "Cognitive Schema Theory and the Perse-

verance and Attenuation of Unwarranted Empirical Beliefs," *Communication Monographs* 49, June 1982, pp. 115–126. For an article exploring the nature, function, and scope of emotional appeals, see Michael J. Hyde, "Emotion and Human Communication: A Rhetorical, Scientific, and Philosophical Picture," *Communication Quarterly* 32:2, Spring 1984, pp. 120–132.

15. Irving L. Janis and Seymour Feshbach, "Effects of Fear-Arousing Communications," *Journal of Abnormal and Social Psychology* 48, 1953, pp. 78–92.

16. Michael Eliot Howard, "America and the Wider World," *Vital Speeches of the Day,* July 1, 1984, p. 557.

17. For an examination of how one politician adapted to his audience's attitudes, see David Zarefsky, "Subordinating the Civil Rights Issue: Lyndon Johnson in 1964," *Southern Speech Communication Journal* 48, Winter 1983, pp. 103–118.

18. Anson Mount, speech before Southern Baptist Convention, in Wil A. Linkugel, R. R. Allen, and Richard Johannessen (eds.), *Contemporary American Speeches,* 3d ed. (Belmont, Calif.: Wadsworth, 1973).

19. Harriet J. Rudolf, "Robert F. Kennedy at Stellenbosch University," *Communication Quarterly* 31, Summer 1983, pp. 205–211.

20. Roger Aden, "The Forgotten Victims," *Winning Orations, 1984* (Interstate Oratorical Association, 1984), p. 55.

21. Classroom speech presented December 14, 1976.

12

Humorous and Special Occasion Speaking

Humor: An Introduction

We study humor within the realm of public speaking for two reasons. First, humor is the main component of one of the most common forms of special occasion speaking, after-dinner speaking. Secondly, humor can be injected into a wide variety of informative and persuasive speeches. According to the experts, "Humor can show that you have a complete mastery of your subject."[1] It can also make a dull message more interesting, and therefore more effective.[2] We should point out, however, that humor is definitely not appropriate for all speeches. Appropriateness, in fact, is one of the three requirements that you have to consider before using humor in a speech.

Requirements for Humor

It is easiest to discuss humor by borrowing examples from professional comedians as well as professional speakers. A word of caution is appropriate: The goal of this discussion is not to make you a professional entertainer. We take professionals as examples only because it pays to learn from the best.

    The requirements for humor include levity, originality, and appropriateness.

Levity

Levity is the quality of being light. "Funny" is not the key word in humor. "Light" is the key word. A speech to entertain does not take itself altogether seriously. It deals with the serious in an absurd manner or with the absurd in a serious manner.

For example, marital strife, poverty, and religion are serious topics; but who can help laughing when Flip Wilson tells his story about the wife of the poor minister who comes home with her third new dress of the week? "The devil made me buy this dress," she screeches. "He pulled a gun, and he threatened me, and he made me sign your name to a check. . . ."[3] It is difficult to keep a straight face when we see that many frightening subjects in an absurd light.

Originality

Routines like Flip Wilson's "The devil made me do it" have become classics. Classic jokes, however, are not the most effective tactics for an amateur speaker seeking to entertain. For example, take Henny Youngman—please.[4] It is funny when he says, "My grandson complains about headaches all the time. I tell him, Larry, when you get out of bed, feet first. . . ."[5] The same line might not be funny if you said it.

Anecdotes of your own about strange experiences, strange people, or unique insights into everyday occurrences are the best ingredients for a speech to entertain. "Original" in this sense does not mean "brand new." It means "firsthand" or "derived from the source." Take Bill Cosby's anecdote "Hofstra":

> The truth of the matter is that it didn't take much to play for Temple at the time that I was playing because we had lost twenty-seven games in a row, and we played against real weak teams . . . they all killed us. Especially Hofstra. Hofstra beat us 900 to nothing. In their street clothes. They wiped us out. Vassar wouldn't even play us, that's how bad we were. . . . So I'm going to give you some insight about what happens in a loser's locker room.
>
> We were gonna play against Hofstra . . . and when you play for a team like Temple you got nothing to do except pace up and down in the locker room and say, "Boy, I sure do hope I don't get hurt. I almost made a tackle last week. I must have been crazy. . . ."
>
> I played on the second team, which was actually the nut squad. These are the guys who can play, but they're afraid. They don't want to go out there. So they do nutty things, like put their helmet on sideways, look out through the ear hole; some guys got on scuba outfits, no shoes, and an ice skate. . . .[6]

The unpleasant feeling of facing overwhelming odds is one that we all encounter from time to time. It is a relief to see that feeling burlesqued in this manner; but Cosby's story is funny because it is original. It is him. He has not borrowed it. He has not just made it up, either. He has probably been telling the story, in some form, since his college days. Each time he tells it he recognizes some new twist or phrase or facial expression that makes people laugh more, and he incorporates it into the anecdote. The anecdote becomes part of him. It just would not be as effective for anyone else.

There are two lessons here: (1) Original anecdotes are funny because they are best suited to the speaker, and (2) original anecdotes are funny because they are not original in the sense of being "brand new." They are tested, tried, and true. A comedian who does a "bit" knows it is funny. Comedians test their humor in all their interactions, and they do not get up in front of an audience with an unproved product. This second lesson is probably the more important one. Test out your anecdotes first.

Appropriateness

Humor must be appropriate to the audience, the speaker, and the occasion. Be careful telling Polish jokes to the Kasimir-Pulaski Social Group, or drunk jokes at an Alcoholics Anonymous meeting. Joan Rivers's comments on Elizabeth Taylor might not be appropriate for an audience of Taylor's fans, or anyone who is weight conscious:

> Is Elizabeth Taylor fat? Oh, grow up! This woman has more chins than a Chinese phone book. She has a walk-in belly button. She got stuck between the arches trying to get into McDonald's! Oh yes! Absolutely![7]

To be fair, we should add that Joan Rivers also makes potentially inappropriate comments about svelte starlets ("Bo Derek is so dumb she studies for her pap test") and herself ("My body is falling so fast my gynecologist wears a hard hat.").

Consider how appropriate Woody Allen's "lecture" on "The Origin of Slang" would be for an audience of students studying any facet of human communication:

> How many of you have ever wondered where certain slang expressions come from? Like "She's the cat's pajamas," or "to take it on the lam." Neither have I. And yet for those who are interested in this sort of thing I have provided a brief guide to a few of the more interesting origins.

> Unfortunately, time did not permit consulting any of the established works on the subject, and I was forced to either obtain the information from friends or fill in certain gaps by using my own common sense.

> Take, for instance, the expression "to eat humble pie." During the reign of Louis the Fat, the culinary arts flourished in France to a degree unequaled anywhere. So obese was the French monarch that he had to be lowered onto the throne with a winch and packed into the seat itself with a large spatula. A typical dinner (according to DeRochet) consisted of a thin crepe appetizer, some parsley, an ox, and custard. Food became the court obsession, and no other subject could be discussed under penalty of death. Members of a decadent aristocracy consumed incredible meals and even

dressed as foods. DeRochet tells us that M. Monsant showed up at the coronation as a wiener, and Etienne Tisserant received papal dispensation to wed his favorite codfish. Desserts grew until the minister of justice suffocated trying to eat a seven-foot "Jumbo Pie." Jumbo pie soon became *jumble* pie and "to eat a jumble pie" referred to any kind of humiliating act. When the Spanish seamen heard the word *jumble,* they pronounced it "humble," although many preferred to say nothing and simply grin.[8]

Some Techniques of Humor

There are many techniques of humor. *Physical humor* includes pratfalls, pies in the face, dressing in outlandish outfits, and walking into walls. Perhaps fortunately, physical humor is not of much use to the average public speaker. There are several more cerebral techniques that can make your own experiences or insights entertaining.

Humorous Description

Humorists have to be sensitive to the scenes in life that sound funny when they are recounted later. They look at life more observantly than everyone else, and point out things that are, upon examination, a little out of whack. In the sample speech on page 270, Tim Muehlhoff told how he expected a traditional welcome on his first visit home from college. Instead, he said he found this scene:

> . . . There was my mother wearing Jordache Jeans, with blue streaks in her hair, and a button that said "Nuke the Whales." My dad was wearing a sequined Sergeant Pepper uniform, sunglasses, and one black glove. They were both dancing to Michael Jackson's "Thriller."

Of course, the humor in that passage does not just rely on description—there is also a suggestion of exaggeration, our second technique.

Exaggeration

Exaggeration—magnifying a description beyond the truth—is one of the most effective humorous techniques. You could begin a speech with this exaggeration:

> In order to prepare today's speech I read 27 books, interviewed 36 experts, ran 14 carefully controlled experiments, and surveyed the entire population of Tanzania. I worked on the speech for over a year, taking only short breaks for sustenance and catnaps. During that time I have lost considerable weight as well as my entire life's savings, and my wife has run off with a stevedore from San Diego. I am proud to tell you, though, that it was all worth it, for today I am fully prepared to explain to you *Why Ice Floats.* . . .

A speaker recently overstated the condition of Washington, D.C., this way:

> As municipalities go — Washington is going. . . . It has been said that Washington has more people out of work than any other city in the country, but fortunately most of them are employed by the federal government. A recent survey showed that 10 percent of the population was on welfare, 30 percent on unemployment, and the rest on tranquilizers.[9]

Representing something as *less* than what it is (understatement) is another form of exaggeration:

> I had a difficult time investigating this topic. I tried researching it at our library, but it was closed. Someone had checked out the book.

The chairman of the board of Exxon Corporation used second hand understatement recently in a speech before the Economic Club of Detroit:

> I promise to be brief. I'm told that Mrs. Frankfurter used to complain about the lengthy speeches the Justice made. "There are two things wrong with Felix's speeches," she once said. "One is that he always strays from the subject. The second is that he always returns to it." Well, I'll try to stick to the point, at least.[10]

The fact is, any library has more than one book, and Justice Frankfurter was a fine speaker. However, understatement made both examples funny.

Incongruities

Incongruities (statements that are out of place or inconsistent) can also inject humor into a speech. Herbert S. Richey, the chairman of the board of directors of the United States Chamber of Commerce, recently began a speech with an incongruity:

> Thank you for that most generous introduction. I'd like to have a copy, if one is available . . . so I can show it to my wife occasionally.[11]

Elreta Alexander, a district court judge, used the same type of humor in her address to a high school commencement. After thanking her audience for a warm welcome, she said:

> Viewing you in your radiance, I am impelled to respond as did a witness in court after I repeatedly admonished him to look at the jury as he testified. I finally ordered, "Mr. Witness, will you please address the jury!" He nodded, turned to the jury, and said, "Howdy."
>
> Howdy, all you beautiful people. Your presence is encouraging.[12]

Thomas A. Vanderslice, an executive of General Electric Company, recently borrowed an incongruity from Casey Stengel:

I am told that Casey Stengel, on reaching one of his supernumerary birthdays, was asked, looking back on his long life in baseball, what would he have done differently.

The "Old Perfesser" thought a bit, and said: "If I'd have known I was going to live so long, I'd have taken better care of myself."[13]

Incongruities, like any other form of humor, must relate directly to your topic to be effective in a speech. For example, Vanderslice followed his anecdote about Casey Stengel with a smooth transition into his topic:

My remarks today are dedicated to the proposition that this country, and our form of government, will be around for a while yet, and we'd better take good care of what we have.[14]

Word Plays

A play on words allows you to create humor by manipulating language. One way is to place an unexpected ending on a familiar expression:

Where there's a will, there's a lawsuit.

Another way is to change a word or two in a familiar expression:

You can lead a man to college, but you can't make him think.

You can also rearrange words in some nonsensical way:

I showed that wiseguy; I hit him right in the fist with my eye.

Or just use a common word or expression in an unexpected way:

I get so tired of putting my cat out at night. I wish he would stop playing with matches.

A *pun* is a special type of play on words. It uses a word or expression to emphasize different meanings (such as when you introduce a dentist as a man who looks down in the mouth) or uses a word that sounds like another word (a girl's best friend is her mutter).

Puns should be handled carefully in a speech. They are usually clever rather than funny. They "fool" people rather than entertain. They make people groan, rather than laugh. Therefore they are a high risk. For example, the punch line of the following anecdote relies entirely on the effect of five puns strung together mercilessly at the end:

There was once a scientist who won a million-dollar government grant to see what would happen when a mammal mated with its own tenth-generation offspring. The first step in this research was to find a mammal that could survive ten generations and still be interested in mating. The scientist had heard of a type of porpoise that lived in a lake in central Africa. The porpoise reportedly lived for so long that the natives called it "the whale that will not die." The scientist went to Africa, where he was told that the immortal whale was considered sacred and that he would have to wear an equally sacred myna bird on his shoulder to ward off evil spirits. He hired a native guide for the 500-mile trek into the wilderness. When he had almost reached his destination he found his path blocked by a dead lion. The native guide warned the scientist not to step over the animal, since it belonged to the state. The scientist stepped over it anyway, and was immediately arrested for *transporting a myna across state lions for immortal porpoises.*

Some audiences might be angry with you if you took that much time for a pun. People have a tendency to think that puns are the lowest form of humor, unless they think of them first. Still, puns can be used sparingly for humorous effect as long as they do not interfere with your message.

Satire

Satire (humor based on the exposure of human vice or folly) is considered a much higher form of humor.[15] One example of this technique is Lily Tomlin's characterization of "Ernestine of the Telephone Company." Ernestine, harassing customers between snorts and "ringie-dingies," exposes the impersonal treatment we sometimes receive from public utility companies. When Ernestine tells one customer that the phone company has been recording his phone conversations because he owes them $23.64, she responds to his protests,

> Privileged information? (snort) . . . Oh, that's so cute. No, no, no, you're dealing with the telephone company. . . . We are omnipotent.

Later, Ernestine declares to another customer,

> When you anger me you anger the phone company and all the power necessary to tie up your lines for the next 50 years![16]

One speaker used satire this way:

> Some of you may be familiar with the three least credible sentences in the English language.

> They are: First, "Your check is in the mail."

> Second, "Of *course* I'll respect you just as much in the morning."

> And finally, "I'm from the government and I'm here to help you."

Satire, as much as any other type of humor, has to be handled carefully. It has to be appropriate to the speaker, the audience, and the occasion.

No matter what type of humor you use, you should follow three rules during your presentation:

1. Do not, under any circumstances, *try* to be funny. Some of the best humor is accidental. Be light, be original, and be appropriate, but let the fun take care of itself.

2. If you do get a laugh, do not step on it. Wait until the laughter has hit its peak and is beginning to subside before you resume speaking.
3. If you do not get a laugh, keep going as though nothing had happened.

Sample Speech

The following speech won first place for after-dinner speaking in the 1984 National Forensics Association National Tournament. It was given by Tim Muehlhoff, a student at Eastern Michigan University who has a knack for seeing the funny side of things.

The Best Is Yet to Be

Tim Muehlhoff
Eastern Michigan University

Comments

The introduction establishes the style and tone of the speech: It will be uniquely personal and filled with humorous descriptions, exaggerations, and incongruities. We have to listen carefully to catch all of them.

Humorous description, with more than a little satire on current fashions. "Nuke the Whales" is a humorous combination of left-wing and right-wing slogans.

Gary Hart's politics and Michael Jackson's theatrics are both satirized (cont. on p. 271)

1 After two long months of school, after having my phone service cut off by AT&T, and after coming to the rude realization that "Our Friend the Beaver" was not a suitable term paper topic for an advanced zoology class, I decided to surprise my parents with a restful weekend visit. On the long bus ride home, I imagined what it would be like to go home. I pictured myself opening the side door and smelling hot cornbread baking. There, standing by the stove, would be my 52-year-old mother dressed in an apron. And when she'd hear me come in she'd turn, just like in "The Sound of Music," and say, "Father, come quick, our youngest has come to visit." There would be my father, dressed in a cardigan sweater, smoking a pipe (my father doesn't smoke a pipe, but I always picture him with one). He would stop petting our golden retriever (we don't even have a dog, but it's all part of the picture), come into the kitchen, and shake my hand and say, "Welcome home, son."

2 When I actually arrived home and stepped through the door, I got the biggest surprise of my life. There was my mother wearing Jordache Jeans, with blue streaks in her hair, and a button that said "Nuke the Whales." My dad was wearing a sequined Sergeant Pepper uniform, sunglasses, and one black glove. They were both dancing to Michael Jackson's "Thriller."

3 Questions jumped into my mind. What had happened to them? Had Martians kidnapped them, and left not so cleverly designed imitations? Had they spent too long trying to figure out Gary Hart's foreign policy? When I finally got them to quiet down, persuaded my father to take off his black glove and stop talking like a girl, I asked them what was going on. My parents said that they had simply realized that they weren't getting any younger, and decided to do something totally different and crazy. For the first time I thought about old age. How hard it must be for my parents to grow old. I also

Comments

here, and the satire leads smoothly into the thesis statement of the speech.

A preview of main points (even an entertaining speech has to say something).

Satire on a TV commercial.

Exaggeration of his father's physical state.

Humorous description.

Classic incongruities.

More humorous description, with a quick satire on parental clichés.

Transition to second main point.

More humorous description, overstatement, and satire.

TV commercials are almost always appropriate targets for satire.

---

realized that growing old was going to be an experience I was going to share with them. And if we were going to get through this okay, I needed to know more about the aging process and how to cope with my aging parents. So I went to the library. While I was in the library I figured what the heck, why keep this to myself? So here I am.

4   Basically the aging process is broken up into three parts: acceptance, denial, and settling. Acceptance is what most of our parents are going through right now. This stage is when they first realize they are getting old. The body starts to slow down, the hair starts to thin and gray. I remember when my mother found her first gray hair. She let out a scream so loud from the bathroom that we thought someone had taken the whitener out of the Final Touch. And my dad was changing too. He started to lose some of his physical ability. "Honey, the leaves are raked and would you please call an ambulance?"

5   All around the house you start to notice the tell tale signs of old age. In the closet you see products like Porcelana, Ben-Gay, and caffeine-free Squirt. In the living room, the love seat has been replaced by a La-Z-Boy recliner with a built-in vibrator. In the morning you see your dad's old familiar smile, except it's in a glass in the bathroom and he's in the kitchen. The hardest thing about Acceptance is that you go through it with your parents. You see them change. Our parents are no longer infallible. Dad isn't the strongest man in the world and Mom sometimes makes mistakes. "Mom, why is there a pork roast in the washing machine?" "I don't know son, but I think I'm broiling your shirt."

6   Probably worst of all, our parents begin to say "old people things" like, "When I was a kid, we walked five miles to school with the wind blowing in our face, in a blizzard, in ten feet of snow."

7   "What are you trying to tell me, Dad, you were stupid?"

8   My dad still wasn't too old to put this scar on my head.

9   It must be scary for our parents to know they are getting older. It's scary to watch that happen to someone else. So your parents are scared, you're scared, so you both move into Denial.

10   Denial is when our parents rebel against the idea of becoming an aging relic. They set out to show not only you, but themselves that they can be just as young as the rest of us. Dad tries to emulate your modern lingo, "Hey dude, what's cooking, Blood?" Mom tries to come to you on your own wavelength, "Son, your father and I have decided to snort some of that marijuana we have been hearing about." Your father, in an attempt to cover up the aging process, buys some Grecian Formula so that the people at work will say, "Wow, John's hair was snow white a month ago, but now it's jet black, and we didn't notice because it happened *so* gradually." Whom are we kidding? I could gradually grow a third arm, but when it comes in, people are going to talk.

11   It's not only our parents who deny growing old; as sons and daughters we deny they're growing old too. We take our parents out to do young things. We take our mom to the disco. We drag our dad to the arcade to play

Comments

a game of Pac Man, which inevitably evokes a response similar to something like, ''This is really asinine, son.''

12   We say stupid things like, ''You're not getting older, you're getting better.'' ''Hey Mom, for a hot tomato, you sure are well preserved.'' On birthdays we buy our fathers silly cards with exotic women on them, who say, ''You just turned 50, and I think you're foxy.'' What in the world is my 52-year-old father, who has been happily married for 26 years, ever going to have to say to a big-bosomed woman in a leather bikini? ''Hey, want to help fix the lawn mower?''

Greeting cards are satirized here.

Third main point.

13   The last stage is Settling. Settling is when your parents realize that old age is here to stay and it's not that bad. They're adjusted, they're satisfied. It's *you* that has the problem. You're just not the main part of their life any more. They have other things to do. So sometimes on a Friday night when you call, the phone's busy or nobody's home. That's hard for us to take, so when you finally do get them on the phone you find yourself sounding awfully familiar. ''Mom, Dad, how come your never come over anymore? You never write; you never call. What, there's no phone where you live? I tried to be a good son. Maybe when I'm gone you'll realize just what a son you had, and you'll wish you had spent more time with me.'' When you hang up the phone you can't believe you've said those things. The reason you've said them is because you've gotten older too.

Another satire of parental clichés — this one using the incongruity of role reversal.

Smooth transition to conclusion.

14   Everybody gets old. It's a natural progression. Someday, you might find yourself an aging parent, facing the same situations your parents are in now. You'll be saying things to your kids like, ''We're not getting any younger, you know. This is a very difficult and confusing time for us. Look, why don't you talk to Old Man Muehlhoff's kid? He knows about these kinds of things.''

15   Now you know about them too. Our parents are passing into a transition period that can be one of the most rewarding times of their lives. By understanding and sharing all the little traumas of settling in, we can become closer to them than ever before.

A strong conclusion, with a humorous description rich in overstatement and incongruity. It even leaves you with a serious point to remember.

16   So the next time you surprise your parents with a restful weekend visit and they're dressed in the linen yelling ''Toga, toga, let's party little dude,'' don't panic. Your parents have just embarked on life's ultimate trip. Don't be left behind; go along with them. ''The best is yet to be.''

Special Occasion Speaking

The term ''special occasion speaking'' is reserved for speeches that are not primarily informative or persuasive in nature, and are not presented as part of our jobs or everyday routine. This type of speaking is done at a special event, such as a wedding, a memorial service, or a banquet honoring a special person.

Obviously, there are more ''special events'' than we could hope to cover in depth in the remainder of this chapter. There are a few events that happen so often, however, that it is worth our while to discuss them here.

They include after-dinner speaking, introductions, presentations, acceptances, and speeches of commemoration.

After-Dinner Speaking

After-dinner speeches such as "The Best Is Yet to Be" are given at parties, club meetings, and banquets, with the main purpose of entertaining the audience. There will probably be some sentiment or idea underlying the entertainment, but it is important to keep it light. No one is eager for great profundity on a full stomach. An after-dinner speech is usually expected to be humorous, also; but you do not have to be humorous to be entertaining. The word "entertain" derives from the Latin word *tenere,* meaning "to hold." Entertainment is anything that holds your audience's attention by making your message interesting or pleasant for them. An assortment of stories and anecdotes about your audience, for example, will suffice as long as they are presented genially, in a manner that suggests that you yourself are having a good time.

Introductions

A second common type of special occasion speaking involves the introduction of another speaker. When you are called upon to introduce a speaker, there are certain rules to keep in mind. The first and most important rule is that the speaker being introduced is the star, not the introducer. This rule underlies all the others.

Be brief. The audience, no matter how enthusiastic, has a limited store of patience, and that patience should be primarily reserved for the speaker. The speaker has a right to feel short-changed if you use up too much of the audience's listening energy. The British statesman Arthur Balfour once demonstrated the consequences of an overly long introduction. After a 45-minute introduction he got up and said,

> I'm supposed to give my address in the brief time remaining. Here it is: 10 Carleton Gardens, London, England.[17]

Show respect and appreciation for the speaker, without going overboard. It is all right to list the speaker's major accomplishments, but do not gush. It would only embarrass a speaker to be introduced as "the world's greatest authority on . . ." or any other obvious exaggeration.

Find out in advance what the speech will be about, and *"set your audience up"* for it. If you were introducing someone who was speaking on the topic of organized crime, you would not be laying it on too thickly if you said:

> Our speaker tonight will discuss a subject that affects all of us every day, even though it stays generally hidden from public view. It causes our taxes to go up. It adds to the cost of what we buy. Worst of all, it threatens our personal safety and that of our families — indeed our very freedom. It

causes untold damage to human lives and human health, yet its revenues are estimated to exceed the net profit of all the Fortune 500 corporations combined. Our speaker will tell us about organized crime in America.[18]

Adapt your remarks for the audience and the occasion. Years ago, when the humorist Will Rogers introduced the presidential candidate Franklin Roosevelt at the Hollywood Bowl, he said:

> Governor Roosevelt, you are here tonight the guest of people who spend their lives trying to entertain. This great gathering is neither creed nor politics, Jew nor Gentile, Democrat nor Republican. Whether they vote for your or not — and thousands of them won't, never mind what they tell you — every one of them admires you as a man. Your platform, your policies, your plans may not meet with their approval, but your high type of manhood gains the admiration of every person in this audience.[19]

Thus Rogers acknowledged both his audience and the political occasion of the speech.

Above all, *make sure that what you say is entirely accurate.* The most embarrassing type of introduction is one in which the speaker's name is mispronounced or some piece of information is incorrect. Whenever possible, it is a good idea to read your introduction, in advance, to the person who is to be introduced.

Presentations

One common type of introduction introduces the speaker as the winner of an award. In a presentation, all the guidelines above still apply, plus you have to explain briefly the significance of the award.

Here is how actress Diana Muldaur presented a special award to Bob Hope at the 1984 Emmy Awards ceremonies:

> Each year the board of governors of the Academy of Television Arts and Sciences selects a candidate to receive its most prestigious accolade, the Governor's Award. The recipient of this year's award is a man whose career in television is so monumental in terms of length and public acceptance that he is truly unique in his field. Many labels have been attached to him over the years by fans, television critics, and heads of state. President Kennedy called him "America's most prized ambassador of good will throughout the world" when he awarded him the Congressional Gold Medal. Other Presidents from Roosevelt to Reagan have been on the receiving end of his brilliant wit, but still saw fit to make him the most decorated civilian in the United States. . . .
>
> Tonight we honor him . . . for his contribution to television. . . . Bob Hope has been delighting television audiences with his magnificent humor for thirty-five years now, and we're certain that he will continue for many more. For his ability to make us laugh during the good times and laugh even harder during the bad times we owe him a great debt. He is an ageless wonder and for all of us, Hope springs eternal. Ladies and gentlemen, the recipient of this year's Governor's Award, Mr. Bob Hope![20]

Acceptances

An acceptance speech is two-fold: you show your appreciation for the award and thank the people who gave it to you. With an acceptance speech you walk a fine line between self-aggrandizement and humility. This is how Robert Keeshan, television's "Captain Kangaroo," handled his acceptance of a recent award:

> I am deeply honored by this recognition, the Distinguished Communications Recognition Award. I am mindful that this award is not given annually, but is bestowed only when the trustees feel it is appropriate to do so, and that makes me humble. Although this is a great personal experience, I take pleasure in knowing that this award is a recognition of my work of the last thirty-five years, in television for children, and elsewhere as an advocate for young people.
>
> I cite with gratitude the words of Dr. Jimmy Allen in announcing this award. "He has strengthened the best that is in each of us, forged the universal values of the spirit, families, parenting . . . contributing to a better future for our country."
>
> Those words of Dr. Allen go to the heart of my work and outline my dream for the future of our nation. It is the bedrock of my philosophy that our future is in our children, in the environment that we provide for them, and in the quality of our nurturing. It is also bedrock that every child in America is the child of every American adult and that each of us who has escaped the rigors of childhood is responsible for the nurturing of young America.[21]

It is important to adapt your acceptance to the occasion. It is extremely important, for example, to know how many other speakers there will be and how long you will be expected to speak. In an awards ceremony like the Academy Awards, the dozens of recipients are each expected to be as brief as possible. However, in the ceremony for Captain Kangaroo, he was the only recipient and was expected to give a full speech. Therefore he used his acceptance remarks as a transition to his ideas on "the nurturing of young Americans."

Speeches of Commemoration

Speeches of commemoration honor the memory of a person or event. Their purpose is to keep a memory alive, so the choice of language is extremely important. One of the most famous commemorative speeches is Lincoln's Gettysburg Address. This speech's language is so inspiring that schoolchildren are still required to memorize it.

One common type of speech of commemoration is the eulogy, which honors a person who is recently deceased. Honest emotion is especially important with this type of speech; trite, oversentimental, or cliché language will rob the occasion of its dignity. Speak honestly even when the person being eulogized is in some way controversial, as in the case of "Baby Fae," the infant who died three weeks after receiving the

world's first animal–human heart transplant. In her short life this infant
had touched many hearts, as her struggle for survival was captured on a
television news clip. Marie Whisman, the heard nurse of the hospital unit
where Baby Fae lived and died, had this to say at the infant's memorial
service:

> We wish you could have seen our smiles, but they were hidden by those
> green masks that you by now had become so accustomed to. You brought
> joy to so many. The video you starred in won you worldwide popularity. A
> casual stretch and a yawn will never be forgotten. While the press was
> printing that you were grasping at lines and tubings, we knew you were
> also grasping and holding our fingers. Through this touching we tried hard
> to convey to you the love and caring of the many letters and gifts that were
> arriving from all over the nation. You were really a sweet-dispositioned
> baby. . . . It was impossible not to love you.[22]

Summary

This chapter dealt with humor and special occasion speaking.

Humorous entertainment has three requirements: (1) it should be
light, although not necessarily funny; (2) it should be original, although
not necessarily brand new; and (3) it should be appropriate to you, your
audience, and the occasion. There are many techniques for humor, including humorous description, exaggeration (representing something as
much more or less than it is), incongruities (statements that are out of
place or inconsistent), word plays (manipulated language), and satire
(pointing out vice or folly).

Humor is the main ingredient in after-dinner speaking. Other types
of special occasion speaking include introductions, presentations, acceptances, and commemorations. All of these types have guidelines based on
adaptation to the audience, speaker, and occasion.

Questions/Assignments

1. Humor can be used to capture audience attention on a serious topic. Is such a
   tactic effective, or is humor sometimes counterproductive? Cite examples to
   support your answer.
2. Suppose you were the master of ceremonies for a banquet in your home town,
   and that you had the money and the influence to invite any famous comedian.
   Considering the audience and the occasion, which humorists would you want
   to speak? Why? Which people would you *not* consider as entertainers? Why?
3. To understand the idea that humor must be original to the speaker, think about
   two comedians you enjoy, and consider the nature of their humor. Which
   anecdotes suitable for one of these people would be inappropriate for the
   other? (For example, what elements of Joan Rivers's humor would not be
   appropriate for Johnny Carson?) Explain your answer.

4. Observe an awards ceremony, either on campus or through the mass media (such as the Emmys or Oscars). Pick out one presentation and one acceptance that you find most effective. Explain your choices.

Notes

1. Donald H. Dunn, "The Serious Business of Using Jokes in Public Speaking," *Business Week,* September 5, 1983, p. 93.

2. See Dorothy Markiewicz, "Effects of Humor on Persuasion," *Sociometry* 37, September, 1974, pp. 407–422.

3. Flip Wilson, "The Devil Made Me Buy This Dress," Little David Records, Los Angeles, Calif.

4. For those of you born too late, this clever phrase refers to Youngman's most classic line: "Take my wife — please." Like most humor, if you have to explain it, it is not funny.

5. "Take My Wife — Please," *Newsweek,* February 2, 1976, p. 75.

6. Bill Cosby, "More of the Best of Bill Cosby," Warner Bros. Records, Inc., Burbank, Calif. By permission of Bill Cosby.

7. From comments by Rivers on the "Tonight" show and in other appearances. See, for example, *Newsweek,* October 10, 1983, pp. 58–60.

8. Woody Allen, *Without Feathers* (New York: Random House, 1975), pp. 206–207. By permission of Random House Inc.

9. Lee Loevinger, "Is There Intelligent Life in Washington?" *Vital Speeches of the Day* 43, January 1, 1977.

10. C. C. Garvin, Jr., "Recognizing Today's Realities: Where is the U.S. Energy Policy?" *Vital Speeches of the Day* 43, December 1, 1976.

11. Herbert S. Richey, "The Theologians of Freedom," *Vital Speeches of the Day* 43, December 1, 1976.

12. Elreta Alexander, "Reflections for a Graduate," *Vital Speeches of the Day* 42, August 1, 1976.

13. Thomas A. Vanderslice, "The Vital Need for Technology and Jobs," *Vital Speeches of the Day* 43, December 15, 1976.

14. *Ibid.*

15. Experimental evidence into the effects of satire is somewhat inconsistent. There is some evidence to suggest that if an audience is initially favorable to a speaker's position, both the message and the speaker will be evaluated more favorably when satire is employed. See L. Powell, "Satire and Speech Trait Evaluation," *Western Journal of Speech Communication* 41, Spring 1977, pp. 117–125. However, if listeners tend to be neutral or in opposition, satire is either at best ineffective, or at worst, counterproductive. See N. Vidmar and M. Rokeach, "Archie Bunker's Bigotry: A Study in Selective Perception and Exposure," *Journal of Communication* 24, 1974, pp. 36–47.

16. Ellen Cohn, "Lily Tomlin: Not Just a Funny Girl," *New York Times Magazine,* June 6, 1976, p. 91.

17. James C. Humes, *Roles Speakers Play* (New York: Harper & Row, 1976), p. 8.

18. Adapted from introduction to William French Smith, "Combatting Organized Crime," *Vital Speeches of the Day,* February 1, 1984, pp. 229–231.

19. From *The Autobiography of Will Rogers,* Donald Day, ed. (Boston: Houghton Mifflin, 1977).

20. Diana Muldaur, presentation to Bob Hope, Emmy Awards, September 24, 1984.

21. Robert J. Keeshan, "The Nurturing of Young America," *Vital Speeches of the Day,* May 15, 1983, pp. 465–467.

22. Marie Whisman, quoted in *New York Daily News,* November 18, 1984, p. 2.

PART FOUR

Special Circumstances

13

GOOD MORNING, AND WELCOME TO BROOKLYN COLLEGE PRESENTS TODAY, OUR GUESTS

Speaking Through the Electronic Media

Why Study Media Skills?

The electronic media, like Rodney Dangerfield, sometimes have a difficult time getting respect. One critic claims that television is called a "medium" because nothing on it is ever well done. Another critic calls radio "junk food for the ears," and so on. Say what you will about radio and television (and their sister technologies of audio recording and videotaping), they are powerful and plentiful in today's society. We need to study these media, and the skills behind their use, if for no other reason than to understand their effect upon us.

Another reason we study speaking through radio, television, and recording devices is to see how the principles of speech preparation relate to these contexts.[1] This insight, in turn, helps us recognize how they relate to still other contexts, such as writing.

There are more than theoretical reasons for studying media speaking skills. Opportunities for "regular people" to speak before radio microphones or television cameras are increasing dramatically. In many occupations, the ability to speak effectively through audiovisual media will determine professional success. Let us take a look at some of the ways that the paths of public speakers are crossing with media technology.

Communications Careers

With the explosion of our audiovisual technologies, opportunities are increasing for articulate speakers to become communications professionals. Professional recordings for home use are offering everything from "novels on tape" to video dating services, while radio and cable television talk programs on local issues are becoming increasingly popular. Although it is still as difficult as ever to become a network star, the fragmentation of our radio and television media has created a wealth of new opportunities for high-paying, rewarding careers. Every talk show needs a host; every panel discussion needs a moderator.

Public Relations

With the current legal and technological state of our communications media, any citizen can become a spokesperson for a company or for a public interest cause. Take the case of editorial replies on commercial television channels: under current law, radio and television stations are required to deal with both sides of controversial issues.[2] To achieve this balance, among other ways, station personnel present the station's view and then open up their studios for replies from responsible speakers for the opposing view. If you feel strongly about an issue, you might have the opportunity to air your views in this way.

If you do not have the opportunity to air your views on a commercial channel, you still might do so over the new cable public-access channels. Most cable television operators are required by their communities to provide at least one channel on a first-come, first-served basis.

Corporate Video Networks

Many large United States corporations are now establishing their own in-house video networks that link offices, brokers, shareholders, and major customers. Businesses are spending $13 billion a year on video paraphernalia.[3] The most common use for this equipment is *teleconferencing,* which means conducting business meetings through video hookups. These meetings might involve a handful of executives in different cities, or hundreds of participants. Corporations need not own their own equipment for teleconferencing — 1000 of the largest United States hotels offer teleconferencing services. Almost one million business meetings per year are now held by teleconferencing.[4]

Corporations are also producing video cassettes for their stockholders, for securities analysts, and for customers. One executive warns all his colleagues that they must learn to use video. "If you don't," he tells them, "the initiative will go to others who are adept and clever enough to embrace a new medium that offers results that your background and training cannot deliver."[5]

Audiovisual Training

Corporations are also becoming more interested in training their employees by videotape. An entire consulting industry has sprung up for just this purpose.

It is not just in the professional world that media are used as educational tools. Audiovisual recording can also be a powerful teaching tool at all academic levels, especially when it is used to provide feedback about the acquisition of a skill such as public speaking.[6] For years, video playbacks of speech assignments were the province of high-priced communication consultants, but now many schools and universities are equipped to play back speeches presented in class. These exercises are often a revelation for the student: "Did I really sound like that?" "Did I really keep sticking my hand in front of my mouth like that?" One objective of the current chapter, then, is to make these playback exercises, if available, as productive as possible.

The first step in acquiring media skills is to recognize the differences between mediated and face-to-face public speaking.

Mediated versus Face-to-Face Public Speaking

The differences between mediated and face-to-face speaking require some adaptations. For one thing, mediated communication is almost always a collaborative effort, requiring a certain amount of coordination and cooperation. Message preparation tends to be a more complex process. The mediated message itself is usually delivered without the benefit of direct feedback. This fact leads to an interesting, apparently paradoxical, set of differences:

Mediated messages tend to be more accurate. When you are preparing to record something for posterity, or at least for a large, diverse, and unseen audience, you tend to be very careful in all the stages of message preparation. You research your ideas, make your language choices, and practice your presentation more thoroughly than you would for a less formal occasion. Audio and visual recordings put the speaker's entire being, personality, appearance, and intelligence on the line. Everything is there for the receiver to hear and see, and as more than one newscaster has pointed out, "the camera never blinks."

However, *mediated messages tend to be less understandable than face-to-face messages.* This apparent paradox is caused by the lack of direct feedback in mediated communication. Even though the message itself might be more accurate, the audience has more opportunity to twist that message through selective attention, perception, and recall.[7] Media speakers cannot respond to puzzled or blank looks, nor can they rectify misunderstandings in a question-and-answer period.

These two major differences, combined with the collaborative effort that is necessary and lack of feedback, are why we have to approach the speechmaking process differently for a mediated presentation. Whether we are using a home recording device or a fully-equipped studio, we must adapt the various steps of message preparation.

Audience Analysis and Adaptation

The most common mistake when speaking over the broadcast media is to visualize a "mass audience." You should visualize a specific audience of a few individuals if you want your speech to be effective. If you are speaking over radio or television, the station personnel will be able to tell you what type of individual makes up your audience during the time you are speaking. Local stations subscribe to ratings services that not only tell them how many people listen to their station at a particular hour, but how old those people are, whether they are male or female, and what economic bracket they are in.[8] All of this information can be valuable for your audience analysis, and you should make use of it.

For television, the typical audience at home can be visualized as three people, sitting about 10 feet from the screen. The television audience is usually involved but fickle; if you grab their interest they will pay close attention, but if not they will switch channels quickly. (These people, by the way, would never think of getting up and leaving the room if you were speaking to them in person.) You should also remember that your audience will have to contend with all the noise and distractions of their households.

The radio audience can usually be visualized as one person, doing something else while listening as a secondary activity. The radio listener usually is not paying careful attention to what you have to say unless you provide motivation.

The final word of advice in audience analysis is as follows: Mass audiences are *always* made up of different types of people; make sure you give your topic universal appeal.

Supporting Material

It makes sense, in media speaking, to be as conscientious as ever in your choice of supporting material. You should adapt some forms of support, however. For example, when you use statistics it is suggested that you round off large and detailed figures. Use expressions such as "about," "approximately," "nearly," "almost," and "at least." Instead of "a one hundred percent increase," say "doubled." Instead of $501,214,784.74, say "about one-half billion dollars."

Language

For radio, make your descriptions of things that listeners cannot see extremely precise. Sometimes precise vocabulary is not sufficient—you have to choose terms your audience will understand. Take the following description from a standard encyclopedia:

> Its long hair grows thick on top, and soft and furry underneath. Its colors are brown and white, black, white and tan, gray, and all white. It has a long, narrow head and ears that stand up straight but droop at the points. Its bushy tail curls up at the tip. It stands about 22 inches at the shoulder, and weighs from 50 to 75 pounds.[9]

Now, that description is precise and specific, but most audiences would have a difficult time recognizing that you are describing a collie. It would be better simply to say "a dog like Lassie."

Also, it is important to "write for the ear" when you are preparing a speech for either radio or television. The Associated Press instructs its broadcast reporters to "think in terms of sound" and read their sentences aloud as they write them:

> This procedure will enable you to spot awkward phrases, involved sentences, and unclear passages. Almost automatically you will write better . . . without full realization of any technical principles that may be involved.[10]

"Writing for the ear" means avoiding words and phrases that tend to be confusing when they are only heard, and not seen. For example, the expression "twenty sick sheep" is virtually indistinguishable over the radio from "twenty-six sheep." The United Press International radio style manual suggests, "Don't ever say *a* million. The *a* makes it come out *8* on the air. Say *one* million."

Finally, veteran broadcasters warn that you should know the correct pronunciation of each word you use. If it is a foreign word, they suggest that you find a native speaker or call the consulate.

Delivery

Many of the factors of delivery are more important in mediated than in face-to-face delivery, because mediation tends to magnify mistakes. Verbal mannerisms such as "anduh" and "y'know" sound worse over the radio than in person. Physical mannerisms such as scratching your scalp or playing with your ears look worse on television.

Pitch, rate, and volume are still important considerations in media speaking. Most professional radio and television announcers have deep voices. There is not much you can do about your basic pitch, but if you tend to be high-pitched, control it as much as possible. No matter what your pitch range, it is suggested that you always try to speak in the lower half of your register.

Problems with rate are often exacerbated in media speaking because time limits are usually imposed. You still have to remember that too rapid a rate can lead to incomprehensibility (especially after your voice has been filtered through various forms of transmitting and receiving equipment), whereas too slow a rate can lead to boredom.

Volume, however, is a different consideration for media speakers than for face-to-face speakers. A public speaker's natural tendency is to project the voice to the camera or microphone. Actually, the camera and microphone bring you "up close" through amplification, so you should speak at the same volume as you would for a one-on-one conversation.

The idea of "being conversational" is important. You should be animated and lively; nothing is worse than a monotone. The biggest tip-off that an amateur is speaking is a sing-song recitation. Most professionals advise that it is necessary to make yourself sound "larger than life" by being extra enthusiastic. This "larger than life" attitude is necessary for a number of reasons. First, just being in a studio surrounded by unfamiliar equipment and activities is enough to inhibit anyone's natural effervescence and vitality. Add the fact that in radio you are no more than a disembodied voice, flattened out by studio acoustics, and on television you are a flattened-out, two-dimensional image filtered through electronic equipment, and you have a performance that loses a great deal in the process of transmission.[11]

It is also necessary to sound natural, but most professionals insist that overdoing it will be less of a problem than flatness. One expert says, "You will not need to be told to avoid, as remedies, the extremes of vocal caricature in radio and 'hamming it up' or 'mugging' on television. Your natural reserve will usually suppress any tendency to these extremes."[12]

However, one possibly negative side effect of "larger than life" media speaking is a strange placement of emphasis within sentences. Dwight Bolinger calls this tendency the "network tone of voice."[13] Bolinger points out that emphasis should be placed on words that convey important or unexpected ideas, but media speakers tend to emphasize words almost randomly, especially near the ends of sentences. Watch out for emphases such as these:

The windstorm is predicted to reach hurricane *status* today.

("Status," says Bolinger, adds no meaning — it is simply a carrier in this sentence.)

The fire melted the telephone lines in the *area*.

("Area" is not important or informative here.)

The most important thing to remember is to be natural. When developing your "media voice," you do not have to sound like someone else. You only need to sound like an articulate, carefully prepared version of yourself.

Movement and Gestures

Movement can be somewhat hampered when you are wired to the various forms of machinery that the media necessitate. When you are wearing a microphone, for example, it is important not to scratch yourself anywhere near it — the result sounds surprisingly like a giant buzz saw ripping

The actual studio experience is seldom the glamorous event it appears to be on the screen.

through the studio. If you are speaking in front of a standing mike, you have to be careful not to move out of its range. You cannot keep talking as you bend over to pick up a prop under your desk, for example.

Your movement is also somewhat circumscribed when you are on camera. It is difficult for a camera operator to adjust to sudden movement, especially when that movement is unexpected. It is important to "telegraph" your moves before you make them; say something like, "Now let us move over to exhibit A," or "To understand this next point, we have to move to the chart I have set up over here." Once you telegraph your move, it is important to move as slowly as possible (while still seeming natural), to give the camera operator time to adjust.

Gestures also tend to be more modest on television, because it is an "intimate" medium. Television speeches consist mostly of close-ups, so a gaze or a raised eyebrow can be more important than a broad gesture.

Developing Media Skills

The question students who want to break into the media most often ask is, "How do I learn to do what Dan Rather (or Barbara Walters, or Johnny Carson) does?" The answer is that it takes years of experience and quite a few lucky breaks to make it to the top. There are, however, a number of specialized "media skills" you can develop. They include taking advantage of the medium, microphone technique, script formatting, and using prompting devices.

Take Advantage of the Medium

When we say "take advantage of the medium," we mean let the medium do what it does best, whether that medium is a homemade cassette or a network broadcast. In a way, this skill has been stressed throughout this book, because effective delivery in face-to-face public speaking really means taking advantage of the "medium" of face-to-face speaking.

Your first question should be, "What is the correct medium for my message?"

Audio recording, for example, is an effective medium for education. With a tape recorder you can replay a particular part of a message over and over again. You can even include "self tests" and instruct your listeners to replay a portion of the tape if the test proves that they missed a point somewhere. Suppose, for example, that it is your job as a meteorologist for a city parks system to orient all the summer part-timers who do not have your background in meteorology. You might explain the different types of cloud formations and then say:

> At this point you should be able to name ten different types of clouds. Put your tape player on "pause" now and see whether you can list all ten types. . . . Finished? If you got stuck on any of the cloud types, rewind this tape to the previous section and replay my explanation of cloud types. If you were able to name all ten, let's go on to the next section.

There is something else to remember when using audio recording devices: the human imagination plays a more important role in the reception of audio-only messages than in the reception of face-to-face speaking or the visual media. Use this difference to your advantage; allow the imagination of your audience members to take flight by using sound effects. You can crackle a piece of bunched-up cellophane to create the sound of a fire, and crush a styrofoam cup in your hand to create the sound of a ship hitting an iceberg. Kitty litter in a shoebox, tilted sideways next to a microphone, makes a terrific landslide. Most people have no trouble recreating hurricanes and bomb blasts by making the noises with a microphone placed close to their mouths.

Television, on the other hand, is a visual medium. Use the visual component. You can be more than a "talking head" when you appear on television. Photographs, slides, charts, and graphics can be used to good effect.

Microphone Technique

You should become familiar with the various types of microphones. A *lavaliere "mike"*[14] is a small microphone that is usually either hung around your neck or clipped to your clothing. Sometimes there are two of these microphones on one clip, so if one goes dead for any reason, the sound engineer can switch to the other. The engineer will position this microphone on your body so you can speak naturally and still be heard. Essentially you can forget about this type of microphone, provided you remember not to scratch yourself near it or thump it with a gesture.

In a radio studio you will generally use a *stationary microphone* placed either in a stand on the desk in front of you or in a larger stand on the floor. Either way, a stationary microphone will be about one foot in front of you, a little beneath the level of your mouth. Remember that the function of the microphone is to *amplify* your voice, not just to pick it up. It will not be necessary to bend over and get closer to the microphone in order to talk into it; it is best to speak naturally, *over* the mike instead of *into* it.

With a *"boom mike"* (the kind that is suspended over your head from a crane) the best idea is to ignore it; speaking to a boom microphone will defeat its purpose, which is to be unobtrusive.

Before you begin speaking, the audio engineer will ask you to speak in order to set the microphone level. Speak at a normal volume during this procedure, or the engineer will have to make adjustments in the middle of your speech, which may cause your audience to miss part of it.

Just as it is important not to move toward the microphone, it is important not to move too far away, out of range. If you have to move out of range — to pick up something you are about to discuss, for example — you have to stop talking to do it. Some microphones are "directional," which means that they will pick up your voice only if you are in front of them. Ask in advance what the pickup pattern of your microphone is.

There are two exceptions to the rule of not moving away from or toward your microphone. During your speech, if you are going to raise your volume suddenly for dramatic effect, then you have to back away from or move to the side of the microphone. If you are going to lower your volume, also for some type of effect, then you have to move toward the microphone. However, this type of technique is tricky, and it is not suggested without a good deal of practice.

You have to be careful of plosive consonants — *p, t,* and *k* — that are delivered directly into the mike. These consonants can cause a distracting "popping" noise. This can be partially eliminated with the use of a "pop" filter, a bulblike attachment on the front that filters out sudden air blasts. You also have to watch out for the sibilants — *s, z, th,* and *sh* sounds, which produce high frequencies and could therefore cause a whistle.

The best way to assure effective microphone technique is to experiment before the speech until you are satisfied with the results.

Scripting

When speaking on radio or for audio recording, you can use the manuscript style of presentation described in Chapter 9. You can mark words you want to emphasize and, if it seems to help, the best places to pause and take a breath. Remember that if you read your speech from manuscript, you have to avoid the "recitation" effect. Make sure you read as if you were saying those words for the first time, in a conversation with a friend.

You can roughly time out your script by figuring each line of ten words as three seconds of speaking. Precision timing comes through rehearsal, but keep in mind that most people speak faster in the studio than while practicing at home. If you are operating under strict time limitations, you might "back time" your manuscript, marking on each paragraph how much time you need to deliver the rest of the speech. That way you can slow down or speed up as necessary as you go along. For example, you can adjust your rate of speaking if you hit the "one minute" mark and discover that you have two minutes left, or thirty seconds. Many experts suggest that you keep an extra anecdote or an all-purpose extra point in reserve in case you need a filler.

Be careful as you move from one page of your script to another. The microphone will pick up and amplify the sound of the pages turning. If you make any changes in your script, do not cross out parts of sentences or words — cross out the whole thing and then write the new sentence or word clearly above it.

Part of the reason you bring a manuscript of your speech to the radio station with you is so the sound engineers will have their starting and stopping cues. Therefore, if you are speaking from memory or brief notes, you should at least supply the engineers with the first and last lines of your speech, as well as any cues for movements or sound effects within the speech.

Scripting is especially tricky for television, because there is so much going on in the studio at one time. Video has to coordinate with audio; the control room has to coordinate with the studio; the engineers have to coordinate with the production personnel. Because of this complexity, a special type of script format is used for television, in which the audio appears on the right side of a split page and the video appears on the left. Your speech, written out in the split-page format, might look like the sample on the next page.

The split-page format is important for the collaborative effort of studio television production. However, because you are now on camera, you might prefer to use notes rather than a full manuscript. If you do so, you will still need to provide your director with a split-page script, with any lines that act as cues clearly marked and written out in full. If you do use a manuscript for a televised speech, *do not use white paper*. White paper reflects too much light and plays havoc with color cameras. It will also be difficult for you to read under studio illumination. Yellow, pink, or blue paper works better for both speaker and camera. Manuscript pages can be so distracting to a television audience, however, that most speakers use some kind of prompting device.

Sample Split-Page Script

Video	*Audio*
	Speaker:
Camera 1: Close-up of speaker.	And so, if you agree with me that this waste of human life cannot continue, please write to the following address:
cut to	
Camera 2: Medium shot of speaker and visual aid.	(read address on card)
cut to	
Camera 3: Close-up of visual aid.	That's (repeat address)
cut to	
Camera 1: Close-up of speaker.	Thank you very much.

Prompting Devices

Cue cards (sometimes derisively referred to as "idiot cards") are large pieces of stiff white paper, held by the floor manager or an assistant, with your notes or manuscript written on them in large, dark letters. For a manuscript speech on cue cards, the floor manager holds the cards so that the line you are reading is right next to the lens of the camera into which you are looking. As your speech progresses, the card is moved up until you have read all lines next to the lens. Then the floor manager hands that card to an assistant and aligns the next card with the lens in a similar manner. In this way, your eyes always look as directly as possible at the lens. This procedure enables you to simulate eye contact with your audience.

Cue cards can contain manuscript, outlines, or speaking notes. When cue cards hold brief notes, they can be placed anywhere off camera where the speaker can glance at them, and they need not be moved and aligned as the speech progresses. Many monologists, such as Johnny Carson, use cue cards with just an outline, to act as a reminder of the sequence of the items being presented from memory.

Cue cards are not easy to use. If you decide to use them, make yours well in advance of your studio date so you can practice extensively with them at home. Take a full-size (22 × 28 inch) piece of oaktag or poster-board and cut it in half lengthwise. You will have the long thin (14 × 22) card that is recommended; the narrow card will allow you to read the copy a little at a time, thereby minimizing the unnatural eye movement that reading causes. Write the material on the card with a dark, thick, felt-tipped pen, in letters 2 to 3 inches high.

You might also have the opportunity to use a *teleprompter.* The teleprompter is a sophisticated piece of equipment that enables a speaker to read copy while looking straight into the camera lens. One type of teleprompter accomplishes this impressive feat as follows: a closed-circuit camera in the back room photographs the typed speech from regular typing paper. A monitor above the studio camera is positioned to show the speech on a one-way mirror directly in front of the lens. Thus the speaker reads the speech off the one-way mirror but appears to be looking the audience squarely in the eyes.

The test of teleprompter proficiency is in eye movement. A beginner's eyes will be obviously moving from side to side while reading. A professional's eyes will seem steady.

Your Wardrobe

As a visiting speaker, you will not need to be knowledgeable about the engineering and production equipment of the station. However, you should realize how this equipment affects your performance.

Electronic equipment generates heat as it operates, and if it gets too hot it simply *stops* operating. For this reason a broadcast studio must be kept cool, even on the hottest of summer days. Of course, in a television studio the hot lights often more than compensate for the air conditioning, so it is difficult to know what temperature to expect. The best advice is to dress in layers, and shed or add as many as are called for.

What you wear on television is determined by image, illumination, and design. Most experts advise against flashy, faddish clothing and warn that you have to dress according to the message that you want to get across. Perhaps you feel more comfortable in jeans, but if you are speaking on a complex political issue, a dark suit would be more appropriate. You should also avoid colors with high contrast. The television camera has a limited contrast pickup, so it has problems with white blouses under black coats. The camera will also accentuate contrasts between skin and clothing; if you are very pale, you will appear even paler with dark clothing. If you are dark-skinned, light clothing will make you appear even darker. Blacks especially have to be wary of light clothing, because the camera's contrast pickup will tend to wash out facial features in the dark areas. Moreover, your clothing has to coordinate with the set design. If you clash too violently, the set designer will threaten suicide; if you wear the exact color of the set, you will tend to disappear into it. One television executive tells how this apparently minor consideration—blending into the set—once affected history:

> One of the costliest clothing mistakes in television history occurred during the 1960 presidential debates. Richard Nixon showed up for the broadcast wearing a light gray suit which was almost identical in color and brightness value to the light gray set. The insufficient contrast between Nixon in the foreground and the gray background set contributed to his overall poor appearance, which, in turn, adversely affected viewer perceptions and cost him the debate.[15]

You should wear solid-colored clothing. If you wear patterns at all, they should be bold, simple patterns. Very fine patterns such as herring-bones, checks, and small plaids cause an interference with the television's scanning lines, and cause an unpleasant visual vibration that is known as a *"moiré effect."*[16]

Television's flattening of the three-dimensional image tends to make you look heavier on camera. If you do not need the extra weight, you should stay away from bulky clothing or clothing with broad horizontal lines.

In light of all these considerations, it is advisable to bring an extra set of clothes to the studio with you, just in case.

If you are offered makeup before your appearance, accept it. Often women want to retain their street makeup, but it is not designed for high-intensity studio illumination and does not photograph well. Men often decline to be made up because they do not think it masculine. Richard Nixon made this mistake in the 1960 debates—he did not use makeup, and the audience disliked his heavy beard, pale skin, and the dark circles under his eyes. Men should remember that television makeup is designed only to make them look natural on camera. For one thing, the color camera has a tendency to accentuate the natural red, yellow, and green tones in skin pigmentation. For another thing, cameras have the tendency to bring out minor blemishes that might not be noticeable to the naked eye. Cameras also wash out eye detail and accentuate discoloration under the eye. Television makeup for men is mostly just the application of a base to smooth out skin tone and reduce shine.

Legal and Ethical Considerations

Anything that affects vast numbers of people the way mass media do in the United States is bound to entail some ethical considerations. Take news, for example: not only do newscasters have to worry about objectivity, accuracy, and fairness as journalists do, but they also have to worry about visual excitement and depth of coverage. Critics are continually condemning television newspeople for choosing news items on the basis of how much flashy videotape footage they have—a gory accident and interviews with crying relatives might get more air time than a congressional hearing that affects millions of citizens. Local televised news especially has been accused of a callous lack of concern for privacy when it comes to interviews, especially the "ambush" (unannounced, uninvited) interviews. Critics also berate televised news as a "headline service" that does not provide the necessary depth to allow viewers to understand the day's events.

Broadcast entertainment also receives its share of criticism: there is too much sex and violence, too much stereotyping of women and minorities, too little realism, and often a total lack of logic to the plots. Broadcast advertising gets the heaviest criticism: it is assailed, sometimes rightly, for a lack of truthfulness. This dishonesty might be visual as well as verbal, as when the photography for a floor wax commercial implies that the product can make the floor shine like a mirror. Sometimes the deception is literal, as when a shaving cream company claimed that its product could soften sandpaper so the sand could be shaved off. Unfortunately, they proved their claim by shaving wet sand off a piece of glass. Television commercials are assailed also for implying and suggesting miracles. ("Wow," says the handsome hunk, "where have you been all my life?" "Why, I've been living next door to you for sixteen years," says the beautiful girl. "You finally noticed me because I just used Product X.") Television commercials get the heaviest criticism when they direct their psychological messages toward children.

All of these ethical issues, and ethics in general, should concern you if you plan to speak through the media.

Some ethical issues, of course, cross over the line between ethics and legality. Libel and slander are such issues. Both libel and slander are forms of defamation, which is "a false statement about a person which tends to bring that person into public hatred, contempt, or ridicule or to injure him in his business or occupation."[17] Slander is generally spoken defamation, whereas libel is written defamation. In most states, anything presented over the mass media is subject to libel laws.

Notice that a libelous statement is a *false* statement. Your best defense against libel, therefore, is to speak the truth when you speak of others over the mass media. The only other standard defense of concern to us here is "fair comment." Fair comment means that you are acting as a critic, and you are evaluating someone's performance by stating your own opinion. Therefore, if you were a theater critic, you could say that actor X spoke his lines as though he were under the influence of drugs. That statement is your opinion. However, you could not say that actor X was obviously using drugs, unless you knew that to be a fact. Between fact and opinion, however, is an ambiguous area, and it is best just to stay away from it.

Summary

This chapter dealt with media speaking skills, a topic that is becoming more and more important as career possibilities open up in radio, television, public relations, corporate video, and audiovisual training. Many of the principles of public speaking apply to mediated speaking with minor adaptations. Principles in this category include audience analysis and adaptation, forms of support, language, and delivery. Mediated messages are generally more accurate but less understood than face-to-face communication. These differences necessitate the learning of certain media skills, including taking advantage of a medium's capabilities, microphone technique, script formatting, and the use of prompting devices such as cue cards and teleprompters.

Ethical considerations include avoiding deception in advertising, stereotyping in entertainment, and invasion of privacy when reporting news, as well as the legal issues of libel and slander.

Questions/Assignments

1. Analyze any speech from *Vital Speeches* or any other source. What adaptations would you want to make to present that speech over television, as opposed to face-to-face?
2. It is mentioned in this chapter that broadcasters are required to cover both sides of controversial issues. Listen to an editorial over one of your local stations. Tape it if possible. How could this editorial have been improved?
3. Identify a television or radio speaker you think is particularly effective. What qualities make this speaker effective?
4. Familiarize yourself with one radio or television commercial. How do the producers of this commercial take advantage of the medium they are using? How would the same message have to be adapted if it were presented one-on-one between a salesperson and a customer?
5. Listen to two news broadcasts, one local and one network. What problems in inflection (the "network tone of voice") can you identify, as discussed on page 287?

Notes

1. Researchers are becoming increasingly interested in what audiovisual media can tell us about other communicative contexts. See, for example, Robert Cathcart and Gary Gumpert, "Mediated Interpersonal Communication: Toward a New Typology," *Quarterly Journal of Speech* 69:3, August 1983, pp. 267–277. The authors believe that "the exclusive identification of the media with mass communication has restricted understanding of the symbiotic relationship of the media and interpersonal communication."
2. The "equal time law," Section 315 of the Communications Act of 1934, requires broadcasters to give equal opportunity to opposing political candidates. The fairness doctrine is a Federal Communications Commission policy that requires stations to devote a reasonable amount of time to discussion of controversial issues and to see that opposing points of view are aired. For a further discussion of these regulations see Sydney Head and Christopher Sterling, *Broadcasting in America,* 4th ed. (Boston: Houghton Mifflin, 1982), especially Chapter 17, "Freedom and Fairness in Broadcasting."
3. John F. Budd, "Video: A Corporate Communications Tool," *Vital Speeches of the Day,* July 15, 1983, p. 593.
4. *Ibid.*
5. *Ibid.*
6. The effectiveness of video training has been widely supported. See, for exam-

ple, Gregory W. Sharp, "Acquisition of Lecturing Skills by University Teaching Assistants: Some Effects of Interest, Topic Relevance, and Viewing a Model Videotape," *American Educational Research Journal* 18:4, Winter 1981, pp. 491–502. However, the effectiveness of video training does remain controversial under some conditions. See W. L. Marshall, Liane Parker, and Bonnie J. Hayes, "Treating Public Speaking Problems: A Study Using Flooding and the Elements of Skills Training," *Behavior Modification* 6:2, April 1982, pp. 147–170.

7. Research indicates that 25–33 percent of what is seen on television is miscomprehended. See David C. Schmittlein and Donald G. Morrison, "Measuring Miscomprehension for Televised Communications Using True-False Questions," *Journal of Consumer Research* 10:2, September 1983, pp. 147–156.

8. For a description of how ratings work, see Eugene Foster, *Understanding Broadcasting* (Reading, Mass: Addison-Wesley, 1982), especially Chapter 11, "Ratings." See also, "Nielsen Report on Television." This brochure, which is published annually, is available at no charge from A. C. Nielsen Company, Nielsen Plaza, Northbrook, Illinois 60062.

9. "Collie," *World Book Encyclopedia* (Chicago: Field Enterprises Educational Corporation, 1962).

10. *Associated Press Broadcast Stylebook,* cited in Arthur Wimer and Dale Brix, *Workbook for Radio and TV News Editing and Writing,* 4th ed. (Dubuque, Iowa: Wm. C. Brown, 1975).

11. Lee J. Dudek, *Professional Broadcast Announcing* (Boston: Allyn & Bacon, 1982), p. 10.

12. *Ibid.*

13. Dwight Bolinger, "The Network Tone of Voice," *Journal of Broadcasting* 26:3, Summer 1982, pp. 725–728.

14. "Mike" and "mic" are both short for "microphone." Equipment is usually labeled "mic." Many writers prefer the slang "mike" because it looks friendlier and less technical.

15. Alan Wurtzel, *Television Production,* 2d ed. (New York: McGraw-Hill, 1983), p. 459.

16. Herbert Zettl, *Television Production Handbook,* 3d ed. (Belmont, Ca.: Wadsworth, 1976), p. 322.

17. Arthur Wimer and Dale Brix, "Advice from the Lawyers — Slander and Libel," in *Workbook for Radio and TV News Editing and Writing,* 4th ed. (Dubuque, Iowa: Wm. C. Brown, 1975), p. 275.

14

Speaking in Groups

Many public speaking classes involve group assignments. Sometimes these projects entail group research, but usually they will be either *group discussions* or *group presentations*. Even if your class does not include such an assignment, you may still be involved in group work in the criticism and discussion of classroom speeches. Later in life, you might preside over meetings or serve on a panel. This chapter provides a brief overview of some of the concepts that are essential to successful joint discussions and presentations.

Leadership Styles

Shared leadership increases member commitment and satisfaction in group discussion. In some cases, it increases group output.

There are two ways to share leadership. One is to have no designated leader, and the other is to have a designated leader who is willing to share responsibility. Because most discussion groups have designated leaders or moderators (chosen by the group or by an outside authority), it is a good idea to examine traditional styles and responsibilities of group leadership.

Authoritarian Leadership

Traditionally, three leadership styles are identified. The first is authoritarian leadership, in which the leader controls everyone. The authoritarian leader is concerned mostly with efficiency—getting the job done as quickly and easily as possible—and therefore seeks compliance rather than commitment from the other group members. Interaction in a group with an authoritarian leader goes something like this:

> Authoritarian Leader: All right, today we're going to discuss the pros and cons of moving the national capital to Lebanon, Kansas. Mary, you start.
>
> Another group member: May I say something first?
>
> Authoritarian Leader: Not just yet. You'll get your turn.

Unfortunately, chances are that when the other group member finally gets a turn, the comment the leader suppressed will no longer be appropriate. The group will never hear that contribution.

Laissez-Faire Leadership

The second leadership style is the permissive or laissez-faire style of leadership. This type of leader does not guide the group in any way. The laissez-faire leader sometimes relinquishes leadership responsibility in favor of being "just another member" or, even more passively, just an observer of the group. This style encourages spontaneity among group members, but often leads to disorganized and confusing discussions.

Democratic Leadership

The third style is democratic leadership. The democratic leader encourages all members to contribute and interact, while at the same time keeping them on the topic. Interaction in a group with a democratic leader goes like this:

> Democratic Leader: We're going to discuss the pros and cons of moving the national capital to Lebanon, Kansas. Would someone like to start by listing one of the disadvantages of the move?
>
> Mary: Could we start with the advantages? I feel pretty strongly about this . . .
>
> Democratic Leader: Fine, let's start with the advantages.
>
> Mary: I feel like it's been a long time since Americans have had a dramatic national breakthrough to cheer about. Well, here's something that will excite everyone. Let's move Washington!
>
> Another member: At least Kansas is in the geographical center of the country.
>
> Yet another: Yes, but the cost of such a move would be tremendous, in terms of both money and the disruption of government services.

Democratic Leader: This is great. By my count, we have two advantages and one disadvantage so far. Let's go into them in a little more depth. . . .

At its best, democratic leadership will be just as efficient as authoritarian leadership and will stimulate spontaneity just as well as laissez-faire leadership. For this reason, it is the preferred type of leadership in most discussion groups. Still, you should recognize that the other styles have their place. Military units are still most comfortable with authoritarian leadership, and therapy groups that attempt to have members "come out of their shells" are most effective when handled by a laissez-faire leader.

Leadership Functions

Discussion moderators are well advised to share leadership responsibility with the group. Still, by accepting the title of "moderator" they take on the responsibility of making sure that certain things get done. These things include the matters that have to be handled *before* the group meets, such as securing a room, making sure the lights and temperature controls work, and notifying all the group members. The traditional leadership functions also include responsibilities *during* the group discussion: controlling traffic, resolving conflicts, reviewing progress, and maintaining an agenda.

Traffic Control

Traditionally, the moderator takes on the responsibility of regulating *who* talks, *when,* and for *how long.* Part of traffic control is encouraging discussion from all members; therefore, if one member tends to monopolize the group's time, the leader is expected to inhibit that member in some way. (The leader might say, "That's a good idea, Fred, and your anecdote about summer camp certainly proves it. But let's see what some of the others think.") If a member does not contribute in any way, the leader is expected to draw that member out. Sometimes this work requires a sensitivity to nonverbal cues. Members who want to speak might not say so. They might just look puzzled or exasperated. At such times those members should be specifically invited to speak. ("Did you have a question, George?," or "Martha, did you want to add something?")

Sometimes traffic control is enhanced by the physical arrangement of the group. People sitting across from each other, for example, tend to interact more. People physically isolated from the group — such as two members in the back of the room, alone — will tend to form a clique and interact with themselves rather than with the rest of the group. A circle is considered the ideal physical arrangement for group interaction.

Conflict Resolution

When conflict becomes *dysfunctional,* the leader is expected to help the group move beyond it. Some conflicts are functional: arguments over ideas and opinions that are leading to increased understanding, for example, are good. Other conflicts stifle group activity. For example, if two group members begin arguing over who did the most work in the last group they both belonged to, the leader might have to step in and say, "Let's not dwell on past history. This is a new group, and a new opportunity for success."

Review Progress

The leader stresses progress toward goals, and periodically reviews that progress. ("So far we've accomplished _____ , _____ , and _____ . According to the goals we've agreed upon, we still have to accomplish _____ .")

Establish and Maintain an Agenda

The discussion leader organizes an agenda, which is a plan of group activities. For example, if you have an assignment to give a group presentation, your agenda for your first group discussion might look like this outline:

I.   Introduce group members
    A.   Areas of interest
    B.   Areas of expertise
II. Establish group goals
    A.   Requirements for the assignment
    B.   Norms for the group
        1.   How often to meet
        2.   When and where to meet
        3.   Time limits for meetings
        4.   Attendance requirements for members
        5.   Other
III. Choose topic for presentation
IV. Discuss topic
    A.   Analysis of topic
    B.   Division of labor among group members
V.   Explore avenues of research
    A.   Library research
    B.   Interviews
    C.   Surveys/experimentation

Notice that the agenda is organized in outline form, according to the principles of outlining presented in Chapter 6.

The Standard Agenda

Different group situations require different agendas. One list of activities is based on John Dewey's process of reflective thinking (see Chapter 3). This *standard agenda* can be used as a model for many types of problem-solving groups. It has five parts:

1. Defining the Problem. Included under the first step might be the identification of the group's goals: "This group will present a discussion of United States foreign aid and how it might be made an effective part of our foreign policy."

2. Analyzing the Problem. Now the background, causes, and effects of the problem are discussed. The problem might be broken up into sub-problems at this stage. Criteria for solutions are determined. For example, the group might determine that their suggestions for the improvement of foreign aid must be practical in light of our recent relationships and subsequent foreign policy problems with the following countries: Iran, Nicaragua, Mexico, and Cuba.

3. Proposing Solutions. Group members might suggest that foreign aid should be made contingent upon free elections, constitutional reforms, human rights, clean government, and the willingness of countries to repay debts to the International Monetary Fund.

4. Testing Solutions Against Criteria. Next, the group's suggestions would be tested against their practicality in dealing with Iran, Nicaragua, Mexico, and Cuba.

5. Selecting Final Solutions. The group will choose those solutions that pass the test of their criteria for their final presentation.

Hidden Agendas

Organizing group work around stated agendas helps keep *hidden agendas* from interfering with group efficiency. Hidden agendas are plans, usually based on individual needs, that are not discussed openly. Examples of hidden agendas include one member's plan for revenge against another member. You cannot always stop hidden agendas, but you can operate efficiently in spite of them if you have a stated agenda to keep the group on the track.

Making Group Presentations

The preceding discussion refers to groups that are working to get something done, such as solving a problem or preparing a presentation. These groups generally meet in private, but when their work is complete, their final presentation is made publicly. A specific format is helpful in a public presentation. The most common formats are *formal* and *informal panel discussions,* either one of which could be followed by an *audience forum.*

The Informal Panel Discussion

In an informal panel discussion, the participants are prepared to be knowledgeable on their topic, but they do not make formal presentations. The atmosphere of an informal panel discussion encourages interaction and spontaneity; participants often interrupt each other and exchange heated comments. They are often on a first-name basis with one another, so they might joke occasionally also. In spite of the informality, this type of panel will often discuss serious matters, such as community planning.

After a panel discussion the audience may be invited to ask questions and make comments to the panelists. At that point the panel discussion becomes a *forum.*

The suggested procedure for an informal panel discussion is as follows:

1. The chairperson introduces the topic and the panel members.
2. The chairperson then poses a question to one of the panel members.
3. All members discuss the question informally.
4. The chairperson "controls traffic," making sure that each panelist is given a chance to complete a thought before the next panelist begins speaking, asking specific questions when the interaction seems to falter.
5. The chairperson clarifies, summarizes, restates, or paraphrases ideas if necessary.
6. At the end of the allotted time, the chairperson summarizes the discussion.
7. If a forum is scheduled, the audience is invited to ask questions or comment. The chairperson controls the audience "traffic," also.

The Formal Panel Discussion

In a formal panel discussion each participant gives a prepared presentation. The suggested procedure for a formal panel is as follows:

1. The chairperson introduces the topic and the panel members in the order in which they will speak.
2. The members then make their formal presentations. Although they may refer to each other, they do not interact during the presentations.
3. The chairperson generally supplies transitions from one participant to the next. However, in one variation the members supply the transitions themselves as part of their conclusions. This variation, if prepared carefully, can result in an exceptionally smooth presentation.

4. The chairperson, or the final speaker, summarizes the discussion. If scheduled, the audience forum begins.

Summary

Traditional leadership styles include authoritarian leadership (I'm-the-boss-so-do-as-I-say), laissez-faire leadership (permissive), and democratic leadership (in which everyone participates and the leader supplies guidance). Traditional leadership responsibilities include traffic control, conflict resolution, recording and reviewing progress, and establishing and maintaining an agenda.

The agenda is a list of group activities, arranged according to the principles of division, coordination, and order. The standard agenda is used for problem-solving and lists the following activities: definition of problem, analysis of problem, proposing solutions, testing solutions against criteria for solutions, and the selection of the final solution. Stated agendas help thwart hidden (that is, undiscussed, personal) agendas.

An understanding of underlying dynamics such as these helps make group work more productive.

The most common formats for group presentations are formal and informal panel discussions, either one of which could be followed by an audience forum.

Questions/Assignments

1. Groups are very prevalent in our society. What groups have you been involved in? Do you consider them successful groups? Why or why not?
2. Different leadership styles might be most effective in different situations. Name one group situation in which each of the leadership styles (authoritarian, laissez-faire, or democratic) might be most effective.
3. Divide into groups of three to five, with an observer for each group member. As the group proceeds with any task, keep a record of the effect of nonverbal behavior, showing the behavior and its disposition on a graph such as this:

Behavior	*Disposition*
Fidgeting; quizzical expression	Ignored
Drumming loudly on desk top with fingers	Other members look annoyed; no one asks for the reason for this behavior.
Clearing throat; raising hand	Other members become silent so participant may speak.

Index